Religion and the State

Religion and the State

Europe and North America in the
Seventeenth and Eighteenth Centuries

Joshua B. Stein and Sargon G. Donabed

LEXINGTON BOOKS
Lanham • Boulder • New York • Toronto • Plymouth, UK

Published by Lexington Books
A wholly owned subsidiary of The Rowman & Littlefield Publishing Group, Inc.
4501 Forbes Boulevard, Suite 200, Lanham, Maryland 20706
www.rowman.com

10 Thornbury Road, Plymouth PL6 7PP, United Kingdom

British Library Cataloguing in Publication Information Available

Library of Congress Cataloging-in-Publication Data

Religion and the state : Europe and North America in the seventeenth and eighteenth centuries /
[edited by] Josh Stein and Sargon Donabed.
  p. cm.
Includes bibliographical references and index.
ISBN 978-0-7391-7156-1 (cloth : alk. paper) -- ISBN 978-0-7391-7157-8 (electronic)
1. Church and state--Europe--History--17th century. 2. Church and state--Europe--History--18th century. 3. Church and state--United States--History--17th century. 4. Church and state--United States--
History--18th century. I. Stein, Josh, 1944- II. Donabed, Sargon.
  BR735.R443 2012
  322'.109032--dc23
  2012021415

The paper used in this publication meets the minimum requirements of American National
Standard for Information Sciences Permanence of Paper for Printed Library Materials,
ANSI/NISO Z39.48-1992.

Printed in the United States of America

To Suzanne, Amanda, and Sarah, my wonderful daughters-in-law, three.

For Tom Clarke, John Lanci, Mary Joan Leith, Greg Shaw, and Erika Schluntz who introduced me to the study of religion.

Contents

Acknowledgments

First, special thanks to our editors at Lexington Books, Justin Race and Sabah Ghulamali, for accepting the project and answering the myriad questions directed toward them. To the many people at Roger Williams University who have made this conference a success financially: Guilan Wang, Assistant Provost of Global Affairs and Director of the Spiegel Center for Global and International Programs; former Provost Laura de Abruna; and former Interim President Ronald Champagne. To Lydia Serpa, Kay Neves, Joe Carney, Ruth Bazinet, and Tara Norcross for all of their help setting up a fantastic conference that was well received. To Ann Aubrey Hanson for her proofing and copyediting. To our students Emily Masseo, Alice Badger, Meredith Bergen, Anna Dallendorfer, and Sean Stausser for administering both registration and book sales. To the Department of History at Roger Williams for their support, including Laura D'Amore, Autumn Quezada-Grant, Jeffrey Meriwether, Debra Mulligan, Richard Potter, Jennifer Stevens, and Michael Swanson. Last, a heartfelt thank you to all those who attended the conference as observers and as participants.

Foreword

Roger Williams University is named after the English Protestant theologian Roger Williams (1603–1683), who in spring of 1636, along with a number of his followers, founded the Providence (named so for God's providence) Plantation Colony, which provided a refuge for religious minorities. There, civil matters were settled by a majority vote by heads of households, and the concepts of "liberty" and "conscience" were held in great esteem. The London-born preacher, an early proponent of religious freedom and the separation of church and state, established the First Baptist Church of Providence (the first in the United States) in 1639.

Williams was also a student of Native American languages and an advocate for impartial dealings with Native American nations, and a close friend of Narragansett chief Canonicus, who in fact granted Williams the land on which the settlement was built. Various people would flock to Williams's colony in the following years, including dissenting Christians, Jews, and others.

In this tradition of religious freedom and discovery, the History Department at Roger Williams University sponsored the first Church/State conference in 2007, the second in 2009, and the third in 2011. Participants at all the conferences have hailed from around the world, including Spain, Poland, Egypt, Turkey, Israel, Canada, Scotland, and the United States. This book is a result of the most recent conference, the third biennial conference on Church/State relations entitled "Religion and the State: The 17th and 18th Centuries in Europe and America," chaired by Joshua B. Stein, Sargon G. Donabed, and Matt Hedstrom. Speakers included Lawrence Goodheart, University of Connecticut; Rebeca Vázquez Gómez, University of A Coruña (Spain); Steven K. Green, Willamette University; Matthew Hedstrom, University of Virginia; Joy Howard, United States Military Academy at West

Point; Jae Jerkins, Florida State University; Sara Kitzinger, University of St. Andrews (Scotland); Matt McCook, Oklahoma Christian University; Douglas S. Mock, Boston University; Keith Pacholl, University of West Georgia; Julianne Parse Sandlin, Florida State University; Noah Shusterman, Temple University; Brent S. Sirota, North Carolina State University; Holly Snyder, Brown University; Tara Thompson Strauch, University of South Carolina; and Tasdeusz J. Zielinski, Christian Academy of Theology (Warsaw). The conference was honored to host James Hitchcock of St. Louis University, and Gordon S. Wood of Brown University and winner of the 1993 Pulitzer Prize for History as the two keynote speakers.

Joshua B. Stein and Sargon G. Donabed
Roger Williams University, March 2012

Introduction:
Establishing and Disestablishing
Religion in the Atlantic World

Matthew S. Hedstrom and Brent S. Sirota

On December 6, 2007, former Massachusetts governor Mitt Romney, then running for the Republican presidential nomination, gave his so-called "Faith in America" speech at the George Herbert Walker Bush Library in College Station, Texas. Seeking to cement his status as a conservative alternative to Senator John McCain, Romney hoped to reassure Christian voters about his Mormon faith and, in doing so, neutralize the threat to his candidacy posed by former Arkansas governor Mike Huckabee, a Baptist minister and a favorite of evangelical Republicans.[1] In a rather self-conscious emulation of the address given by another Massachusetts politician nearly half a century earlier—Roman Catholic presidential candidate John Kennedy's September 1960 speech to the Greater Houston Ministerial Association—Romney delivered a meditation on the meaning of religious toleration in American history. Above and beyond the *de rigeur* invocations of the founding fathers, the candidate's text dwelt on the bequest of the early modern world, tracing the legacy of the enlightenment on both sides of the Atlantic. Romney invoked the renegade Puritans Anne Hutchinson and Roger Williams, grouping them together with Mormon pioneer Brigham Young, all religious dissenters for whom America had failed to live up to its high purpose as a refuge for tender consciences. Such figures served as confessors for what he called "our grand tradition of religious tolerance and liberty." But when the governor looked toward Europe, he saw only empty cathedrals, "postcard backdrop to societies just too busy or too 'enlightened' to venture inside and kneel in prayer." Romney was, in effect, presenting a curious bifurcation in the legacy of the Enlightenment, which had apparently equipped Americans with wisdom enough to guarantee "the free exercise of religion," but left Europeans possessed only of a deplorable "religion of secularism." Interestingly, Romney blamed "the establishment of state religions in Europe" for this predicament. In the American republic, which proscribed such establishments, religion was cherished as a liberty, while in Europe religion was overthrown as an imposition. In this political and ideological context, Romney's task in College Station was a fairly trick one. He needed to conjure just enough liberalism from the Christian conservatives in the base of his party to accept a Mormon candidate as their standard-bearer, but not so much that it endangered his (already somewhat questionable) *bona fides* as an advocate for the so-called "values" issues dear to social and religious conservatives. He needed an American Enlightenment, not a European one.

The Romney speech vividly demonstrates Faulkner's famous dictum, "The past isn't dead. It isn't even past." The historiography of Church-State relations in America and Europe remains a live cultural, religious, and political issue on both sides of the Atlantic. Even more, Romney's invocation of history illuminates the need for a thoroughly trans-Atlantic approach to the history of Church-State relations in the modern West. In the seventeenth and eighteenth centuries, the formative period for modern Church-State relations, we see vividly the complex interrelationship of developments in England, France, and America. Ever since, historians and political figures, such as Romney, have compared the European and American efforts to discern the proper role of religion in government and government in religion.

Though the "republican" turn in the historiography of the American founding has long abandoned the once unassailable proposition of *Locke et praetera nihil,* the English philosopher continues to loom large in the genealogy of American religious liberty. As citizens, Americans claim the intellectual bequest of Renaissance civic humanists, seventeenth-century English republicans, country Whigs, and Scottish *philosophes,* and yet as possessors of liberty of conscience, somehow we are all still Lockeans. Thus, it was refreshing to encounter a series of papers that examined what might be thought of as a variety of "illiberal" affirmations of the separation of Church and State, in which claims for separation were rooted not in the putatively enlightened languages of individual rights, civic liberty, toleration, or secularism, but rather in conceptions of discipline, priestly authority, and ultramontanism. The separation of Church and State, it must be remembered, preoccupied proponents of enlightenment no less than the agents of European counter-enlightenment.

James Hitchcock's contribution to the volume offers a meticulous overview of the vicissitudes of politics and religion in the polities of post-Reformation Europe. Hitchcock deftly weaves together various narratives of dynastic crisis, religious settlement, and sectarian conflict throughout the sixteenth, seventeenth, and eighteenth centuries. He rightly highlights the paradoxical aspect of religious politics in the period, where faith served as both "the moral foundation for obedience to the state and as the justification for rebellion." His account engages with the major theorists of Church-State relations in the period stretching from the Reformation to the Enlightenment. Significantly, he suggests that the European theorists of toleration, by confining faith to human interiority, were unable to stem the tide of religious indifference unleashed by the Enlightenment. Only the United States, he suggests, was able to reconcile disestablishment and dogma.

Sara Kitzinger's contribution adopts an illuminating theological perspective on the problem of Church-State relations in late sixteenth- and early seventeenth-century England. Supplementing the conventional narrative that considers the magisterial and Erastian form of the established Church of England as something of a political exigency, born of the religious and dynastic instabilities of the Tudor age, Kitzinger presents the Church as something of a theological exigency as well. Setting the English Church amid a wider conversation in the Reformed Protestant world, Kitzinger depicts an Elizabethan and early Stuart Church of England in need of continual insulations from the ecclesiological implications of a rigorous predestinarian theology. In her telling, English predestinarians gravitated toward an ecclesiological vision in which a church comprised exclusively of the godly subsisted under the authority of a strictly ministerial discipline. In rejecting magisterial oversight and the inclusion of the ungodly among the congregation, the English predestinarians embraced an ecclesiology in which Church and State "were potentially segregated." This could by no means be allowed by the defenders of the Anglican establishment and the royal supremacy upon which it rested. And indeed, as Kitzinger shows, Anglican establishmentarians were willing to risk theological ambiguity on the question of absolute predestination in order to defend the church polity. Moreover, as religious and political tensions worsened in early seventeenth-century England, defenders of the magisterial establishment increasingly abandoned the doctrine of predestination altogether. Critics of the Anglican establishment meanwhile resorted to ever-greater spiritualization of the church in order to justify its emancipation from magisterial tutelage. Many, such as Roger Williams, found themselves rehabilitating the fallen natural world to provide some ground upon which a free church might stand.

Brent Sirota's chapter examines the fate of Anglican high churchmanship in the aftermath of the Glorious Revolution of 1688–1689. The displacement of the legitimate, though Roman Catholic, sovereign James II from the English throne in favor of his Protestant son-in-law and daughter posed a seemingly insoluble problem for the conservative wing of the established Church. While a small handful of conservative clergy and laity refused to transfer their allegiance to the new monarchs and suffered the consequences of their "nonjuring," the majority of Anglican high churchmen acceded to the Revolution. Having done so, however, they found themselves bereft of the ideological means of mounting an opposition to the reformist agenda of the new regime. In Sirota's telling, the Anglican high church movement lit upon the language and principles of the so-called "country ideology"—a complex of political and constitutional ideas emphasizing civic virtue and honest governance, well-known to scholars of the eighteenth-century Anglo-American world, at least since the publication of Bernard Bailyn's *The Ideological Origins of the American Revolution* a half-century ago. Employing the language of the "country ideology," Anglican High Church writers sought to embed the rights and privileges of the established Church within a conception of England's ancient constitution. The traditional prerogatives of church and clergy were to be defended against the Leviathan-like fusion of civil and ecclesiastical power embodied in the Revolution state.

Noah Shusterman's examination of the controversy in revolutionary France surrounding the Civil Constitution of the Clergy of 1790 offers an instructive counterpoint to Brent Sirota's essay. In both studies, a reactionary clergy find themselves exposed to the dominion of a sovereign state in which civil and ecclesiastical power had been functionally integrated. In Sirota's analysis of the ecclesiastical politics surrounding the Revolution of 1688–1689, the clerical opposition attempted to circumscribe the sovereignty of the revolutionary state, sheltering the beleaguered Church of England within the liberties of the so-called "ancient constitution." In Shusterman's essay, however, the refractory French clergy, when confronted with the seemingly unlimited sovereignty of the National Assembly over the Gallican Church, opted instead for counter-revolution. Shusterman depicts the crisis as something of a classic Schmittian "state of exception." Whereas the Old Regime could abide the elaborate fiction of political and ecclesiastical cooperation between scepter and miter, the moment of revolution requires a revelation of sovereignty: the church must yield. Shusterman considers its unwillingness to do so a "turning point" in the French Revolution, the foundational resistance upon which the counter-revolution would be erected. From this vantage, it is not surprising that government repression of the counter-revolutionaries in the years 1792–1794 proceeded with such a pronounced anticlerical agenda. In a grim coda, Shusterman invokes the images of the *noyades* and the "republican marriages," the horrific drownings of refractory clergy and nuns, employed against counter-revolutionaries in the Vendée. In these, perhaps, one sees clearly the full amplitude of revolutionary sovereignty exercised without limit against the countervailing powers of the Gallican Church.

Rebeca Vázquez Gómez helpfully bridges the gap between the early modern world and the twenty-first century. Vázquez's chapter examines the legacy of Spain's Catholic denominational past in post-Franco Spanish society. In particular, she examines contemporary efforts on the part of the Spanish state to balance its claims to secularity and the protection of religious freedom in the public sphere. Vázquez highlights the weight of the Catholic past in contemporary controversies regarding Christian, Islamic, and Jewish symbols and attire in public institutions. Authorities often vigorously pursue religious neutrality with respect to minority faiths, while remaining tolerant of the persistence of Christian symbols as part of the historic or artistic heritage of the nation. Vázquez's is a fitting conclusion to the European section of the volume, as it opens up serious questions regarding the aptitude of liberal and enlightenment notions of disestablishment and political secularity in a world in which secularization has either slowed markedly or reversed completely. Once again, Europe must address the concerns of those who fundamentally reject the notion of a public sphere purged of religious practice, values, and discourses.

The historiography of Church-State relations in British North America and the early United States follows many of the same contours as that regarding Europe, as the following essays reveal. In the case of scholarship on the United States, however, we see a particularly powerful liberal master narrative. This narrative frames not merely the Establishment and Free Exercises clauses of the First Amendment to the U.S. Constitution as the inevitable culmination of political contestation between Church and State, but even more looks to the particularly robust and far-reaching post-World War II interpretations of these constitutional provisions as the yardstick by which to measure earlier generations. But as Philip Hamburger, in *Separation of Church and State*, and others have argued, the American experience of Church-State relations has often blended liberal and illiberal impulses, as secularly and religiously motivated constituencies—always unstable categories—have variously cooperated and competed in the public discourse about religion and public life.[2] We must understand the complexities of these crosscurrents if we are to make sense of the larger story of Church-State relations in colonial America and the United States.

The great victories of the Revolutionary period for religious liberty—first the *Virginia Statute for Religious Freedom*, penned by Thomas Jefferson and championed by James Madison, and a few years later the First Amendment to the Federal Constitution—were remarkably far-reaching pieces of legislation, truly unprecedented in scope. The great leaders of the moment certainly saw them that way. George Washington, in his famous 1790 letter to the Jews of Newport, for example, claimed that under the new government, "It is now no more that toleration is spoken of, as if it was by the indulgence of one class of people, that another enjoyed the exercise of their inherent national gifts. The Government of the United States," he wrote, "gives to bigotry no sanction, to persecution no assistance. . . ." Jefferson, not surprisingly, went even farther. Commenting in old age on the Virginia Statute, he noted that his intention was "to comprehend, within the mantle of its protection, the Jew and the Gentile, the Christian and Mahometan, the Hindoo, and infidel of every denomination."

Yet highlighting Washington and Jefferson in this way obscures the very real political battles of the Revolutionary period for religious liberty, and the variety of arguments that were advanced for and against the Constitution and its protections. If Washington and, even more, Jefferson were steeped in the latest philosophies of Anglo-American liberalism, a great many of their countrymen were not, and the debates about Church and State in the founding period—and indeed for the rest of American history—were waged, quite often, in religious terms in addition to classical liberal terms. Article 6, paragraph 3 became the flashpoint. This section of the proposed federal Constitution reads, "no religious test shall ever be required as a qualification to any office or public trust under the United States," and though it elicited little comment at the Constitutional Convention in Philadelphia—little comment among the Washingtons and Madisons, in other words—it set off a firestorm in the states. Eleven of the thirteen states at this time, after all—all but New York and Virginia—had religious tests for holding office, including Rhode Island, where only Protestants could hold office or vote. The ratification fight in North Carolina provides perhaps the best insight into the fierceness of this debate over the secular Constitution. "Let us remember," warned William Lancaster, a Baptist minister and anti-Federalist delegate to the North Carolina ratifying convention about what Article 6 might mean for the future of the Presidency. "Let us remember that we form a government for millions not yet in existence. I have not the art of divination. In the course of four or five hundred years, I do not know how it will work. This is most certain, that Papists may occupy that chair [again, meaning the Presidency], and Mahometans may take it. I see nothing against it."[3]

Papists and Mahometans—Catholics and Muslims—in this formulation stood for the prime exemplars of religious tyranny—often literally understood as antichrist, and certainly as embodiments of religious systems thoroughly and oppressively intermeshed with civil governance. Rev. Lancaster, as a Baptist minister, knew something of this kind of tyranny himself, since Baptists were excluded from public office in England on account of their dissenting faith. Only Protestants, he contended, with their proper theological understanding of the role of individual conscience, could adequately safeguard religious freedom. Catholics and Muslims, on the other hand, would naturally seek to subvert liberty, as the history of the papacy and the caliphate seemed to demonstrate. As a delegate in Massachusetts worried, without some kind of religious test for office, "Popery and the Inquisition may be established in America."[4]

Counter to these concerns, in ratifying conventions across the continent, Federalist delegates dutifully argued on Enlightenment grounds for individual liberties. But many also advanced decidedly more pragmatic arguments, arguments that met these religious concerns head on. Madison himself made it best. One of the reasons he remonstrated against religious assessments in Virginia, he wrote, was because a religious establishment was "adverse to the diffusion of the light of Christianity" and would impede its spread among those "still remaining under the dominion of false Religions." A state church, Madison contended, "at once discourages those who are strangers to the light of revelation from coming into the Region of it; and countenances by example the nations who continue in darkness, in shutting out those who might convey it to them. Instead of Levelling as far as possible, every obstacle to the victorious progress of Truth, [a religious establishment] with an ignoble and unchristian timidity would circumscribe it with a wall of defence against the encroachments of error." The author of the First Amendment and president who ardently defended secularism, to a point that would be inconceivable today, argued for religious liberty because, he felt, it would aid the spread of Christianity in its battle with false religion.

The essays in this volume on Church and State in North America helpfully illuminate, in different ways, the complex interplay of religion and political philosophy that framed these early American deliberations about religion and public life. Lawrence B. Goodheart's essay brings our focus to British colonial America in the seventeenth century, with a study of the law and practice of capital punishment in Connecticut. Goodheart's work locates the Puritan project in New England in the wider context of the Puritan experience in England, but delineates critical departures. Most fundamentally, Puritans in America framed their enterprise in North America as the establishment of a New Israel, and as settlers on a frontier an ocean away from metropolitan England were free to base much more of their legal code on Old Testament models. For these reasons, Puritans in Connecticut deemed a wide array of offenses punishable by death, ranging from murder to witchcraft, adultery, bestiality, blasphemy, and cursing, smiting, or rebelling against a parent. Yet, as Goodheart's essay demonstrates, such provisions were enforced unevenly, a tacit acknowledgement of the challenges of governing a New Israel in the New World. Over the course of the seventeenth century, the law of capital punishment in Connecticut changed to reflect these evolving cultural norms, so that fewer and fewer offenses were deemed capital crimes. These changes, Goodheart suggests, stemmed not only from the impracticalities of the previous system, but also from the decline of Puritan understanding of their society through an Old Testament typology.

The Puritan understanding of their errand in the wilderness as a sacred reenactment of God's covenant with Israel stood in marked contrast to the experience of actual Jews in colonial British America, as Holly Snyder insightfully demonstrates. Her essay addresses the political and civic rights granted to Jews in Rhode Island, the colony long regarded as the most liberal in its religious tolerance. Rhode Island history, Snyder contends, has too often been read through the lens of Roger Williams's writings on liberty of conscience rather than through the colony's actual practices regarding religious freedom. Here Snyder offers the illuminating example of the 1762 denial of naturalization to two Jews who had resided in the colony for seventeen years, and, more compellingly, the withholding of voting rights from Rhode Island Jews until 1798. This backdrop places not only the legacy of Roger Williams in a new light, but also the famed 1790 letter of George Washington to the Jewish congregation in Newport. In this letter Washington affirmed that the new nation gave "to bigotry no sanction," and yet the Jews of Newport, we see, rightly knew better, as they were denied in their home state what the new Federal Constitution afforded. In fact, as Synder writes, "The Charter of 1663, with its provision for liberty to protect Rhode Island against the 'enemies of Christianity,' remained as the founding instrument of Rhode Island statehood—a posture which would not be finally, and irrevocably, abandoned until the adoption of a State Constitution in the 1840s." The case of the Jews of Rhode Island provides a starkly clear example of "the extent to which 'Liberty of Conscience,' as articulated by Roger Williams, was put into practice," and therefore of the limits of religious freedom in colonial America.

Tara Thompson Strauch shifts our attention to the pivotal decade between the Declaration of Independence and the ratification of the federal Constitution, a period when states served as critical laboratories of democracy. In particular, she describes the fascinating and little-studied legal and theological debates in various states regarding the swearing of oaths. Removing oath requirements for public service, many feared, would allow Muslims and Jews to become full participants in civic life, while narrowly constructed oaths would bar Quakers, Mennonites, and other pious Christians from service, for irrelevant theological reasons. The debates over oaths at the state level, in this way, manifested the same tensions and fractures as did the simultaneous debates regarding the ratification of federal Constitution—an effort to balance religious liberty with the desire to protect the privileged status of Protestant Christianity. Underlying the argument in favor of oaths was the assumption that individual virtue, an absolute necessity for a democratic polity, required religious faith, often assumed to include, at a minimum, a belief in a future state of rewards and punishments. (In practice, the theological basis for virtue was often understood much more narrowly as essentially requiring adherence to Protestant Christianity in some form.) Eventually, however, Gov. William Livingston of New Jersey and others began to offer Madisonian arguments against oath requirements for public officials, opining, in Strauch's characterization, "that true Christian citizens could only exist in a state which did not require a certain denominational affiliation." Those Anglicans and Lutherans accustomed to European state churches often supported oath requirements, but soon the adherents of dissenting traditions— not only Quakers and Mennonites, but Baptists and Methodists as well— came to see oath provisions as assaults on freedom of conscience, and in that way ultimately inimical to religion. As in the matter of the Constitution itself, only the presumption that the United States would remain Christian in fact, if not strictly in law, allowed the coalitions of dissenters and deists to argue persuasively against oath requirements.

Keith Pacholl, like Strauch, likewise focuses on the early national period and the ongoing debates about the proper public role of religion in a moment of rapid disestablishment. Pacholl's essay addresses the role of education— especially through early American periodical literature—in instilling notions of civic virtue in the American reading public. Periodicals offered a powerful mechanism for the moral formation of Americans in the era between the founding of the republic and the emergence of widespread public education systems in the states. In fact, as Pacholl notes, Americans at the end of the eighteenth century had "a higher per capita readership of periodicals than anywhere else in the Atlantic world." Periodical writers frequently reminded readers of the increased need for virtuous citizens in a self-governing and religiously disestablished nation. This moral formation, Pacholl notes, reflected prevailing Enlightenment notions of "rational Christianity," a faith reconciled with science in the vein of the Scottish Common sense philosophy. Begun in childhood, a reasonable, pragmatic education would prepare boys for political leadership and girls for the duties of "republican motherhood." At the same time, periodical writers stressed the principles of religious toleration as an ethical requirement of rational Christianity. Beyond arguing for virtue and toleration, Pacholl notes as well the simultaneously argument in the periodicals for the cultivation of science and reason as similarly necessary for the survival of the republic. In these ways, Pacholl finds in the mass circulation periodicals a wide-ranging discourse about the proper place of religion and education in the early national period.

The concluding essay of the American section of this volume, like the concluding essay of the European section, takes a step back from the controversies of the seventeenth and eighteenth centuries and examines matters of Church and State closer to our own times. Matt McCook does this through a detailed examination of contemporary debates about the religious character and intentions of the Founding Fathers. This debate, he notes insightfully, typically sheds more light on the religious, cultural, and political faultlines of the late twentieth and twentieth-first centuries than on those of the founding period. McCook groups contemporary writers on religion and the founding into four broad categories: secular polemicists, Christian polemicists, strict-separation academics, and accommodationist academics. McCook helpfully delineates the major scholars and works in each of the four categories, and concludes this essay—and this volume—with a call for a publicly engaged historical scholarship that will bring standards of evidence and reason to bear on this critical, important national matter. As Mitt Romney's 2007 speech reveals, how we understand and, critically, *compare*, the religious and political histories of Europe and the United States continues to shape our ongoing debates about Church and State. This interdisciplinary volume aims to shed critical historical light on these still-pressing matters.

REFERENCES

Hamburger, Philip. *The Separation of Church and State.* Cambridge, MA: Harvard University Press, 2002.

Kramnick, Isaac, and R. Laurence Moore. *The Godless Constitution: A Moral Defense of the Secular State.* New York: W.W. Norton, 1996, 32.

Luo, Michael. "Romney, Eye on Evangelicals, Defends His Faith," *The New York Times*, December 7, 2007.

Spellberg, Denise A. "Could a Muslim Be President? An Eighteenth-Century Constitutional Debate." *Eighteenth-Century Studies* 39, no. 4 (Summer 2006): 485.

NOTES

1. Michael Luo, "Romney, Eye on Evangelicals, Defends His Faith," *The New York Times,* December 7, 2007.

2. Philip Hamburger, *The Separation of Church and State* (Cambridge, MA: Harvard University Press, 2002).

3. Quoted in Denise A. Spellberg, "Could a Muslim Be President? An Eighteenth-Century Constitutional Debate," *Eighteenth-Century Studies* 39:4 (Summer 2006), 485.

4. Isaac Kramnick and R. Laurence Moore, *The Godless Constitution: A Moral Defense of the Secular State* (New York: W.W. Norton, 1996), 32.

Chapter One

Church and State in Early Modern Europe

James Hitchcock

From the beginning, the Protestant Reformation was intimately involved with politics in that it was ultimately governments—emperor, kings, nobles, town officials—who determined which religious movements would prevail. In the Peace of Augsburg of 1555,[1] after a rebellion of the Lutheran princes, the Holy Roman emperors Charles V and Ferdinand I conceded to each prince the right to determine the religion of his subjects, a concession sum-marized by the famous principle *cujus regio, ejus religio* (Whose realm, his religion). Those unwilling to accept the religion of their rulers were permit-ted to emigrate, since it was thought that each territory ought to be religiously homogeneous. Tolerance was granted reluctantly, but it was the first time that any European state officially had recognized the religious diversity of its subjects. The Augsburg settlement worked relatively well for more than half a century[2] until a combination of events provoked the Thirty Years' War,[3] the last and greatest of the religious wars, in which, as always, religion and politics were held together in an inextricable grip.

In 1618, the Hapsburg prince Ferdinand was elected king of Bohemia and announced his intention of imposing the minority Catholic faith on a relig-iously diverse society. A revolt followed, but Ferdinand was able to enforce his claim, even though the Protestant princes of the empire rallied in support of the Protestant claimant, Frederick the Elector of the Rhine Palatinate. Ferdinand was also soon elected Holy Roman Emperor and undertook the strict enforcement of the Peace of Augsburg, which had excluded Calvinists. (By 1618, only one of the princely electors of the empire was a Lutheran, while three were Catholic and three Calvinist.) He also sought the return of all Catholic Church lands taken since 1555. Other factors—notably the inde-

1

pendence of the United Provinces from Spain—also complicated the strug-
gle. Religion provided an often murderous passion for the antagonists in the
Thirty Years' War, but policy ruled. Ferdinand sincerely wanted to promote
the Catholic faith. But that also strengthened his power, which even the
Catholic princes feared would grow at their expense; this made them cautious in supporting him.

Several times Ferdinand was close to victory, but each time the Protestant
cause was saved by foreign intervention—first by Lutheran Denmark, then
by Lutheran Sweden, finally by Catholic France, whose foreign policy was
implacably anti-Hapsburg, demonstrating that when religious and political
interests conflicted, the latter prevailed. (The popes found themselves in the
untenable position of relying on the Habsburgs to support the Catholic faith,
while often opposing Hapsburg interests, because of the Hapsburgs' continuing designs on Italy.[4]) During its final decade, the war was essentially fought
between the two leading Catholic powers—France and Spain—on German
territory.

In 1648, Ferdinand III had to acquiesce in the Peace of Westphalia,[5] a
group of treaties that, like Augsburg, marked a victory for the princes, who
retained disputed church lands and who, in practice, retained the right to
determine the religion of their subjects, although in theory the treaty guaranteed liberty of conscience. Calvinists were now included. Pope Innocent X
condemned the treaty,[6] but a number of German bishops were territorial
princes who pursued their own interests above those of the church. The
prince-bishops of Trier, Mainz, and Cologne were electors of the empire, and
the Catholic duke of Bavaria was one of the major beneficiaries of the peace.
The princes set about consolidating their power according to the terms of the
peace agreement and, although they generally promoted religion among their
subjects, they also brought the churches under their control.[7] Shortly after
religious war in Germany was brought to an end by the Peace of Augsburg in
1555—primarily because Catholic France intervened—religious war erupted
in France itself, a war that would last for almost forty years, subjecting the
kingdom to disruptions suffered by no other country in the sixteenth century.[8] Officially the French crown committed itself to suppressing the French
Calvinists (Huguenots). But much of the time events were beyond royal
control.

The queen mother, Catherine de Medici, and her three sons, each of
whom ruled briefly and died young, attempted to retain control over the
situation by formally upholding the Catholic faith while allowing semitolera-
tion of the Huguenot minority, a policy that allowed the ultra-Catholic family
of Guise to accuse the reigning Valois of betraying the faith. The religious
wars in France were therefore three-sided—the crown, the Guises, and the
Huguenots. Cousins of the Valois, both the Guises and the Huguenot Bourbon families had designs on the throne, which both justified in the name of

religion. (The infamous St. Bartholomew's Day Massacre of 1574 may have been a ploy by Catherine and her son Charles IX to embroil the Guises and the Bourbons in a war of mutual extermination.) The Guises had the support of Philip II of Spain, for whom religion and politics conveniently came together in his desire both to promote the Catholic faith and to weaken France. Both sides employed assassination, and in 1589, a Dominican friar killed Henry III, whom the assassin considered overly tolerant of the Protestants. This ended the Valois dynasty and brought the Huguenot Bourbon Henry IV to the throne, although the Guises, with Spanish support, continued the war for a few more years. Henry subsequently became a Catholic, supposedly uttering the famous remark, "Paris is worth a Mass."

In 1598, he issued the Edict of Nantes, which, along with the Peace of Augsburg, was the most important attempt to deal with the religious divisions of the age. Huguenot nobility were given complete religious freedom in their own domains, certain cities were designated as places of free worship, and there was to be no discrimination in the universities and the various state bureaucracies. Most remarkably, the Huguenots were permitted to fortify their cities against any attempt to violate the edict.

Henry IV showed himself a faithful Catholic[9] and the terms of the edict were respected. However, partly because he was contemplating war with Catholic Spain, he was assassinated by a Catholic fanatic in 1610. The edict was, in a sense, an advance on the Peace of Augsburg, in that it envisioned Catholics and Protestants actually living side by side in some places. But the story of Henry IV showed that it was still thought impossible that a monarch should rule over a people most of whom were of a different faith from himself. The decrees of the Council of Trent were not officially accepted in France until after Henry IV's death, and then only by the clergy, not the monarchy, since the kings wanted as free a hand as possible in dealing with the religious divisions of the kingdom.[10]

For almost twenty years (1624–1642), Cardinal Armand de Richelieu[11] was the power behind the French throne. Personally devout, he pursued policies in which religious considerations had no place, although he invoked the divine authority of the king to silence criticism. Among other things, he dampened the zeal of the Catholic *devots*,[12] who opposed the toleration of Huguenots and France's support of the German Protestants. Richelieu made war on the Huguenots, personally accompanying the royal armies and destroying the Huguenot fortresses, but this was mainly because of the Huguenots' semi-independence from royal control. The provisions of the Edict of Nantes granting them religious toleration remained in effect.

Sixty years later, Louis XIV departed from the pragmatism that had governed royal policy for more than a century and revoked the edict,[13] an act that sent numerous Huguenots into exile, although many remained—always in danger of persecution—and even occasionally achieved prominence in national life. The official Assembly of the Clergy condemned the use of force against the Huguenots, and even Jacques-Benigne Bossuet, the dominant bishop and theologian of the age, doubted its wisdom. Pope Innocent XI congratulated Louis on his action but privately thought it unwise and ineffective.[14]

Louis perhaps acted mainly because religious toleration seemed to show that he did not have full control of his kingdom, but he perhaps also had a sense of guilt that he was a less than exemplary Catholic.[15] Such guilt, if indeed Louis experienced it, exemplified one of the paradoxes of monarchy—the king ruled over all his subjects, but the clergy had the obligation to rebuke the king for his moral failings. Louis endured chastisement from the pulpit, briefly banishing one of his mistresses from court after a priest refused her absolution. For a time, he endured blunt sermons delivered by the courageous Archbishop Francoise Fenelon, but Fenelon was later banished from court and became an open critic of royal power.[16] Louis consistently nominated bishops for political reasons, many of whom were absentees from their dioceses, and fell into a protracted conflict with Pope Innocent XI over the royal claim to collect the revenues of all vacant dioceses.[17] During that dispute the Assembly of the Clergy issued the Gallican Articles, according to which the king was not subject to any higher authority "in temporal things" and could not be deposed. The pope was supreme in "spiritual matters" but limited by the laws of the kingdom. Innocent condemned the articles and refused to confirm the king's nominees to a number of vacant dioceses, but his successor subsequently approved the nominees and conceded the king's right to collect the revenues. The articles were officially withdrawn but continued to be influential. Louis's ceaseless drive for territory caused much of Europe to unite against him,[18] especially after he invaded the Rhine Palatinate and oppressed its Calvinist inhabitants.[19] The English, the Dutch, and some Germans saw the issue as partly religious, but at times the coalition also included the Catholic Hapsburgs.

For more than a century, religion and the state in France were locked in a complex relationship because of the Jansenist movement,[20] which originated in Flanders with the bishop after whom it was named. It was a Catholic movement that was condemned as a kind of quasi-Calvinism in its emphasis on human sinfulness and its seeming denial of free will.

At various times Jansenism was condemned by the pope, by the Sorbonne, and by the crown, and each time the Jansenists' response was to reformulate their teachings, a strategy that led merely to further condemnations, culminating in a 1713 decree by Pope Clement XI that some French bishops refused to accept.[21] As the battle escalated, the Parlement of Paris made use of Jansenist grievances, without sharing Jansenist beliefs, in order to increase its authority over church affairs, a way both of affirming Gallicanism and of putting limits on royal power. The Jansenists were thus allied with the Parlement in attempting to check royal authority, with the Gallicans in rejecting much of papal authority, and with the lower clergy in undermining episcopal authority. They managed to build a quasi–underground network, including an effective clandestine press, and waged a propaganda war against both civil and ecclesiastical authorities.

The Jesuits were Jansenism's greatest antagonists[22] and at the same time themselves the target of increasing hostility on the part of Catholic monarchs[23] because they were directly subject to the pope. They were dubbed Ultramontanists because their loyalty was "across the mountains" (the Alps). In 1761, the Parlement forbade the Jesuits to accept new members and closed its schools, and a few years later Jesuit involvement in the Caribbean trade led to their being sued by various creditors, which gave the Parlement an opportunity to urge their expulsion from France as enemies of the crown. Louis XV reluctantly agreed because he needed the Parlement's help in his chronic financial troubles.

Mary Stuart returned to her native Scotland as queen in 1561, having been widowed by Francis II of France and suspected of being under the influence of his mother Catherine de Medici. The Presbyterian movement had firmly established itself during her absence, and both her Catholicism and the byzantine intrigues at her court led to a rebellion that forced her to flee to England.[24] The kirk, organized along Presbyterian lines that might be considered republican, was independent of both the crown and the weak system of episcopacy that survived in Scotland.

In Spain, the Inquisition continued, under royal control.[25] Protestantism was virtually unknown and the influence of skeptical ideas was minimal, so that its chief targets were *conversos* suspected of remaining faithful to Judaism or Islam. In 1609, the crown decreed the expulsion of all Muslims remaining in the kingdom. When Charles V abdicated at the time of the Peace of Augsburg, he divided his empire, placing the Netherlands under Spain.[26] The Netherlands over time had become the most religiously diverse society in Europe, including a majority of Catholics—along with Calvinists, Lutherans, Anabaptists, and Jews—all of whom were tolerated as long as they were economically productive.

From faraway in Spain, Philip II attempted to consolidate his rule, including a draconian attempt to suppress heresy. The various religious groups did not necessarily respect one another, but all of them, including the Catholics, resented Spanish rule. As Philip's oppression deepened, resistance mounted under the leadership of some of the nobility, especially William of Orange, a lukewarm Catholic who became a Lutheran and eventually a Calvinist, since the Calvinist burghers of Holland, although only a small minority of the whole population of the Netherlands, were the backbone of the resistance. The estates of the northern Netherlands formally deposed Philip for having mistreated his subjects. Most Catholics probably supported the revolt, which was more political than religious. But as the rebellion succeeded, Calvinists began to see it primarily in religious terms. Mobs attacked Catholics, something that Orange opposed, although for the sake of public order he acquiesced in a temporary ban on Catholicism in some of the northern provinces. The southern provinces—roughly modern Belgium—were, in turn, motivated to make peace with Philip. As the split between north and south became unbridgeable, William of Orange was assassinated by a Catholic in 1584, but by that time the northern provinces had successfully repulsed the Spanish, who were eventually forced to agree to a truce. Although the United Provinces remained the most religiously tolerant nation in Europe, extending tolerance even to Jews, Catholics, and Anabaptists, this tolerance was limited to the right to practice their faiths in private. Such groups could not have houses of worship and were excluded from public life.[27] Complete tolerance was not extended even to Protestants. In the early seventeenth century, the Reformed church was deeply split between orthodox Calvinists and Arminians[28] (a school of theology based on the teachings of Dutch theologian Jacob Arminius, for whom it is named), who were accused of smuggling elements of free will and human merit into their account of salvation.

In 1618, the Synod of Dordrecht (Dort) condemned Arminianism and attempted to expel its adherents from the church. The condemned fought back under the designation of Remonstrants. Jan van Oldenbarnevelt, the advocate of Holland, and Count Maurice of Nassau, son of William the Silent, were ranged on opposite sides in the dispute, which was as much about princely versus republican dominance as it was about religion. Although Calvinists were still a minority in the United Provinces, Maurice triumphed by espousing the anti-Remonstrant cause, and Oldenbarnevelt was executed. The expiration of the Netherlandish truce with Spain was one of the causes of the Thirty Years' War, and at the end of the war, Spain was forced to recognize the permanent independence of the United Provinces, while the southern Netherlands remained Catholic under Hapsburg rule.

Along with the United Provinces, Poland was the most tolerant state in Europe in 1600.[29] There was a great deal of anti-Hapsburg feeling, and Lutherans, Calvinists, and others had settled in the kingdom. The monarchy was elective, the nobles had great power, and successive kings showed no desire to persecute heretics. After 1573, each new king had to swear to protect the religious liberties of his subjects, although this extended only to the nobility. Toleration was also officially limited to Trinitarians. Both a schismatic Calvinist group dubbed the Arians and the followers of the Italian Unitarian Faustus Socinus, who settled in Poland, were suppressed in the course of the seventeenth century. Hungary had a similar history, moving from a religiously diverse, tolerant society after the Reformation to an enforced Catholicism a century later, much of the enforcement being the work of the German emperors.[30]

It was in England that the complex relations between church and state had the most far-reaching consequences in the seventeenth century. From the beginning, the English Reformation was an act of state, with bewilderingly contradictory religious changes decreed by successive monarchs and parliaments. During the reign of Elizabeth I, the dissident Anglicans, who came to be called Puritans, increasingly objected to the episcopacy and to religious ritual, both of which they saw as unbiblical and "papist."[31] But the crown itself authorized those things, so that the Puritan stance seemed to be an implicit rejection of the royal supremacy, to which defenders of these *adiaphora*—things neither forbidden nor required by Scripture—appealed. The bishops were the appointed agents of the crown, their office established by statute and required for the sake of good order, so that those who rejected *adiaphora* were therefore seen not as exercising legitimate freedom but as disobedient subjects.

The Puritans agitated in Parliament for further religious changes, which Elizabeth bluntly rejected. They also engaged in a pamphlet war, much of it from the safety of the Continent, attacking episcopacy and advocating either a congregational or a presbyterian system of church government. But by the mid-1580s, the movement had lost much of its energy. Those Elizabethan Puritans called Separatists, from whom the New England Puritans derived, explicitly rejected the royal supremacy and the idea of an established church. A few were put to death as traitors.

Catholics under Elizabeth occupied a precarious position. Officially outlawed, they were sporadically fined for not adhering to the Church of England, to which many conformed on an occasional basis.[32] However, especially after Pope Pius V excommunicated Elizabeth in 1570 and released her subjects from their obedience, all priests were viewed as traitors and if caught were hanged, often along with the lay people who harbored them. There were a few abortive plots against the crown, some with the aim of putting Mary Stuart on the throne. In 1605, disappointed that the new king, James I, had not substantially lessened their burdens, a small group of Catholics conspired in the Gunpowder Plot to annihilate both king and Parliament.[33]

Ironically, although James ascended the throne of Scotland because his mother had been overthrown in a rebellion that was as much religious as political, he was a strong proponent of divine-right monarchy[34] and detested the boldness with which the Presbyterian clergy presumed to rebuke their king.[35] At the beginning of his reign in England, he accurately perceived that the Puritan clergy were independent-minded, uttering his famous warning, "No bishop, no king."

James took much direct interest in religion, involving himself in the last executions for heresy in England in 1612, when two anti-Trinitarians were burned, and commanding the translation of the Bible that came to be known by his name. But like other monarchs of the age, James did not allow religion to dictate his foreign policy. In the face of parliamentary demands to the contrary, he gave only slight assistance to the French Huguenots and to his son-in-law Frederick of the Palatinate, and he outraged many people by seeking an alliance with Catholic Spain.[36]

The split between the monarchy and the Puritans came to a head under James's son Charles I,[37] particularly under Archbishop William Laud,[38] who emphasized precisely the things the Puritans most detested—the authority of bishops and ritual worship. Laud attempted to enforce and even extend practices that the Puritans considered popish, and those who attacked him in print were severely punished. Charles was in agreement with Laud's policies and saw attacks on his archbishop as attacks on the royal supremacy itself. When, at Laud's urging, the *Book of Common Prayer* was introduced into Scotland, it provoked rebellion that soon escalated into the Bishops' War north of the border. In 1640, this necessitated Charles calling Parliament, for the first time in eleven years, in order to finance the war. Years of frustrated grievances—some religious, some secular—suddenly exploded.[39] The king was confronted with a firestorm of demands, which included the execution of Laud for treason, an action in which Charles passively acquiesced. When negotiations between king and Parliament broke down completely, both sides took to arms in a civil war, during which Parliament effected the dismemberment of the Anglican Church while leaving open the question of what would replace it. The New Model Army,[40] heavily composed of ardent Puritans fighting against what they considered an evil monarchy, was itself a religious community. Gambling and other common soldierly vices were banned, and troopers heard daily sermons and marched into battle singing psalms.

Parliament won the war and, after complex political maneuvering, Charles was beheaded. Over the centuries, kings had sometimes been killed, but for the first time in history a king was formally executed, treason being defined no longer as an offense against the king but as an offense against the kingdom. The execution of the king and the abolition of the monarchy could only be justified as the will of God. A split then developed between Parliament, many of whose members were Presbyterians who would have preserved a limited monarchy, and the army, many of whom were Independents or Congregationalists and favored some republican form of government. Both favored a state church but disagreed as to its form, and some Independents supported religious toleration.[41]

Oliver Cromwell, the general who successfully pushed for the king's execution, became a kind of mediator between Parliament and the army; when he found Parliament intractable, he did not hesitate to dissolve it on his own authority and hold new elections, in one instance allowing the Puritan clergy to nominate those eligible to serve. But as parliamentary government failed, Cromwell assumed more and more authority, in the semimonarchical role of Lord Protector, pursuing policies that might be called theocratic. Like Calvin, the Puritans believed that the glory of God required that the customs of society be brought as far as possible into conformity with the divine law, especially through the regulation of public morals, in ways that gave rise to the popular meaning of the word *puritan*. Both Presbyterians and Independents favored a state church while disagreeing as to its form. But England no longer had such a church, and the uncorking of religious enthusiasm and the abolition of episcopal authority led to a instantaneous proliferation of religious groups that might be broadly called Puritan.[42] Cromwell tolerated all of them, including Quakers and other radical groups, and he invited the Jews back into England after almost four centuries. Parliament sometimes pushed him to be less tolerant, and he in turn, pointing out that England no longer had laws against heresy, faulted Parliament for its severe punishment of a Quaker accused of blasphemy. But Cromwell did not tolerate Anglicanism and Catholicism. During the war, he dealt brutally with Catholics in both England and Ireland, and in Ireland he began the policy of seizing the lands of the Catholic nobility and settling English and Scottish Protestants in their place.[43] Once again, religion did not dictate foreign policy. Despite their long-standing mutual sympathy, England and the United Provinces twice went to war under Cromwell, in rivalry over international trade.[44]

At the Restoration, Charles II[45] proposed a policy of limited religious tolerance, but the staunchly Anglican Parliament rejected the idea and Dissenters (non-Anglican Protestants) were barely tolerated. (A few Anglicans advocated tolerance, even for Catholics.[46]) Officially, Catholics were not tolerated at all, and several were put to death in the fraudulent Popish Plot,[47] a miscarriage of justice that Charles permitted. But he became a Catholic on his deathbed, made a secret agreement with Louis XIV to restore England to the Catholic Church, and successfully fended off attempts to deny the throne to his Catholic brother James.

James II[48] sincerely desired religious tolerance (he was a patron of William Penn), but he encountered trouble; in 1688 he attempted to achieve it by royal edict, without parliamentary agreement, and arrested seven bishops who refused to promulgate his decree.[49]

When his wife gave birth to a son, thereby ensuring a Catholic succession, some of the leading men of the kingdom invited his Protestant daughter Mary and her Netherlander husband William to take the throne, and James fled to France.[50]

As with the conversion of Henry IV of France, James's overthrow illustrated the belief that a monarch could not rule over a people most of whom were of a religion different from his own, although several German princes of the time in fact did so. (The Calvinist elector of Brandenburg gave Lutheranism a preferred place in his domains.) Several bishops and a number of other clergy (the Nonjurors), even though they had opposed James's policies, felt bound by their oath of obedience to him and refused to take the same oath to William III and Mary II. They were removed from their offices.[51]

After the Glorious Revolution of 1688, toleration of Dissenters was extended so far as to allow them to have "meeting houses" and to open schools, although they were still excluded from public life and there were numerous restrictions on their conduct. Catholics were still officially outlawed but were usually not prosecuted. At the same time, the Anglican Church attempted as far as possible to encompass Dissenters. Laud's "high church" policies were abandoned, and an increasingly latitudinarian theology prevailed.[52] The Restoration of the English monarchy did not help the Irish. Priests were outlawed and often persecuted by the British crown, but they came to replace the aristocracy as the leaders of Irish society, closely associating the church with liberation from English rule.[53] France was by no means the only place where the Catholic Church was under attack in the eighteenth century.

The Enlightenment's contempt for tradition of all kinds appealed to self-consciously enlightened rulers, who reorganized their realms in order to centralize their power and make it more efficient, a goal to which the church, and especially the papacy, was an at least passive obstacle.[54] Most of the "enlightened despots"[55] were not hostile to religion as such but thought of themselves as effecting reforms that would bring the church into harmony with the age. In accord with the Enlightenment idea that the purpose of religion was the improvement of society, the monastic orders were a special target, because the contemplative life seemed idle and unproductive. (Nursing orders of nuns were tolerated.)

Writing under the name of Justinus Febronius,[56] a German bishop revived late-medieval conciliar theories, making the pope merely a kind of presiding officer in the church and holding that diocesan bishops received their authority directly from Christ. In 1768, the diocese of Pistoia,[57] under the authority of the grand duke of Tuscany, officially espoused Jansenist doctrines about salvation, decreed the use of the vernacular in the liturgy, and proclaimed its essential independence from the papacy.

The Holy Roman Emperor Joseph II (1765–1790)[58] especially thought of himself as an enlightened despot and interested himself in religion to the point that he was dubbed "the sacristan emperor," even decreeing the number of candles on the altar at Mass, a policy of control of the church that came to be called Josephinism. Joseph II closed 700 monasteries, pruned the liturgical calendar (too many holy days interfered with productive labor), redrew diocesan boundaries, forbade the publication of papal bulls, and undertook supervision of the Catholic schools, including seminaries for the education of priests.

Portugal, during the ministry of the Marquis de Pombal,[59] took the lead in attacking the Jesuits. When an attempt was made on the king's life in 1758, Pombal blamed the Jesuits and effected their wholesale expulsion or imprisonment. One by one, Catholic states began expelling the Society of the Jesuits,[60] and in 1773, Clement XIV acquiesced in the suppression of the society, something that went completely against the papacy's interests and thereby demonstrated its impotence. Ironically, the Jesuits remained officially in existence only in Protestant Prussia and Orthodox Russia, whose rulers did not recognize the papal decree and valued the society's educational work.

The Protestant Reformation confronted European Christians of all kinds with the dilemma of how to relate to a ruler who presumably had his authority from God but who professed a false religion and even persecuted true believers. Sebastian Castellio of Basel[61] was one of the very few the Reformation leaders to advocate general toleration, first formulating the argument that would later become the basis of the religious (as distinct from political) case for tolerance—centuries of theological controversy showed that some things simply could not be known and certain passages of Scripture were simply opaque. There should be no persecution over nonessential beliefs, although it was precisely such beliefs that caused the most persecution.

Religious groups should be judged by their moral effects, not their doctrines, Castellio urged. Sincerity of conscience did not prove the validity of a belief, but such sincerity was necessary, because "I must be saved by my own faith and not that of another." A mistaken belief might serve as the foundation of a good moral life, although even Castellio thought that certain ideas should not be allowed to be preached. The Anabaptist David Joris[62] held similar views, especially emphasizing the wholly inward nature of religion, so that externals should not be a cause of conflict. Rather than persecution, suffering is the mark of the "true church."

The right of rebellion was taken to its farthest point in Scotland, where it justified the overthrow of Mary Stuart. John Knox, the Presbyterian leader—in a tract aimed at Mary Stuart, Mary I of England, and Catherine de Medici— appealed to Scripture to deny the legitimacy of any female rule.[63] (Published a year before she ascended the throne, it logically also caught Elizabeth I, to whom Knox had to explain that he meant only Catholic queens.) But the right of resistance almost always rested on belief in the truth of one's own faith and the falsehood of the ruler's and thus did not encompass general tolerance. Knox and other Scots advocated a theocratic state, to be established by force if necessary. George Buchanan[64] justified the overthrow of the queen by an appeal both to historical precedent and to a theory of contract between ruler and ruled, which in time became the basis of most arguments for the limitation of monarchy. Although some theory of divine-right monarchy was generally held in the seventeenth century, some theorists proposed that the religious character of the royal coronation ceremony itself bound the king to certain obligations to his subjects, just as his baptismal vows bound him to obligations to God.[65]

The men at the French court who favored religious tolerance for the sake of civil peace came to be called the *Politiques*.[66] Some of them made a strong argument for royal authority, in defense of the king's right to tolerate heresy, and over time *Politique* thought tended toward royal absolutism as the only guarantor of civil peace. In particular, rulers were not to be subject to spiritual authority. (Their critics, seeing this as mere political realism, recalled that Catherine de Medici was Italian and therefore dubbed them Machiavellians.)

Like the *Politiques*, William Barclay,[67] a Catholic Scot who lived in France, considered insurrection and civil war the greatest evils. But he went beyond the pragmatism of the *Politiques* and defended royal authority against those who would limit it, including his fellow Catholics, using the familiar arguments from Scripture and tracing all subversive ideas back to John Wyclif and other heretics. Jean Bodin,[68] the most important political theorist of the age, seems to have privately doubted the teachings of religion and to have believed that ultimate truth was unknowable. Publicly he was associated with the *Politiques*, giving to the state an absolute sovereignty that included the authority to grant religious toleration. Huguenot apologists devised various theories of limited monarchy, according to which the king's authority derived from the people and was subject to restraint by the magistrates.[69]

The anonymous *Vindiciae contra Tyranos* (1579),[70] probably written by Philippe Du Plessis de Mornay, posited a contract between the king and God, which the king forfeited if he was unfaithful. Making use of a restricted permission only cautiously allowed by John Calvin, the author of the *Vindiciae* justified rebellion if it was carried out by the "magistrates," a term construed to include the nobles who led the Huguenot resistance. On the other side the Catholic League—supporters of the Guises—also put forth theories of limited monarchy, of the right of resistance, even of tyrannicide, because the Valois kings were not maintaining the Catholic faith as they should.[71]

The Dutch jurist Johannes Althusius[72] described society as a hierarchy of semiautonomous communities, beginning with the family and culminating in the state, and he, too, allowed the people to recall power given to their rulers. But Althusius also held that the "true church" alone should be recognized in the Commonwealth and should be promoted by the authorities, and he apparently assumed that Calvinism was that church. The "true and pure religion" was not to be established "by a majority of the citizens . . . but by the Word of God alone." Atheists or "libertines" should not be tolerated, according to Althusius. Jews and papists could be tolerated but should be segregated and not allowed to have houses of worship. Heretics should be excluded from public life; but if a heretic were elected, the "orders" should instruct him in the true faith. There could be coercion of external actions, even to the point of expulsion from the Commonwealth, but not of matters of belief, because religious persecution caused civil disorder, as shown in France and other nations. There should be no schism over theological issues that were not fundamental to the faith. Althusius's Commonwealth was theocratic in that each precept of the Decalogue was political, to be translated into civil law, with the civil magistrates regulating both morals and the enforcement of ecclesiastical decrees. "Sound worship and fear of God" were the bases of peace and good order, although conscience was given by God to men in order to understand the law, and even a heathen could be an upright man in civic life. The ruler made a contract with God and, again following Calvin, Althusius held that the "ephors" should rebuke the a magistrate who strayed from his duty;; in extreme cases, they might even "impede" his tyranny, as happened in the Netherlands under Philip II.

Another Netherlandish jurist, Hugo Grotius,[73] an exile from his native country after the fall of Oldenbarnevelt, also based the state on natural law, which, he said, exists in order to fulfill the needs of its people. He held that natural law, which is known by reason, could exist even without God, but law is based on the divine will and God is the ultimate vindicator of justice, without whom justice would not be seen to triumph. He punishes evildoers in eternity and often in time as well. Unusual for his time, Grotius included Catholics in a proposed great reunion of all Christians.[74]

The Portuguese-Dutch Jew Baruch Spinoza,[75] who was expelled from the synagogue as a suspected atheist, saw the state as an arrangement in which a multitude of individuals each sought their own self-interest. There was to be no coercion in matters of religion, but the state was to maintain peace among the various religious groups.

The German jurist Samuel Pufendorf[76] held that in entering into the social contract, people did not surrender their religious beliefs. He favored a state church, with clergy appointed by the government, but there was to be no coercion of belief.

In England, by contrast with Scotland, most theologians upheld the royal supremacy in religion, a claim they thought had been usurped by the pope.[77] For Richard Hooker,[78] who became the principal Anglican apologist, England was a single Commonwealth under a divinely appointed ruler, the established church was one embodiment of that Commonwealth, and ecclesiastical laws were binding on all subjects. However, Hooker also held a contractual theory, according to which any form of government is theoretically possible and the consent of the community could in principle be rescinded. Human beings are guided primarily by reason, implanted by God. Far from the *adiaphora* being an area of prudential freedom in the church, Hooker held that they required decisions by the authorities for the sake of good order.

Those who rejected episcopacy or clerical vestments in the name of Scripture were not exercising legitimate freedom but were merely disobedient subjects. But while Hooker demanded uniformity of practice and church polity, he favored limited toleration of theological opinion, because some truths were unknowable and controversy was therefore destructive. The church should require adherence only to a basic creed common to all Christians.

Puritan ideas were, of course, quite different. The Separatist leader Robert Browne,[79] who subsequently returned to the Anglican Church, advocated religious toleration on the grounds that the state had no right to interfere with the church, which was the gathered body of true believers. The Separatists advocated only passive resistance to authority, but a few Separatist leaders were hanged as traitors for denying both the royal supremacy and the idea of an established church.[80] As the Puritans pondered the ultimately insoluble problem of how to serve two monarchs—the divine and the human—those whom they regarded as the epitome of false religion, the Catholics, were wrestling with the same dilemma.

The Italian Jesuit Robert Bellarmine[81] refuted the theory of the divine right of kings as expounded by James I, primarily in order to affirm papal authority over monarchs but in the process offering cautious validation of the will of the people. According to Bellarmine, although the pope had no direct authority in temporal affairs, he alone had authority directly from God and could depose monarchs who interfered with the spiritual welfare of their subjects, from whom the ruler had received only delegated authority. The Spanish Jesuits Juan de Mariana and Francisco Suarez[82] were even more direct in justifying popular sovereignty, positing government as growing out of a state of nature, based on human needs and therefore deriving from a contract between ruler and ruled. Mariana condemned Henry IV of France as a tyrant in the classic sense and explicitly justified tyrannicide. The English Jesuit Robert Parsons[83] claimed that the king's entire duty was the welfare of his subjects, of which their religion was the most important, and that dereliction of that duty meant that he was no longer king. Anticipating the Protestant Stuart succession in England, Parsons asserted that the traditional laws of succession, which were merely man-made, were to be abrogated in the interests of religion.

Puritan theory of resistance to the crown came to a head under Charles I and Laud. The lawyer William Prynne,[84] whom Laud severely punished, placed the authority of Parliament above that of the king, who was the servant of his people and could be judged by the natural law. But in time, the Presbyterians, including Prynne, became more favorable to royal authority in the face of what they considered dangerous religious radicalism.

John Milton,[85] addressing Parliament during the Civil War, went even farther than Castellio in employing arguments that seemed to question the very possibility of religious truth. Good and evil grow up inextricably mixed, so that what might be harmful to one person might be profitable to another, and a heretic is one "who believes the truth only because it is told to him." The Golden Rule was to continue seeking the truth. The perfection of the church, therefore, consisted of many different sects and groups, just as a building consisted of many different pieces. God caused the truth "to appear in places we do not expect, and He causes great commotions." But Milton also warned Parliament that it should not tolerate either popery or "open superstition," because both sought to overthrow the state.

The Leveller movement[86] emerged in the New Model Army and had its roots in radical Independency, although many of the Independents came to distrust it and argued for strong government, including coercion in religious matters. John Lilburne, the principal Leveller spokesman, condemned monarchy as a form of idolatry and, after falling afoul of Parliament, attributed sovereignty to the nation at large. The Levellers opposed Cromwell and agitated for a more democratic government. Some Levellers (although not Lilburne himself) argued for some kind of redistribution of property and even for a version of communism, based on the belief that such had been the case at the time of the creation of the world. Gerard Winstanley called Christ "the head Leveller," favored toleration even for Catholics, and proposed that the clergy confine their teachings to those things that could be learned from nature. In the religious tropical jungle of the Commonwealth and Protectorate, every kind of Christian sect flourished. The Fifth Monarchy Men,[87] who took their name from the Book of Daniel, expected the imminent Second Coming of Christ and sought to hasten it by military means, if necessary.

Thomas Hobbes,[88] the most important political thinker of the age, was suspected of atheism, partly because he tried to base his political philosophy ultimately on a purely material foundation—the laws of motion. Although he justified strong government, even tyranny, he did so on a naturalistic basis, depriving kingship of its millennia-old religious aura. Much of his text of *Leviathan* was taken up with a lengthy discourse on the authority of Scripture, but in some passages Hobbes seemed to offer a wholly naturalistic explanation of religion. Too often, people mistook religion for "divinity," he complained, by which he meant the authority of the clergy. Hobbes denounced the Presbyterian clergy for "preaching up rebellion" to their own advantage, using dishonest means to do so. The universities that produced the seditious preachers were to England what the wooden horse had been to the Trojans. But the Anglican bishops had also erred in rejecting papal monarchy but continuing to claim that they themselves received authority from Christ's apostles. True religion ought to be a quiet waiting for Christ's Second Coming, eschewing all theological disputation, endeavoring to lead a good moral life, and obeying the laws of the king, which are also the laws of

God. Hobbes may or may not have been a religious believer. By implication, he seemed to enjoin obedience to the official religion, irrespective of its truth.

John Locke[89] was the principal theorist of tolerance in the age of the Glorious Revolution, famously urging freedom for all forms of Christianity except Catholicism, which he accused of being politically subversive, and also excluding atheists from the Commonwealth because they could not swear trustworthy oaths. Much of Locke's argument was pragmatic, such as his expectation that religious groups that showed subversive tendencies (but not, apparently, Catholics) would become loyal subjects if they were tolerated.

The Commonwealth existed only to help men advance their "civil interests," and neither God nor the people had given the magistrate any authority over men's souls. Nothing that was lawful in private life—ceremonies involving bread and wine, for example, or wearing certain clothes—could be lawfully forbidden in public. No one could demand a particular polity for the church without showing "very express and positive commands of Christ," which in reality they could not do. The fact that theological disputes continued even among those who agreed about church polity showed how uncertain such beliefs really were and gave people legitimate room to choose. Membership in the church should depend on the acceptance of only those things the Holy Spirit had explicitly revealed as necessary for salvation. "Man-made" doctrines should not be imposed on the Scripture, the meaning of which was plain to all sincere Christians. Such impositions were the only true heresy, so that tolerance was precisely the mark of the true church. Men were not nearly so zealous in rooting out vice as they were in combating what they considered false doctrine, even though it was vice, not doctrine, that damned the soul. No man could allow his religion to be chosen for him by another, since religion was a matter of "inward persuasion of mind" and could not be subject to external coercion.

But even though Locke allowed the political community to recall its grant of authority to its sovereign, he insisted that no individual could disobey the command of a lawful government, even if that command was thought to be in error. Perhaps the most important aspect of Locke's thought about religion was his definition of a church as "a free and voluntary society," which was by no means a self-evident claim in an age when all nations had official state churches. The only discipline for religious error was exclusion from the church. Locke wrote in part to refute Robert Filmer,[90] who offered a traditional defense of monarchy as divinely ordained. Locke denied that the authority of a father over his children was applicable in politics and claimed that the idea of divine-right monarchy was unheard of prior to "the divinity" (that is, certain clergy) of the age just previous to his own.

Jacques-Bénigne Bossuet was the most important apologist for divine-right monarchy in the late seventeenth century. The title of his book, *Politics Drawn from the Very Words of Holy Scripture*,[91] was self-explanatory in citing the kings of the Old Testament as models for later monarchies, but he also cited the infidelities of the Hebrew kings and insisted that kings must obey the law.

The French Calvinist Pierre Bayle, an exile in Holland, was suspected of being a secret nonbeliever, since in his great *Dictionary*[92] he emphasized the innumerable disagreements among religious individuals and groups and the difficulty of knowing certain truth.

Against the revocation of the Edict of Nantes, he advocated complete religious tolerance, including Catholics and Muslims, based on liberty of conscience, a position that many of his fellow Huguenots rejected. But conscience, in turn, had to be subject to the judgments of reason, and Bayle candidly raised the perplexing question of the authority of conscience to dictate tyrannicide or persecution, concluding that each person had an obligation to follow conscience, but that the authorities also had an obligation to punish such actions.

Church–state relations in early modern Europe were complex, shifting, and paradoxical, with religion serving both as the moral foundation for obedience to the state and as the justification for rebellion. At no other time in history was it more obvious that religion both unites and divides. Some of those who supported strong monarchy expected the monarch to enforce a single official religion, while others resisted royal authority precisely in order to claim religious freedom for themselves. Some supported strong monarchy so that the monarch would tolerate religious diversity, while others resisted royal authority precisely because the monarch permitted such diversity. In the period prior to the French Revolution, there were few if any comprehensive theories of human rights, but there were many assertions of religious liberty, which thereby became the historic basis of all other rights.

Advocates of religious tolerance on theological grounds offered arguments that they considered virtually self–evident—true Christians suffered but did not persecute; true religion was inward; religious beliefs were uncertain and readily disputed; unanimity of belief was not necessary; morals had primacy over dogma. In the long run, their arguments prevailed in religious circles, but the arguments inevitably worked against them at the time because they seemed to imply that tolerance required religious indifference. Could tolerance then be extended to those deemed to be intolerant? The theorists of tolerance did not transcend religious differences, as they claimed, but in a sense formulated a new kind of orthodoxy. It was first in the United States—and for a time only there—that full civil tolerance was seen as compatible with the religious dogmatism of both individuals and organized churches. In early modern Europe, toleration was almost always granted for pragmatic secular motives, chiefly the avoidance of religious strife—believers being forced by the state to live with their differences.

But absolute rulers also granted tolerance precisely because they did not want a church with authority of its own. Subjects freed from obligations to an official church might thereby more readily conform to the requirements of the centralizing state, a process that began with the enlightened despots and culminated in the French Revolution and the "laicizing" states of the nineteenth century.

REFERENCES

Abercrombie, N. J. *The Origins of Jansenism*. Oxford: Clarendon Press, 1936.

Allen, J. W. *A History of Political Thought in the Sixteenth Century*. London: Methuen, 1951.

Althusius, Johannes. *Politics*, translated by Frederick S. Carney. Boston: Beacon Press, 1964.

Bangert, William V., S. J. *History of the Society of Jesus*. St. Louis, MO: Institute of Jesuit Sources, 1986.

Barclay, William. *De Potestate Papae* (English translation Menston, UK: Scholar Press, 1973).

Bayle, Pierre. *Dictionary Historical and Critical*. Oxford: Voltaire Foundation, 1989.

———. *Political Writings* (ed. Sally L. Jenkinson). New York: Cambridge University Press, 2000.

Bellarmine, Robert. *De Laicis. Treatise on Civil Government* (tr. Kathleen E. Murphy). New York: Fordham University Press, 1928.

Blanning, T.C.W. *Joseph II and Enlightened Despotism*. New York: Harper and Row, 1970.

Bodin, Jean. *Six Books of the Commonwealth*, translated by M. J. Tooley. Oxford: Blackwell, 1967.

Boussuet, Jacques-Bénigne. *Politics Drawn from the Very Words of Holy Scripture*. Translated by Patrick Riley. Cambridge, UK: Cambridge University Press, 1990

Boyer, Richard E. *England's Declarations of Indulgence*. Paris: The Hague, 1968.

Brailsford, H. N. *The Levellers*. London: Cresset Press, 1961.

Breslaw, Marvin A. (ed.). *The Political Writings of John Knox*. Washington, DC: Associated University Presses, 1985.

Brown, Harold E. *Juan de Mariana and Early Modern Spanish Religious Thought*. Burlington, VT: Ashgate, 2007.

Browne, Robert. *The Writings of Robert Harrison and Robert Browne* (Albert Peel and Leland H. Carlson, eds). London: Allen and Unwin, 1953.

Buchanan, George. *Critical Edition of G. Buchanan's Baptiste*, edited by Stephen Berkovitz. New York: Garland, 1972.

———. *Dialogue Concerning Laws and Kingship among the Scots*. Edited by Roger A. Mason and Martin C. Smith. Burlington, VT: Ashgate Publishing Limited, 2004.

Capps, B. S. *The Fifth Monarchy Men*. Totowa, NJ: Capps Publishing, 1972.

Carlton, Charles. *Archbishop Laud*. New York: Routledge Kegen & Paul, 1987.

Carrier, Irene. *James VI and I*. New York: Cambridge University Press, 1998.

Carroll, Stuart. *Martyrs and Murderers*. New York: Oxford University Press, 2009.

Carswell, John. *The Descent on England*. New York: John Day Co., 1969.

Castellio, Sebastian. *Advice to Desolate France*. Edited with an introduction by Marius F. Valkhoff, translated by Wouter Valkhoff. Shepherdstown, WV: Patmos Press, 1975.

———. *Concerning Heretics*. New York: Columbia University Press, 1935.

The Catholic Encyclopedia, VI. "Febronianism." New York: Robert Appleton Co., 1909.

Church, William F. *Richelieu and Reasons of State*. Princeton: Princeton University Press, 1970.

Collinson, Patrick. *The Elizabethan Puritan Movement*. Berkeley, CA: University of California Press, 1971.

Conyers, A. J. *The Long Truce*. Dallas: Spence Publishing, 2001.

Cragg, Gerald. *From Puritanism to the Age of Reason*. Cambridge, UK: Cambridge University Press, 1950.

Daniel-Rops, Henri. *The Church in the Eighteenth Century*. New York: Dutton, 1964.

———. *The Church in the Seventeenth Century*. New York: Image Books, 1961.

Diefendorf, Barbara B. *Beneath the Cross: Catholics and Huguenots in Sixteenth-Century France*. New York: Oxford University Press, 1991.

Donaldson, Gordon. *The Scottish Reformation*. Cambridge: Cambridge University Press, 1960.

Doyle, William. *Jansenism: Catholic Resistance to Authority from the Reformation to the French Revolution*. New York: St. Martin's Press, 2000.

Du Plessis De Morney, Phillippe. *Vindiciae contra Tyranos* 1579. Translated by George Garrett. Cambridge: Cambridge University Press, 1994.

Figgis, J. N. *Studies of Political Thought from Gerson to Grotius*. Cambridge, UK: Batoche Books, 1916.

Filmer, Robert. *Patriarca*. Oxford: Oxford University Press, 1949.

Fischlin, Daniel, and Mark Fortier, ed. *The True Law of Free Monarchies and Basilikon Doron*. By James VI/I. Toronto: Centre for Reformation and Renaissance Studies, 1996.

Fitzgerald, Brendan. *Seventeenth-Century Ireland*. Totowa, NJ: Barnes and Nobles Books, 1989.

Franklin, Julian H. (ed.). *Constitutional and Resistance Treatises in the Sixteenth Century*. New York: Pegasus, 1969.

Geyl, Peter. *The Revolt of the Netherlands*. New York: Barnes and Noble, 1958.

———. *The Netherlands in the Seventeenth Century*, I. London: Benn, 1961.

Gooch, George Peabody. *English Democratic Ideas*. Cambridge, UK: Cambridge University Press, 1927.

Goubert, Pierre. *Louis XIV and Twenty Million Frenchmen*. New York: Pantheon Books, 1970.

Grotius, Hugo. *De Imperio Summorum Potestatum* (English translation). Boston, MA: Brill Academic Publishing, 2001.

Hamilton, Bernice. *Political Thought in Sixteenth-Century Spain*. Oxford: Clarendon Press, 1963.

Hatton, Ragnhild (ed.), *Louis XIV and Europe*. London: Macmillan, 1976.

Hill, Christopher. *The World Turned Upside Down*. New York: Maurice Temple Smith, 1972.

Hobbes, Thomas. *Leviathan* (ed. Richard Tuck). Cambridge, UK; New York: publisher, 1991.

Hogge, Alice. *God's Secret Agents*. New York: Harper Collins Publisher, 2005.

Holborn, Hajo. *A History of Modern Germany: 1648–1840*, II. New Jersey: Princeton University Press, 1964.

———. *A History of Modern Germany: The Reformation*. New Jersey: Princeton University Press, 1959.

Hooker, Richard. *The Laws of Ecclesiastical Polity*. Cambridge, MA: Belknap Press of Harvard University, 1977–1982, four volumes.

Hutton, Ronald. *Charles II*. New York: Oxford University Press, 1989.

Joris, David. *The Anabaptist Writings of David Joris*, tr. Gary K. Waite. Scottdale, PA: Herald Press, 1994.

Kamen, Henry. *Inquisition and Society in Spain*. Indianapolis: Indiana University Press, 1985.

———. *The Rise of Toleration*. London: Weidenfeld & Nicolson, 1967.

Kenyon, John P. *The Popish Plot*. New York: St. Martin's Press, 1972.

Kirby, Ethlyn William. *William Prynne*. New York: Russell & Russell, 1972.

Kishlansky, Mark. *The Rise of the New Model Army*. Cambridge: Cambridge University Press, 1980.

Knecht, R. J. *The French Civil Wars, 1562–98*. New York: Longman, 2000.

Lamont, William M. *Marginal Prynne*. London: Routledge & Kegan Paul, 1963.

Locke, John. *Two Treatises on Government. Epistola de Tolerantia*. New Haven, CT: Yale University Press, 2003.

Lynch, John. *Spain under the Hapsburgs*, II. New York: New York University Press, 1969.

Mason, Roger A. (ed.). *John Knox on Rebellion*. New York: Cambridge University Press, 1994.

Miller, John. *James II*. New Haven, CT: Yale University Press, 2000.

Miller, S. J. *Portugal and Rome*. Rome: Universitá Gregoriana, 1978.

Milton, John. *Aeropagitica*. New York: AMS Press, 1971.

Mousnier, Roland. *The Assassination of Henry IV*. London: Faber and Faber, 1973.

Parker, Charles H. *Faith on the Margins*. Cambridge: Harvard University Press, 2008.

Parsons, Robert A. *A Conference about the Right Succession to the Crowne of England*. Menston, UK: Scholar Press, 1972.

Pearse, Michael T. *Between Known Men and Visible Saints*. New Jersey: Associated University Presses, 1994.

Pufendorf, Samuel. *On the Nature and Qualification of Religion in Relation to Civil Society* (tr. Jodocus Crull). Indianapolis, IN: Liberty Fund, 2002.

Richardt, Aimé. *Fenelon*. Paris: In Fine, 1993.

Root, Ivan. *Commonwealth and Protectorate*. New York: Schocken Books, 1966.

Russell, Conrad. *The Causes of the English Civil War*. New York: Oxford University Press, 1990.

Scott, H. M. (ed.). *Enlightened Despotism*. Ann Arbor, MI: University of Michigan Press, 1990.

Sharpe, Kevin. *The Personal Rule of Charles I*. New Haven: Yale University Press, 1992.

Sonnino, Paul. *Louis XIV's View of the Papacy*. Berkeley, CA: University of California Press, 1960.

Spellman, W. M. *Latitudinarians and the Church of England*. Athens, GA: University of Georgia Press, 1993.

Spinoza, Baruch *Cogita Metaphysica* (English translation). Indianapolis, IN: Thoemmes Press, 2002.

———. *Letters to Friend and Foe*, translated by Dagobert D. Runes. New York: Philosophical Society, 1966.

Straka, Gerald M. *Anglican Reactions to the Revolution of 1688*. Madison, WI: The State Historical Society of Wisconsin, 1962.

Treasure, G.R.R. *Cardinal Richelieu and the Development of French Absolutism*. New York: St. Martin's Press, 1972.

Trimble, William Raleigh. *The Catholic Laity in Elizabethan England*. Cambridge: Harvard University Press, 1964.

Van Kley, Dale K. *Jansenists and the Expulsion of the Jesuits from France*. New Haven, CT: Yale University Press, 1975.

Vierhaus, Rudolf. *Germany in the Age of Absolutism*. New York: Cambridge University Press, 1988.

Wilson, C. H. *Profit and Power* (London, New York: Longmans, Green, 1957).

Wilson, Peter H. *The Thirty Years War: Europe's Tragedy*. London: Penguin Books Ltd., 2009.

NOTES

1. Hajo Holborn, *A History of Modern Germany: The Reformation* (New Jersey: Princeton University Press, 1959), 201–248.

2. Ibid., 249–283.

3. Ibid., 305–360; Peter H. Wilson, *The Thirty Years War: Europe's Tragedy* (London: Penguin Books Ltd., 2009).

4. Henri Daniel-Rops, *The Church in the Seventeenth Century* (New York: Image Books, 1961), 146–149.

5. Holborn, *History*, I, 361–373.

6. Daniel-Rops, *Church in Seventeenth Century*, 146–149.

7. Holborn, A *History of Modern Germany: 1648-1840*, II (New Jersey: Princeton University Press, 1964), 3–67; Rudolf Vierhaus, *Germany in the Age of Absolutism* (New York: Cambridge University Press, 1988).

8. Barbara B. Diefendorf, *Beneath the Cross: Catholics and Huguenots in Sixteenth-Century France* (New York: Oxford University Press, 1991); R. J. Knecht, *The French Civil Wars, 1562–98* (New York: Longman, 2000).

9. Roland Mousnier, *The Assassination of Henry IV* (London: Faber and Faber, 1973).

10. Daniel-Rops, *Church in Seventeenth Century*, 1–117.

11. G.R.R. Treasure, *Cardinal Richelieu and the Development of French Absolutism* (New York: St. Martin's Press, 1972); William F. Church, *Richelieu and Reasons of State* (Princeton: Princeton University Press, 1970).

12. Daniel-Rops, *Church in Seventeenth Century*, 1–117.

13. Pierre Goubert, *Louis XIV and Twenty Million Frenchmen* (New York: Pantheon Books, 1970), 149–162; Daniel-Rops, *Church in Seventeenth Century*, 204–215.

14. Daniel-Rops, *Church in Seventeenth Century*, 204–215.

15. Goubert, *Louis XIV*, 149, 157, 174, 272–276.

16. Aimé Richardt, *Fenelon* (Paris: In Fine, 1993).

17. Paul Sonnino, *Louis XIV's View of the Papacy* (Berkeley, CA: University of California Press, 1960); Daniel-Rops, *Church in Seventeenth Century*, 215–224.

18. Goubert, *Louis XIV*, 193–270; Ragnhild Hatton (ed.), *Louis XIV and Europe* (London: Macmillian, 1976).

19. Holborn, *History*, II, 93–97.

20. N. J. Abercrombie, *The Origins of Jansenism* (Oxford: Clarendon Press, 1936); William Doyle, *Jansenism* (New York: St. Martin's Press, 2000).

21. Daniel-Rops, *Church in Seventeenth Century*, 327–413.

22. Dale K. Van Kley, *Jansenists and the Expulsion of the Jesuits from France* (New Haven, CT: Yale University Press?, 1975).

23. William V. Bangert, S. J., *History of the Society of Jesus* (St. Louis, MO: Institute of Jesuit Sources, 1986), 363–403.

24. Gordon Donaldson, *The Scottish Reformation* (Cambridge: Cambridge University Press, 1960).

25. John Lynch, *Spain under the Hapsburgs*, II (New York: New York University Press, 1969); Henry Kamen, *Inquisition and Society in Spain* (Indianapolis: Indiana University Press, 1985).

26. Peter Geyl, *The Revolt of the Netherlands* (New York: Barnes and Noble, 1958).

27. Charles H. Parker, *Faith on the Margins* (Cambridge: Harvard University Press, 2008).

28. Peter Geyl, *The Netherlands in the Seventeenth Century*, I (London: Benn, 1961).

29. Kamen, *The Rise of Toleration* (London: Weidenfeld & Nicolson, 1967), 119–128.

30. Ibid., 199–201.

31. Patrick Collinson, *The Elizabethan Puritan Movement* (Berkeley, CA: University of California Press, 1971); Michael T. Pearse, *Between Known Men and Visible Saints* (New Jersey: Associated University Presses, 1994); J. W. Allen, *A History of Political Thought in the Sixteenth Century* (London: Methuen, 1951), 210–230.

32. William Raleigh Trimble, *The Catholic Laity in Elizabethan England* (Cambridge: Harvard University Press, 1964).

33. Alice Hogge, *God's Secret Agents* (New York: Harper Collins Publisher, 2005).

34. Daniel Fischlin & Mark Fortier, ed. *The True Law of Free Monarchies and Basilikon Doron*. By James VI/I. Toronto: Centre for Reformation and Renaissance Studies, 1996.

35. Irene Carrier, *James VI and I* (New York: Cambridge University Press, 1998), 48–74.

36. Ibid., 124–139.

37. Kevin Sharpe, *The Personal Rule of Charles I* (New Haven: Yale University Press, 1992).

38. Charles Carlton, *Archbishop Laud* (New York: Routledge Kegen & Paul, 1987).

39. Conrad Russell, *The Causes of the English Civil War* (New York: Oxford University Press, 1990).

40. Mark Kishlansky, *The Rise of the New Model Army* (Cambridge: Cambridge University Press, 1980).

41. Ivan Root, *Commonwealth and Protectorate* (New York: Schocken Books, 1966).

42. Christopher Hill, *The World Turned Upside Down* (New York: Maurice Temple Smith, 1972).

43. Brendan Fitzgerald, *Seventeenth-Century Ireland* (Totowa, NJ: Barnes and Nobles Books, 1989); Root, *Commonwealth*, 154–162.

44. C. H. Wilson, *Profit and Power* (London, New York: Longmans, Green, 1957).

45. Ronald Hutton, *Charles II* (New York: Oxford University Press, 1989).

46. Kamen, *Rise*, 205.

47. John Kenyon, *The Popish Plot* (New York: St Martin's, 1972).

48. John Miller, *James II* (New Haven, CT: Yale University Press, 2000).

49. Richard E. Boyer, *England's Declarations of Indulgence* (Paris: The Hague, 1968).

50. John Carswell, *The Descent on England* (New York: John Day Co., 1969).

51. Gerald M. Straka, *Anglican Reactions to the Revolution of 1688* (Madison: The State Historical Society of Wisconsin, 1962).

52. Gerald Cragg, *From Puritanism to the Age of Reason* (Cambridge, UK: Cambridge University Press, 1950); W. M. Spellman, *Latitudinarians and the Church of England* (Athens, GA: University of Georgia Press, 1993).

53. Fitzgerald, *Seventeenth Century Ireland.*

54. For an extended discussion of this, see A. J. Conyers, *The Long Truce* (Dallas: Spence Publishing, 2001).

55. H. M. Scott (ed.), *Enlightened Despotism* (Ann Arbor, MI: University of Michigan Press, 1990).

56. "Febronianism," *The Catholic Encyclopedia*, VI (New York: Robert Appleton Company, 1909), 23–25.

57. Daniel-Rops, *The Church in the Eighteenth Century* (New York: Dutton, 1964), 353–354.

58. T.C.W. Blanning, *Joseph II and Enlightened Despotism* (New York: Harper and Row, 1970).

59. S. J. Miller, *Portugal and Rome* (Rome: Università Gregoriana, 1978).

60. Bangert, *History,* 363–403.

61. Sebastian Castellio *Advice to a Desolate France.* Edited, with an introduction, by Marius F. Valkhoff. Trans by Wouter Valkhoff (Shepherdstown, WV: West Virginia: Patmos Press, 1975); Sebastian Castellio *Concerning Heretics* (New York: Columbia University Press, 1935).

62. *The Anabaptist Writings of David Joris*, tr. Gary K. Waite (Scottdale, PA: Herald Press, 1994).

63. Roger A. Mason (ed.), *John Knox on Rebellion* (New York: Cambridge University Press 1994); Marvin A. Breslaw (ed.), *The Political Writings of John Knox* (Washington, DC: Associated University Presses, 1985).

64. *Critical Edition of G. Buchanan's Baptiste*, ed. Stephen Berkovitz (New York: Garland, 1972); *Dialogue Concerning Law and Kingship among the Scots*, ed. Roger A. Mason and Martin C. Smith (Burlington, VT: Ashgate Publishing Limited, 2004).

65. J. N. Figgis, *Studies of Political Thought from Gerson to Grotius* (Cambridge, UK: Batoche Books, 1916), 170.

66. Allen, *History*, 280–301, 367–393.

67. William Barclay, *De Potestate Papae* (English translation Menston, UK: Scolar Press, 1973).

68. Jean Bodin, *Six Books of the Commonwealth*, tr. M.J. Tooley (Oxford: Blackwell, 1967); Allen, *History*, 394–444.

69. Allen, *History*, 302–342.

70. Tr. George Garrett (Cambridge: Cambridge University Press, 1994); Julian H. Franklin (ed.), *Constitutional and Resistance Treatises in the Sixteenth Century* (New York: Pegasus, 1969).

71. Allen, *History*, 343–366; Stuart Carroll, *Martyrs and Murderers* (New York: Oxford University Press, 2009), 221–241.

72. *Politics*, tr. Frederick S. Carney (Boston: Beacon Press, 1964).

73. *De Imperio Summorum Potestatum* (English translation, Boston, MA: Brill Academic Publishing, 2001).

74. Kamen, *Rise*, 109. Kamen cites a few other examples on the radical fringes of the Reformation.

75. Spinoza, *Cogita Metaphysica* (English translation, Indianapolis, IN: Thoemmes Press, 2002); *Letters to Friend and Foe*, tr. Dagobert D. Runes (New York: Philosophical Society, 1966).

76. *On the Nature and Qualification of Religion in Relation to Civil Society*, tr. Jodocus Crull (Indianapolis, IN: Liberty Fund, 2002).

77. Allen, *History*, 159–171.

78. *The Laws of Ecclesiastical Polity* (Cambridge, MA: Belknap Press of Harvard University Press, 1977–1982), four volumes. Allen, *History*, 184–198, 231–246.

79. Robert Browne, *The Writings of Robert Harrison and Robert Browne,* eds Albert Peel and Leland H. Carlson (London: Allen and Unwin, 1953).

80. Gooch, George Peabody *English Democratic Ideas* (Cambridge, UK: Cambridge University Press, 1927) 42–44; Figgis, *Studies*, 132.

81. *De Laicis. Treatise on Civil Government*, tr. Kathleen E. Murphy (New York: Fordham University Press, 1928).

82. Bernice Hamilton, *Political Thought in Sixteenth-Century Spain* (Oxford: Clarendon Press, 1963); Harold E. Brown, *Juan de Mariana and Early Modern Spanish Religious Thought* (Burlington, VT: Ashgate, 2007); Allen, *History*, 345–360; Figgis, *Studies*, 180–183, 190–195.

83. *A Conference about the Right Succession to the Crowne of England* (Menston, UK: Scholar Press, 1972).

84. William M. Lamont, *Marginal Prynne* (London: Routledge & Kegan Paul, 1963); Ethlyn William Kirby, *William Prynne* (New York: Russell & Russell, 1972); Gooch, *English Democratic Ideas*, 99–100, 104–105, 143–145.

85. *Aeropagitica* (New York: AMS Press, 1971).

86. C. Hill, *World Turned Upside Down*; H. N. Brailsford, *The Levellers* (London: Cresset Press, 1961); Gooch, *English Democratic Ideas,* 135–140.

87. B. S. Capps, *The Fifth Monarchy Men* (Totowa, NJ: Capps Publishing, 1972).

88. *Leviathan*, ed. Richard Tuck (Cambridge [England]; New York: Cambridge University Press, 1991).

89. *Two Treatises on Government. Epistola de Tolerantia* (New Haven, CT: Yale University Press, 2003).

90. Robert Filmer, *Patriarca* (Oxford: Oxford University Press, 1949).

91. Tr. Patrick Riley (New York, Cambridge: Cambridge University Press, 1990).

92. *Dictionary Historical and Critical* (Oxford: Voltaire Foundation, 1989); *Political Writings*, ed. Sally L. Jenkinson (New York: Cambridge University Press, 2000).

Chapter Two

The Reformed Theologian—The Forgotten Political Theorist? Change and Contest in Theology and Ecclesiology in Late-Sixteenth and Early-Seventeenth-Century Reformed England[1]

Sara C. Kitzinger

The history of ideas has simply been transformed since the crucial work of Quentin Skinner.[2] A leader of the intellectual historians at Cambridge, Skinner offered a new methodology, one that countered an ahistorical approach to theory with a method that engaged the intellectual and practical contexts of the author and text in question—the goal being to "see things their way" without "imposing modern (or postmodern) categories upon past agents."[3] However, as identified by John Coffey, Skinner's own work neglected one significant type of theory or idea, that of religious thought and theology. This negligence, in truth, may have actually sustained the sort of abstract, secular, "whiggish" history that Skinner sought to discourage by ignoring religion's "role in the construction of meaning."[4] Among others, Coffey and Peter Lake have attempted to modify Skinner's contextualist methodology by including religious thought and context within the purview of a history of ideas. The present discussion embraces this methodology, with the intention of exploring the relationship between Reformed theology and ecclesiology and its formative effect on theories of church and state in sixteenth- and seventeenth-century England.

Church of England scholarship has long been dominated by the theory of the church as a *via media*, a halfway house of Roman Catholicism. However, thanks to several contextualist studies over the last thirty years, we are now aware of the English church as a participant in the ongoing European-wide Reformed conversation.[5] Both the Thirty-Nine Articles of Religion and the Book of Common Prayer were heavily influenced by the German divine Martin Bucer and the Italian Peter Martyr Vermigli.[6] Ecclesiologically, the Church of England followed the direction of Heinrich Bullinger and his church at Zurich, which operated according to the central notion in Reformed thought: the separation between things spiritual and things temporal. The Church of England was modeled accordingly, with the magistrate governing those bodily things of the church and Christ governing things ghostly—a double headship. [7]

Still, the importance of the city of Geneva and her godly ministers for the development of reformed ecclesiology should not be discounted. John Calvin and his successor in Geneva, Theodore Beza, implemented a strict disciplinarian ecclesiology based on Calvin's notion of double predestination, which required the church to be limited to the godly and governed by ministerial authority in the consistory (the nonepiscopal, senatorial, egalitarian body of ministers and elders).[8]

Calvin's doctrine of God's double divine decree did not escape inconsistency. Calvin had taught that, given that those who were elected were gifted with faith, those with faith had assurance of salvation.[9] But within the decree of double predestination there lurked implicitly, if not occasionally explicitly, the vexing notion that God had created some men in order to destroy them. How, then, were believers to have any comfort in faith amid such confusion and trouble over the very possibility of assurance? Beza offered an *ordo salutis*, "order of salvation," that sought to remedy this crisis. He posited that Christ had not died for all mankind; his death was only efficacious for those elected. In accordance with the "scholastic method of exposition," Beza placed the doctrine of predestination within the doctrine of God, shifting the moment of election and damnation from *infra lapsus* to *supra lapsus* (i.e., literally, "below" or after the fall to literally "above" or before the fall).[10] The supralapsarian position casts God as having decreed the elect before willing the creation of the world and the Fall of Adam. The ultimate effect was to make predestination the essential point of the life of the church.[11]

No other Englishman emulated and furthered the Genevan scheme more than did Thomas Cartwright—his dedication to consistorial discipline growing only after his withdrawal from Cambridge and relocation to Geneva in 1571. In their assault on the Church of England, Englishmen dedicated to the Genevan-style ministerial discipline had uniquely augmented the Genevan scheme in an exclusive direction.

In his famous altercation with Archbishop John Whitgift, Cartwright accused the English church of failure to allow the true disciplinarian church form as dictated in Scripture—a governance of ministers only. Whitgift denied that church discipline was necessary for salvation or a mark of the "true church," as he could not find a specific order commanded in Scripture by Christ. [12] In contradistinction to the disciplinarian position, the Archbishop defined the church not as limited to the "unleavened bread" of the godly but as a "mixed" institution:

> The visible and external government is that which is executed by *man* . . . and visible ceremonies practiced in that church . . . that containeth in it *both* good and evil, which is usually called the visible church of Christ, and compared by Christ to "a field" wherein both "good seeds" and "tares were sown," and to "a net that gathered of all kind of fishes." [13]

Archbishop Whitgift had supplied Heinrich Bullinger's model of the mixed church, divided into invisible (internal) and visible (external) parts, governed respectively by Christ, the spiritual head, and the magistrate, the temporal head, as in the church of Zurich. The elect were known only to Christ and were effectually the invisible or true church. The church of this world with its material nature consisted of weeds and blossoms alike.

On the other hand, the English "Genevans," such as Cartwright and Walter Travers, authorized by the certitude of God's *supra lapsus* decree, would brook nothing less than ministerial control of such a weighty matter. To be sure, accurate diagnosis of a person's elected status and proper admonishing of persons in an unregulated church-community order proffered little success of a "godly" church. The disciplinarians' adherence to the *supra lapsus* predestination doctrine demanded the rule of the consistory, a ministerial discipline of the church. [14] The church itself was understood strictly as operating in the realm of the spirit. As a matter of fact, the spiritual was fundamentally severed from the material order. [15]

Interestingly, on these two points the Church of England professed the same. The theology of the English church maintained a strict division between spirit and matter; those things invisible were under the authority of Christ, those things visible were under the authority of the king. Because the church, according to an imprecise doctrine of predestination, could indeed subsist as a "mixed" church, Christ governed the true, invisible elect, and the magistrate managed the visible church in all its temporality. [16] The church operated, in effect, under a "magisterial discipline"; church and state were uniquely intertwined.

Conversely, the church under the authority of a "ministerial discipline" supported by a supralapsarian doctrine existed as a body of the saved without the "leaven"—a strictly spiritual existence. A spiritual Christ stood as the master authority at the head, the ministers, his appointed ambassadors. [17] The remainder of temporal human experience was to be governed by the magistrate (though his role as enforcer of the two tables of the Decalogue within the realm continued to present the paradox of a spiritual church of elect within a very physical church-nation. [18]) Church and state, it seemed, were *potentially* segregated.

A torrent of public commentary and uncertainty on account of Cartwright's responses to the archbishop caused the Court of the Star Chamber to restrict the printing of books to approved London and university presses; but it was in the universities that the trouble reached a boiling point. [19] The French émigré Peter Baro, Lady Margaret professor of divinity at Cambridge, had seemingly developed Philipp Melanchton's position regarding the freedom of the human will to sin into a full ability to reject divine grace. [20] Both Richard Hooker as Master of the Temple and Samuel Harsnett, while preaching at Paul's Cross, had similarly attacked the "perseverance of the saints" and the irresistibility of God's grace in the 1580s. [21] Nevertheless the leading Cambridge theologians denounced Baro's position and, by 1595, his colleague William Whitaker, a *supra lapsus* defender, charged him with heresy in the presence of the university heads. The opportune scandal induced a junior scholar, a William Barrett of Gonville and Caius College, to denounce double predestination in his April university church sermon and to advance the notion that a man's damnation was only made possible by his own sin, not through the eternal decree of God. [22] The Cambridge heads labeled the sermon as containing "Romish" sympathies, and Barrett was threatened with expulsion and made to recant, although he later revoked his recantation, much to the outrage of the university authorities. Cambridge itself had become as fervent as the days of the young Cartwright's lectures and a hotbed for disciplinarian rigidity, with particular anxiety over securing a strict predestination doctrine. [23] With the challenge of "free will doctrines" and "conditional predestination," the hysteria over assurance was set aflame. [24]

The Thirty-Nine Articles of Religion closely followed the format of the Second Helvetic Confession—regarded as the authoritative agreement of theology between the French, Swiss, and German Reformed churches—and made no strict commitments to the finality of the regenerate or reprobate nor the *supra lapsus* position. However, the feverish state of the universities prompted the archbishop of Canterbury to call a convocation at Lambeth Palace, notably without magisterial permission, so as to strictly delineate the theological standards by which the universities were bound. [25] This produced a document treating predestination known as the Lambeth Articles, which hold true to the doctrine of the total depravity of man, insisting that men's works unaided by grace are displeasing to God, a view in accordance with both the Articles of Religion and the Second Helvetic Confession. Nonetheless, the first article may be understood to advance a double predestinarian position, perhaps in a *supra lapsus* form. It reads as follows: "God has from all Eternity predestinated some to Life, and reprobated some to Death."[26]

Without a doubt, here the omnipotence of God is preserved against the threat of Baro's notions. However, what is more pertinent for our purposes is the absence of a full-blown Beza-type gloss regarding the cause of damnation. Article 4 states, "Those who are not predestinated to Salvation, shall of necessity be condemned for their Sins"—a mild statement clearly shying away from declaring that God created some men in order to damn them. Yet if those who are damned are so by their lack of true belief and inherent sin, what of the explanation for their lack of belief? Calvin had suggested that God in his justice decreed their damnation, thus inadvertently making God the author of sin; Bullinger sought to explain their damnation "on account of their own guilt" and so inadvertently opened up the possibility of free acts.[27] The combination of a mild double predestination position and damnation based on man's sins without God's decree, flanked by statements guaranteeing the elect assurance of salvation, in essence proposed a dissonance begging for resolution.

Second, the articles oddly reaffirmed notions adduced from the *supra lapus* predestination position, such as the final perseverance of the elect and the fixed categories of regenerate and reprobate, and only served to further whet the appetite of ministerial disciplinarians. Queen Elizabeth instantly demanded that the articles be suppressed. Despite Whitgift's attempts, copies of the articles were made public, thereby fueling the efforts of those anxious for a restructuring of church government on disciplinarian lines in harmony with a scheme of predestination that guaranteed assurance of salvation.[28] As noted by Peter Lake, the situation became increasingly uncomfortable for those theologians who sought to maintain a "magisterial" church discipline *and* a form of double predestination. If strictly adhered to, the soteriological position maintaining the final and certain groups of elected and damned logically called for a ministerial disciplined church and the authority of the consistory. Such a transformation of English society not only stood to possibly topple the authority of the magistrate by an upstart body of popularly confirmed ministers but also would transform the order of the realm into a republican city–state. Lake remarks that such a transition may have amounted to near revolution in England, "the divisive and subversive implications of which Whitgift so abhorred."[29] For those disciplinarians who continued lambasting the English church for her neglect of divine mandate in church discipline, predestination persisted as the foundation of religion.

Reaffirming the consequences of *supra lapsus* predestination, William Perkins, near the turn of the century, issued *A Christian and plaine treatise of the manner and order of Predestination*. He opens his treatise by defending God as innocent of sin but reiterates that the Fall is a consequence of man's sins in much the same wobbly manner as did the Lambeth Articles.[30] Furthermore, he upholds Beza's teaching that Christ died only for the elect, vivifying Beza's "evidential" doctrine of assurance, in which persons look to their works as evidence that they are possessed by the spirit, and so have assurance of their final election.[31] Central to Perkins's consoling doctrine of assurance was a heavy emphasis upon the total depravity of man: "there is no merit before faith; and we do nothing acceptable vnto God before wee have faith."[32] Man's condition is one of determined sin—even Adam in the garden existed in goodness only because God issued forth grace, regardless of Adam's nature. "For that which God doth not hinder, doth therfore come to passe, because hee doth not hinder it; and as no good thing can either bee or come to passe, vnless God make it; so no euill thing can be auoyded, except God do hinder."[33] So naturally wicked is man that God must dispense grace as a restraining device to keep all men somewhat orderly. Says Perkins:

> The restrayning grace is that, whereby the inbred corruption of the hart, is not therby vtterly diminished and taken away, but . . . is restrained . . . that it breake not violently forth into action: and it is giuen onely for a testimonie vnto man, and to preserve order amongst men in a politique societie: and this kind of grace is generall, that is, belonging to all and euery man . . . there is no man, in whom God doth not more or lesse restraine his naturall corruption.[34]

Note especially that "restrayning grace" is given to all temporal men. Perkins presents a second sort of grace dispensed to only some men. Termed "renewing or Christian grace," this gift allows man to "beleeue and repent"; it is the grace that provides him with a new will and secures his final salvation. In his discussion of this binary doctrine of grace, Perkins has replicated the pattern of a severed church and state, according to the ministerial discipline order: two groups of men, separated via flesh and spirit distinctions. For in his natural, unregenerated state, man "is flesh euery iot of him," although after regeneration and the gift of supernatural "renewing grace," man is born anew into the life of the spirit.[35] Ironically, as all good acts require a command of God over man, natural "grace" is conveyed to all in the life of the flesh. "Renewing grace" is reserved only for the elected few governed by the life of the spirit. It is this binary doctrine of grace that subsequent thinkers retain though in a much-altered theological context.

At the time of the accession to the crown of James VI of Scotland as James I, Perkins remained the foremost theological voice. More editions of his works were published between 1590 and 1620 than those of any other author.[36] Enlivened by James VI's reputation as a friend to godly discipline in Scotland, those proponents of Perkins's predestination position presented the new king with several petitions asking for a reformation of the Church in England and an open conversation about church polity.[37] The king called a conference at Hampton Court for such a purpose.

It was there, in January 1604, that John Rainolds, leading disciplinarian, "Cartwrightes scholler,"[38] and president of Corpus Christi College, Oxford, asked James I for the Church of England's doctrine and church order to be "preserved in purity according to God's word."[39] Most significantly, he requested that the "orthodoxal" Lambeth Articles be officially added to the Articles of Religion.[40] Thundering against Rainolds's argument for rigid predestination, the Bishop of London, Richard Bancroft, pleaded with the king to condemn Rainolds's words as scandalous. Though reminding Bancroft that he would hear all arguments, King James was moved to conclude that Reinold's desire for a precise public declaration on predestination could only prove damaging to the stability and order of the church.[41] It was necessary to keep silent on such complex matters, the king warned: "lest on one side, God's omnipotency might be called in question . . . or on the other, a desperate presumption might be arreared, by inferring the necessary certainty of standing and persisting in grace."[42]

It was, in effect, a statement to maintain dissidence within the doctrine, not siding with the certain eternal decree or the free will of man—notably in accordance with the king's insistence upon the viability of disagreement over what he saw as "secondary" doctrines in faith.[43] Moreover, such a doctrinal position guaranteed that no change in church polity toward consistorial governance was needed, magisterial discipline being superior to maintain order and unity.[44] As Elizabeth had done, King James ordered "old, curious, and deep and intricate questions" concerning predestination to be kept from the pulpit to preserve order and peace in the realm.[45]

By the crowning of the second Stuart, Charles I in 1625, the already irritated predestination debate had gained dangerous political import—Holland had fallen into civil war after a dispute concerning final perseverance spread from the universities to local synods and city councils, causing a splintering of the church as well as a military uprising and ending in the death of the grand regent of Holland. The implications for England were too close for comfort, especially as it was a disputation of Perkins's precisian treatise on predestination that began the political avalanche.[46]

Against the order of King Charles I that such questions be rendered silent, a variety of counterarguments and theological creations had spread since the trouble at Cambridge with Barrett and Baro.[47] Craftily painting the Church of England as long unified in matters of grace, former King's College fellow Richard Mountague argued that it was deeply erroneous to hold "That God by his will and inevitable decree, hath ordained from all eternity, who shall be damned, and who shall be saved."[48] In February 1626, Charles I, in order to keep the doctrinal contest out of Parliament and avoid war, called a conference at the Duke of Buckingham's London residence of York House to discuss Mountague's position. One of Mountague's accusers was the master of Emmanuel College, John Preston. Known as deeply committed to pastoral

aids and comfort for the concerned believer, Preston sought to defend the
orthodox Reformed position. He softened Perkins's strict supralapsarian predestination and expanded the application of Christ's sacrifice beyond a final
category of elect, a position known as "hypothetical universalism."[49]

Doctrinally indebted to Bishop James Ussher, Preston posited that, hypo-
thetically, Christ *had* indeed sufficiently died for all; grace had been given to
all who did not reject it, for God loved the world and desired the salvation of
all men, that is, if they themselves did not choose against God.[50] Although it
was miles from Mountague's "Arminian" position, Preston's treatment of
Christ's general atonement, paired with an unusual defense of the ability of
the reprobate to reject Christ's death, had in fact arrived at a position in
danger of flirting with man's ability to accept and reject grace. That is to say
a position that saved the realm of the natural from the rule of total depravity.[51]

In the opening of Preston's posthumously published *Life Eternall,* we are
reminded that God can be apprehended by natural reason.[52] He calls upon the
Apostle's words in Acts that God "is not farre from every one of us: for in
him we live, move, and have our being."[53] In this sense, there are two kinds
of truths: one "wholly revealed and have no foot-steps in the creatures," and
another evident in nature "whereby wee may discerne them"; in other words,
revealed truth and natural truth.[54] God is revealed first by natural truth as a
law written on the hearts of all men. In words dramatically different from
Perkins's, "the workes of Nature are not in vaine."[55] Revealed truth, then,
can act as a confirmation of what a person was persuaded to by the natural;
herein lay a person's assurance of faith.[56] Although hardly original in his
discussion of the natural, in an attempt to make knowledge of faith accessible
to all potential believers, Preston had restored goodness to nature.[57]

Preston maintained the potentially universal application of Christ's death
but allowed man the power to refuse its grace. He turned to nature as a
pastoral device to remind men of the goodness of God, thereby serving as a
confirmation of faith and inducing the acceptance of grace. He had uninten-
tionally overturned Perkins's view of the total depravity of natural man and
supralapsarian predestination and thereby eradicated the logical necessity for
a church government of ministerial discipline by consistory to secure the
godly church of elect. However, although the natural order had been rehabili-
tated, the Reformed dichotomy between grace and nature remained to beget
radical political consequences heretofore unimagined.

Approximately ten years following Preston's death, in 1645, during the
beginning years of the English Civil War, an anonymous pamphlet was published under the title *Ancient Bounds.* Thought to have been written by the
Independent Joshua Sprigge, the argument advanced imitates the dichotomy
set forth by Perkins between church and state.[58] But Preston and others in his
wake had augmented the natural order as established according to its own

law—without Perkins's direct "correcting" law of grace. *Ancient Bounds* elucidated a formula of a stubbornly supernatural church distinct from a natural state. The author explained:

> Christ Jesus . . . hath given several . . . schemes of his dominions . . . of which every man is . . . either of one only or of both . . . of one only, so every natural man (who in a natural consideration is called *microcosmus*, an epitome of the world), in whose conscience God . . . rul(es) him by the light of nature to a civil outward good and end; of both, so every believer who, besides this natural conscience and rule, hath an enlightened conscience carrying a more bright and lively stamp of the . . . power of the Lord Jesus, swaying him by the light of faith or scripture, and such a man may be called *microchristus,* the epitome of Christ mystical.[59]

From this, the author deduced that every natural man is under the jurisdiction of the magistrate, the state being "outward, civil, bodily." The jurisdiction of God is "inward and spiritual."[60] As discussed earlier, this position reiterates the theology of both the Church of England and the Genevan discipline regarding the strict separation between body and spirit. However, this author does not operate within the confines of a totally deprived natural order that is part and parcel of the "pure church" model of the ministerial church discipline associated with Cartwright and Travers. Nor must he limit himself to the mixed-church notion of the magisterial Church of England defended by Whitgift. Instead, the church had been permanently spiritualized.

In tune with the heterogeneity of scriptural hermeneutics characteristic of the chaotic war years, a new scriptural justification against the very notion of a national church had emerged under the rhetoric of toleration. Whereas Cartwright thought he had restored the true church government by returning to the apostolic form, it was argued that he had erred by an incorporation of the Old Testament, erroneously equating the church with the nation of Israel.[61] "Jewish it is to seek for Moses, and bring him from his grave . . . in setting up a National Church in a land of Canaan, which the great Messiah abolished at his coming," argued the separatist Roger Williams.[62] The laws and forms of the Old Testament could not be read as binding without violating the very liberty that is Christ. In this way, Williams managed to avoid problems constitutive of a regional or "state" church—that vexing legal snag regarding if and how much of the Ten Commandments the temporal magistrate was charged with enforcing.

Williams simply concluded that Christ in the new dispensation never named magistrates to be keepers of both tables—all analogies between the old and the new extirpated. "And for Spiritual power they say they have none . . . and then having neither Civill nor Spiritual power from the Lord Jesus to this purpose, how come they to be such Keepers as is pretended?"[63] For Christ "dissolved the Nationall State of the Church, and established a more Sprituall way of worship all the World over."[64] As John Coffey has explained, the deep appeal of primitivism operated to restore a fully and wholly spiritual existence to the church. In this way, Williams had carried the Reformed dichotomy between spirit and matter to its logical conclusion.[65] In the chaos of defining God's eternal decrees, the natural order had been re-deemed and reminded of its own self-contained law, at the expense of the Reformed notion of grace. The moral order was entirely one of natural con-cern, and the church was a voluntary spiritual society. In this context, it was God's wall that had been erected between church and state.

Williams's theory is not exclusively representative of seventeenth-centu-ry political thought. Moreover, theories of church and state continued to be developed through the eighteenth century in the context of ponderings on "origins of government." However, Williams's thought and that of others were undoubtedly progenies of Reformed thought and its complications, not some deliberately secular creation apart from the problems of the day. John Preston, the anonymous author of *Ancient Bounds,* and Roger Williams worked within a theological context energized by the inconsistencies of pre-destination doctrine and their implications for the order of church and state. It was the Reformed dichotomy between grace and nature, spiritual and materi-al, that would remain intellectually continuous, as later made famous by none other than John Locke and his habitués in the New World.

NOTES

1. This essay contains portions of several chapters of the author's active dissertation in early modern history written for the degree of doctor of philosophy at the University of St. Andrews, UK.
2. Quentin Skinner's work on methodology is most accessible in a recently published three volume collection of his essays entitled *Visions of Politics.* See *Visions of Politics,* vol. 1, *Regarding Method* (Cambridge, UK: Cambridge University Press, 2002), esp. chapters 1, 3, 4.
3. John Coffey and Alister Chapman, "Introduction: Intellectual History and the Return of Religion," in Alister Chapman, John Coffey, and Brad S. Gregory, eds., *Seeing Things Their Way: Intellectual History and the Return of Religion* (Notre Dame: University of Notre Dame, 2009), 2.
4. Ibid., 4, 46–55. Charles W. A. Prior also makes a convincing case for "the place of theology amid the language of politics and the nature of early Stuart ideological conflict." See Prior, "Ecclesiology and Political Thought in England, 1580–1603," *The Historical Journal* 48: 4 (2005), 855–884, see 856.
5. A sampling of such works: Torrance Kirby, *The Zurich Connection and Tudor Political Theology* (Leiden and Boston: Brill, 2007), 5–10. Kirby observed that the Church of England has traditionally been cast as a product of "political exigency and pragmatic compromise *rather than* any clear embrace of Reformed theological principle[s]." See also, Peter Lake's sugges-tion that the key to understanding the order and ecclesiology of the English Church is to be found in "the extent and nature of the Christian community." Lake, "Calvinism and the English Church, 1570–1635," *Past and Present,* 114, 32–76, see 39. David Keep suggests the "Zurich"-based thought of Martyr and Bullinger constitutes "par excellence" the thought of the English Reformed Church. See David Keep, "Theology as the Basis for Policy in the Elizabethan

Church," in L.D.G. Baker, ed., *Studies in Church History*, vol. 2 (Oxford, UK: Basil Blackwell, 1975), 265. Peter White offered a refreshing and nuanced conception of the *via media* that expresses the English Church not as a middle point between Catholic and Protestant thought, but between degrees of predestinarian and absolute predestinarian Protestantism. See White, "The Rise of Arminianism Reconsidered," *Past and Present*, 101 (1983), 35–54, see 44.

6. Martyr's formulation of Eucharistic doctrine was "praised by Calvin as the clearest, best formulated orthodox statement of the Reformed position." His formulation was termed "instrumental realism" and sought to reconcile "conflicting positions of Zwingli's anti-realist Sacramentarian memorialism and Luther's hyper-realist consubstantiation." It was Martyr's doctrine that Cranmer used in the Second Prayer Book of Edward VI and was cited in the Restoration Liturgy of 1662. See M. A. Overall, "Peter Martyr in England," *The Sixteenth Century Journal,* 15: 1 (1984), 87–104, 93; Kirby, *The Zurich Connection*, 15. See also, Diarmaid MacCulloch's mention in *The Later Reformation in England, 1547–1603* (Houdmills, Basingstoke, Hampshire, UK: Macmillan, 1990), 69.

7. Bullinger understood the Christian church to be of the same order as the ancient Jewish "Church"—God appointed both prophet and king to lead his people, there being no distinction between the nation and the church. See esp. Kirby, *The Zurich Connection, passim*; J. Wayne Baker, *Heinrich Bullinger and the Covenant: The Other Reformed Tradition* (Athens, OH: Ohio University Press, 1980), passim. In his letters to Queen Elizabeth, Martyr pleaded, "And I beseech you neuer hearken unto them, which faigne that the regard of the reformation of religion belongeth not unto Princes. For the good kings whome I before remembred did not so judge. The holy Scriptures doe not so instruct us, neither did the verie Ethnickes and Philosophers themselues so iudge. Is it the office of a godlie Magistrate to defende onely one, and that the latter table of the lawe diuine? . . . God forbid." See Peter Martyr, "An Epistle to the Most Renowned Princes Elizabeth," in *The common places of the most famous and renowmed diuine Doctor Peter Martyr* (London, 1583), p. 59.

8. Calvin's formulation of this ecclesiastical discipline is commonly known as the "fourfold ministry." A truly reformed church consisted of four orders of ministry for the purpose of discipline: (1) ministers of the Word and testifiers of the Gospel, known as bishops, presbyters, ministers; (2) teachers and doctors of Scripture; (3) elders charged with the supervision and censure of morals; and (4) deacons who cared for the poor by collecting alms and distributing goods. See J. William Black, "From Martin Bucer to Richard Baxter: "Discipline" and Reformation in Sixteenth- and Seventeenth-Century England," *Church History* 70: 4 (2001), 644–673, see 647; and Philip Benedict, *Christ's Churches Purely Reformed: A Social History of Calvinism* (New Haven, CT: Yale University Press, 2004), 87.

9. R. T. Kendall, *Calvin and English Calvinism to 1649* (Carlisle, Cumbria: Paternoster Publishing, 1997), 13–15, 25. Benedict, *Christ's Churches Purely Reformed,* 90. For disagreement between Calvin and Bullinger on this point, see Bullinger's letter to Calvin, cited in Cornelis P. Venema, "Heinrich Bullinger's Correspondence on Calvin's Doctrine of Predestination, 1551–1553," *Sixteenth Century Journal* 17 (1986), 435–450, see 441.

10. Dewey D. Wallace, *Puritans and Predestination: Grace in English Protestant Theology 1525–1695* (Chapel Hill: University of North Carolina Press, 1982), 36–43; Benedict, *Christ's Churches Purely Reformed,* 302.

11. According to this view, the Fall had facilitated God's plan to elect some for salvation and decree others for damnation. Since the regenerate and reprobate were chosen *before* the Fall, the entire economy of salvation, the entire order of the Christian church, concedes to the reality of these fixed groups.

12. "Whether all things pertaining to the outward form of the church be particularly expressed, or commanded in the scripture, or no, is the question that we have now in controversy." And again, "I find no one certain and perfect kind of government prescribed or commanded in the scriptures to the church of Christ: which no doubt should have been done; it had been a matter necessary unto the salvation of the church." John Whitgift, *Works of John Whitgift*, J. Ayre, ed., Parker Society, (Cambridge, 1851) vol. 1, 179, 184.

13. Ibid., 183–184, italics mine.

14. On the matter of predestination, the reformed theologians differed substantially. Calvin followed an interpretation of St. Augustine, which yielded a decree of double predestination (the binary theory of election—some men predestined for heaven, the rest predestined for hell, hence, *double*), as did Peter Martyr and the Polish émigré to London, John a Lasco. Wolfgang Musculus of Augsburg cautiously subscribed to double predestination, but the German Phillip Melanchthon sidestepped it altogether, joining single predestination with an element of free will. Bullinger upheld a definite single predestination and rebuked Calvin for his forceful defense of a double decree, warning him that he had probed further into the mysteries of God than allowed by Scripture. See Alister McGrath, *Life of John Calvin: A Study in the Shaping of Western Culture* (Oxford, UK, and Cambridge, MA: Basil Blackwell, 1990), 95–96; Bard Thompson, "The Palatinate Church Order of 1563," *Church History* 23: 4 (1954), 339–354; Benedict, *Christ's Churches Purely Reformed,* Part 1.

15.   "And agayne who knoweth not that the Byshoppes Office is bounded and limited with spirituall matter and care off sowles/and hath no charge off the common wealth/nor off the state off this life? Or that the Magistrates are carefull for the body and thinges belonging therunto/ The Bishoppes of the sowle and that which apparteineth unto the soule?" Travers later repeats this concern, " . . . the whole authority of the cōnsistory . . . off Correctinge is spirituall,/as proceeding not from the Magistrates but from the Elders off the churche. For as this counsell is Ecclesiasticall/and the court a spirituall court . . . distinguished by S. Paule/from the cyuill courtes and places which the Apostle calleth courtes for thinges belonging to this life) So also the punyshement is speciall and suche as belongeth to the sowle and Conscience/and concerneth not this loife nor those thinges with which the ciuill magistrate is wont to deale." Walter Travers, *A full and plaine declaration of Ecclesiastiall Discipline* (Heidelberg, 1574), 83–84; 161–162.

16. The Articles of Religion made no strict commitments to the finality of the regenerate or reprobate nor the *supra lapsus* position in the same manner as Bullinger's Second Helvetic Confession.

17.   See Travers's explanation of the duties of the ministry: "Elders be such as those officers off the Athenienses were/who had charge to see the lawes kept/or as the Censors of Rome/who exacted and examined euery citezens life accordinge to the lawes. So they marke and obserue euery mans manners/and they them selves doe admonishe men off the lighter faults/and bring the greater to the Consistory . . . they helpe the pastor and take heede that none come unto the lordes supper whose Religion and honestie is not knowen." Travers, *A full and plaine declaration,* 156–157.

18. On this theme, see Theodore Dwight Bozeman's study, *The Precisianist Strain: Disciplinary Religion and Antinomian Backlash in Puritanism to 1638* (University of North Carolina, 2004), chapter 2, esp. page 53: "Presbyterian leaders were nationalistic, nonseparating Dissenters who associated their nation with biblical Israel and upheld the ideal of an inclusive religious establishment." According to Travers and John Udall, the king remained God's steward and was charged with leading the commonwealth in holiness—that is, if he acknowledged the primacy of the Word and its definite dictates for a purified church. If he did not, two awkward insinuations of serious political significance followed: one, either the magistrate should submit to correction by the ministry (ministers and elders of which were *popularly* confirmed as according to the ministerial discipline model), or two, if he did not submit he should be openly disputed. See John Udall's *Demonstration of the trueth of that Discipline* (London, 1588).

19. The order from Star Chamber is reprinted in Edward Arber (ed.), *Introductory Sketch to the Martin Marprelate Controversy, 1588–1590* (London, 1879), 50–51.

20. "Peter Baro, who maintained that by his antecedent will God created all to universal life, although by his consequent will he sentenced to damnation those who rejected the grace he offered—a lucid example of the sort of scholastic distinctions now increasingly driving thought on this question." See Benedict, *Christ's Churches Purely Reformed,* 304. Also John Coffey, *John Goodwin and the Puritan Revolution: Religion and Intellectual Change in 17th-Century England* (Woodbridge, UK, and Rochester, NY: Boydell Press, 2006), 25; ODNB, *Peter Baro*; John Ellis, *A Defence of the Thirty-Nine Articles of the Church of England* (London, 1700), 96.

21. A. F. Scott Pearson, *Thomas Cartwright and Elizabethan Puritanism 1535–1603* (Gloucester, MA: P. Smith, 1966), 253; Benedict, *Christ's Churches Purely Reformed*, 303.

22. Ellis, *A Defence of the Thirty-Nine Articles*, 95–102. See also Nicholas Tyacke, "The Rise of Arminianism Reconsidered," *Past and Present*, No. 115 (1989), 204; ODNB, *William Barrett.*

23. Nicholas Tyacke, *Anti-Calvinists: The Rise of English Arminianism c.1590–1640* (Oxford, UK: Clarendon, 1987), chapter 2; Coffey, *John Goodwin and the Puritan Revolution,* 24–27.

24. Tyacke, "The Rise of Arminianism Reconsidered," 204.

25. Ellis, *A Defence of the Thirty-Nine Articles,* 99–100.

26. Ibid., 104. For a different view, see S. F. Hughes, "The Problem of 'Calvinism': English Theologies of Predestination, c.1580–c.1630," in S. Wabuda and C. Litzenberger (eds), *Belief and Practice in Reformation England* (Aldershot, UK, and Brookfield, VT: Ashgate, 1998), 235–236, although he does not treat the Lambeth Articles.

27. Cornelis P. Venema, "Heinrich Bullinger's Correspondence on Calvin's Doctrine of Predestination, 1551–1553," *Sixteenth Century Journal* 17 (1986), 435–450, see 441.

28. Ellis, *A Defence of the Thirty-Nine Articles,* 101. See Lake, "Calvinism and the English Church," 46: "It was assurance . . . which underwrote that puritan tendency to insist on visible godliness as a qualification for membership of both the church and the Christian community."

29. Lake, "Calvinism and the English Church," 46.

30. Although with the more precise language of a double act reprobation, i.e., 1) desertion of God, 2) damning for man's own fault. Perkins, *A Christian and plaine treatise of the manner and order of Predestination* (London, 1598; published in English in 1606), see esp. 2–6, 33–39, 41–45.

31. "For the Sonne doth not sacrifice for those, for whom hee doth not pray . . . but hee prayethe oneley for the elect and for beleeuers. . . . Therefore the price is appointed and limited to the elect alone by the Fathers decree, and the Sons intercession and oblation." Perkins, *A Christian and plaine treatise,* 18; Kendall, *Calvin and English Calvinism,* 51, 80–82. For Perkins as a leader of the "pietist" "fraternity" and the dominance of evidence-based assurance, see Bozeman, *The Precisianist Strain,* chapters 4 and 5.

32. Perkins, *A Christian and plaine treatise,* 122. See also p. 37; "And every one that is predestinate, is predestinated only by grace, and by Gods mercifull disposition, not for any cause either actuall or priuatiue to bee found in him, whiles hee liveth."

33. Ibid., 42.

34. Ibid., 106–107.

35. Ibid., 108, 155.

36. Benedict, *Christ's Churches Purely Reformed,* 319.

37. Pearson, *Thomas Cartwright and Elizabethan Puritanism 1535–1603,* 389–390. For discussion of James I's support of reformed theology and an active preaching ministry, see Kenneth Fincham and Peter Lake, "The Ecclesiastical Policy of King James I," *Journal of British Studies* 24, No. 2, Politics and Religion in the Early Seventeenth Century: New Voices (April 1985), 169–207, see 173–174.

38. Bishop Richard Bancroft referred to Reinholds and the three other disciplinarian participants at the Hampton Court Conference as "Cartwrightes schollers," noting the late disciplinarian's influence over them. Cartwright was initially to lead the delegation; however, his death prevented his coming. See Pearson, *Thomas Cartwright and Elizabethan Puritanism,* 391, esp. note 2.

39. E. Cardwell (ed.), *A History of Conferences and Other Proceedings connected with the Book of Common Prayer, 1558–1690* (Oxford, UK, 1841), 178.

40. Ibid., 178–179. See also Tyacke, *Anti-Calvinists,* 10.

41. E. Cardwell (ed.), *A History of Conferences,* 181.

42. Ibid.

43. John Platt speaks of James's "Christian eirenical approach," which distinguished between "fundamental articles of belief . . . necessary to salvation . . . upon which all must agree, and those matters of less importance about which genuine differences of opinion may . . . exist." See Platt, "Eirenical Anglicans at the Synod of Dort" in Derek Baker, ed., *Reform and*

Reformation: England and the Continent c1500–1750 (Oxford: Basil Blackwell, 1979), 226. See also Peter White, "The *Via Media* in the Early Stuart Church," in Kenneth Fincham ed., *The Early Stuart Church, 1603–1642,* esp. 223–4; W. B. Patterson, "King James I's Call for an Ecumenical Council," in G. J. Cuming and D. Baker, eds., *Councils and Assemblies: Studies in Church History,* vol. 7, edited by G. J. Cuming and D. Baker (London and New York: Cambridge University Press, 1971) 267–275. Fincham and Lake remind us that James I understood predestination as "a thorny subject on which disagreement was possible yet over which public dispute should be limited." The king also counseled the Synod at Dort to avoid precisian in order to secure political unity. See Fincham and Lake, "The Ecclesiastical Policy of King James I," 189–190.

44.   King James relates his experience with the ministers of Scotland who had pleaded for "Christian liberty to every man" against magisterial authority. The king responded, "I will have none of that; I will have one doctrine and one discipline, one religion in substance and in ceremony." Cardwell, *A History of Conferences,* 198–199.

45.   Ibid., 187.

46.   Christopher Grayson, "James I and the Religious Crisis in the United Provinces 1613–19," *Reform and Reformation: England and the Continent c150–1750,* 195–219; Benedict, *Christ's Churches Purely Reformed,* 305–310.

47.   See *A Proclamation for the establishing of the peace and quiet of the Church of England, 16 June 1626.* "And therefore his most excellent Majesty doth hereby admonish, and also straightly charge and command all his subjects of this realm . . . warily and consciously that neither by writing, preaching, printing, conference or otherwise they raise any doubts, or publish or maintain any new inventions, or opinions concerning religion that such as [are] clearly grounded and warranted by the doctrine and discipline of the Church of England heretofore published and happily established by authority." See J. P. Kenyon (ed.), *The Stuart Constitution: Documents and Commentary* (2nd ed.) (Cambridge, UK, and New York: Cambridge University Press, 1986), 138–139.

48.   Richard Mountague, *A Gagg for the New Gospel, No: A New Gag for an Old Goose* (London, 1624), 107–116, 157–172, 179–183. Note Perkins's argument of Peter and Judas as eternally elected and damned, respectively; see 179. Complicating matters, Mountague had craftily folded into his tracts a divine right justification for Charles I to act without Parliament in matters concerning taxation, causing fierce accusations of an absolutist attack on property rights. See Tyacke, *Anti-Calvinists,* 157–159.

49.   According to Coffey, Preston via Ussher "was concerned that the uncompromising theology of Perkins caused others to react against the Augustinianism of Calvin and the mainstream Reformed tradition." By emphasizing that Christ had died for all, but only prayed for the elect, this position maintained a universal atonement and preserved "the core Calvinist doctrine of absolute predestination." See Coffey, *John Goodwin and the Puritan Revolution,* 25. For a thorough and nuanced account of Preston's application of Christ's death, see Jonathan Moore, *English Hypothetical Universalism: John Preston and the Softening of Reformed Theology* (Grand Rapids, Cambridge: Wm. B. Eerdmans, 2007), esp. chapter 4.

50.   Moore explains that, "Preston insisted that 'the intercession and prayer of Christ doth not fall upon his death, to make that belong to some and not to others.' He implies therefore that the death of Christ belongs, at least in some sense, equally to all without exception." See his *English Hypothetical Universalism,* 101. Moore cites Preston, asserting "there is a sufficiencie in Christ to save all men . . . there is rightousness enough in him to justifie all the world." For this, see Preston, *Riches of Mercy to Men in Misery,* 423 cited by Moore, *English Hypothetical Universalism,* 105.

51.   For a discussion on Preston's treatment of Christ's free offering to all, see Moore, *English Hypothetical Universalism,* 128–134.

52.   Compare this to Perkins's treatment of nature as both corrupt and, in essence, dependent upon grace to operate *naturally,* his terminology of man's "nature" as supernaturally allowed by "restrayning grace."

53.   Preston, *Life Eternall* (London, 1631) 4.

54.   Ibid., 5.

55.   Ibid., 15.

56. Ibid., 19–21, See William Haller, *The Rise of Puritanism*, or, *The way to the New Jerusalem* as set forth in pulpit and press from Thomas Cartwright to John Lilburne and John Milton, 1570–1643 (New York: Columbia University Press, 1938), 171.

57. Man's reason and understanding in his natural state are far from totally corrupted; moreover, they are universal faculties. Faith, as the "lifting up of the understanding," is accessible to all. "Faith, it is but the lifting up of the understanding, by adding a new light to them and it; and therefore they are said to be revealed, not because they were not before . . . but even as a new light in the night discovers to us that which we did not see before, and as a prospective glasse revaleis to the eye, that which we could not see before, and by its owne power, the eye could not reach unto. Preston, *Life Eternall*, 21–22.

58. Barbara Kiefer, "Authorship of Ancient Bounds," *Church History* 22: 3 (1953), 192–196.

59. *The Ancient Bounds, or Liberty of conscience tenderly stated,* modestly asserted, and *mildly vindicated* (London, 1645), reprinted in·A. S. P. Woodhouse, ed., *Puritanism and Liberty Being the Army Debates* (1647–49) From the Clarke Manuscripts, (London; Rutland, Vt., J. M. Dent; C. E. Tuttle, 1992), 247–248.

60. Ibid., 248.

61. Owing to space limitations, a treatment of this development in terms of covenantal theology has been regrettably omitted. For discussion of covenantal theology, national paradigm, and its undoing in spiritualist theology of early mid-century Separatists, see Coffey, "Puritanism and Liberty Revisited: The Case for Toleration in the English Revolution," *Historical Journal* 41: 4 (1998), 961–985, esp. 966–976. See also, Coffey, *John Goodwin and the Puritan Revolution,* 58–61 and chapter 4.

62. Roger Williams, *The Bloudy Tenent of persecution, for cause of conscience, discussed, in a conference betweene truth and peace* (London, 1644), 94. From 1631, Williams had been known as a "godly minister" in New England dissenting circles. He was denied a ministerial position in the church of Salem but preached to the separatist congregation of Plymouth Plantation. See ODNB, *Roger Williams*. For an accessible treatment of the Reformed notion of the Christian church as consonant with Israel, see Bozeman's discussion of the "Israelite paradigm" in *The Precisianist Strain,* 32, 34–35, 45.

63. Williams, *The Bloudy Tenent*, 130.

64. Ibid.

65. Coffey, "Puritanism and Liberty Revisited," 973.

Chapter Three

"The Leviathan Is Not Safely to Be Angered": The Convocation Controversy, Country Ideology, and Anglican High Churchmanship, 1689–1702

Brent S. Sirota

In a letter dated March 3, 1697, William Nicolson, archdeacon of Carlisle, confessed to his friend William Wake, the popular rector of St. James, Westminster, and future archbishop of Canterbury, a certain bewilderment at "the proceedings of some our dissatisfied clergymen, under the present government." A contingent of Anglican clergymen, galvanized by the recent publication of Francis Atterbury's *Letter to a Convocation-Man*, now volubly championed the rights of the Church of England, even at the expense of the prerogatives of its supreme governor. "I always thought," Nicolson reflected, "that the whole of our establishment, and the credit of our Reformation, rested on the doctrine of the [royal] supremacy." And yet, those men who placed the ecclesiastical assemblies of the established church within the purview of the crown were now branded "innovators and enemies to the primitive and apostolical Church." The ecclesiology upon which such accusations were based seemed unfathomable to the archdeacon. "What sort of discipline these men would fix upon at last," he wrote, "is not easily determinable." Yet, poised at the threshold of the bitter and protracted convocation controversy that would engross both men, Nicolson warned Wake that the passions of these men "are now in a violent fermentation, and too headstrong to be brought under the direction of any settled principles whatsoever."[1]

Nicolson was not being obtuse. There *was* something genuinely unsettled about the principles of Anglican high churchmanship at the end of the seventeenth century. The Anglican high church party, traditionally defined by its zeal for episcopacy, ardent royalism, and implacable hostility toward all forms of religious dissent, was undergoing a curious metamorphosis. In the postrevolutionary era, the establishmentarian high church party was evolving from a court to an opposition movement.[2] Of course church opposition to its supreme governor had been a recurrent feature of late Stuart politics, particularly in moments when the crown seemed bent on using its prerogative powers to subvert rather than to uphold Anglican hegemony.[3] Such crises usually prompted the established church to recover, as John Spurr put it, "the 'underlying resources' she possessed in episcopacy." Zealous churchmen, when alienated from the Stuart court, often sought refuge in the apostolic institution of episcopacy as a bulwark against Erastianism—such was the ecclesiological ambidexterity of a church that was at once both catholic and national, *jure divino,* yet established by law.[4] This resilience, never more effective than in the "Anglican Revolution of 1688," was vitiated by the Williamite settlement of church and state that followed the collapse of the Stuart monarchy.[5] In the wake of the Glorious Revolution, churchmen long used to negotiating the tensions inherent within the late Stuart alliance of throne and altar now found themselves strung not between miter and scepter but rather between two pairs of each. The revolution effectively created two competing iterations of the Anglican royalist alliance of crown and church: the exiled James II and the six bishops deprived by Parliament for their continuing allegiance to him, on the one hand, and the revolutionary monarchy of William and Mary and their reconstructed episcopal bench, on the other. In the immediate aftermath of the revolution, the political theology of Anglican high churchmen did not afford them the luxury of any substantive opposition, merely two opposing courts and hierarchies from which to choose. As John Kenyon once described the antinomies of high church Anglicanism, "by the logic of their own theories, they must all be [either] whigs or Jacobites."[6]

Anglican high churchmen then, it would seem, chose Whiggery—or at least, a bloodless approximation thereof. With the not insignificant exception of the half-dozen bishops and some four hundred of their clerical adherents deprived for nonjuring, the overwhelming mass of the Anglican clergy took the oaths of allegiance to William and Mary, retained their cures and offices, and by and large made their peace with the new regime. And in remaining within the establishment, it might be argued, churchmen unenthusiastic about the prospect of further alterations in either church or state were able to ensure a fairly conservative postrevolutionary ecclesiastical settlement. The episcopal polity and doctrine of the Church of England survived the revolutionary crisis intact.[7] The move toward comprehension—that is, the modification of certain terms of communion to reconcile Protestant dissenters to the established church—was soundly defeated. The Test Act, which restricted political and military officeholding to communicating members of the established church, was upheld—even in the face of the new king's desire to open his government to "all Protestants that are willing and able to serve."[8] Of course the Toleration Act passed in May 1689 effectively stripped the established church of its legal monopoly over public worship, but its terms were limited to a narrow indulgence for Trinitarian Protestants, stopping well short of civil equality.[9] Nothing could be done to prevent the painful schism of the nonjurors deprived by the new regime, but this breach remained more of a psychic wound than a legitimate ecclesiastical crisis.[10] More troubling, though, was William and Mary's overhaul of the church hierarchy, made possible in part by the vacancies created by the deprived nonjurors. The new sovereigns elevated no fewer than sixteen men to the episcopal bench in the first two years of their reign alone, overwhelmingly loyal Williamites unperturbed by the revolutionary upheavals in church and state and broadly committed to the monarchs' reformist ecclesiastical agenda.[11]

Clerical acquiescence in the revolution perhaps served to temper the potential radicalism of the postrevolutionary ecclesiastical settlement, but it did so at an enormous ideological cost. The initial acceptance of the revolutionary monarchy of William and Mary and the reconstructed episcopate, however grudging or qualified in conscience, made it exceedingly difficult for churchmen to deny the new regime the full benefit of Anglican royalism. The strictures of Anglican political theology and ecclesiology, predicated above all on the principles of the royal supremacy and episcopacy, severely limited the conceptual resources available for clerical opposition to the crown and to the Williamite bishops. Thus, by the mid-1690s, as their disenchantment with the state of the postrevolutionary ecclesiastical establishment grew, high churchmen found themselves bereft of a language of legitimate opposition— which is to say a language that stopped short of the baldly counterrevolutionary discourses of Jacobitism and nonjuring.[12] The lower clergy, in particular, were hemmed in by the traditional political theology of the established church, which left them little means to oppose their political and ecclesiastical superiors in the revolution's establishment. Clerical opposition, if it was not to succumb to the temptation to maintain the principles of royal supremacy and episcopacy in abeyance on behalf of the exiled crown and the schismatic episcopate, could only proceed by extricating the dissident lower clergy from the civil and ecclesial hierarchies to which they were constitutionally and ecclesiologically consigned. In the later part of William's reign, the lower clergy thus began to refashion their high churchmanship, a courtly ideology par excellence, into something serviceable for legitimate opposition.

Anglican high churchmen at the end of the seventeenth century gravitated toward a robust constitutionalism redolent of an older "country ideology," that shopworn English political commitment to responsible government and the defense of traditional rights and privileges against executive aggrandizement.[13] Churchmen during the reign of William mobilized to secure what they referred to as the "rights of the clergy" against the courtly interests of crown and bishops alike. The lower clergy were, in effect, articulating their own peculiar critique of the growth of the state and its attendant corruptions.

In this, it might be thought that Anglican high churchmanship had been simply swept up in the broader currents of postrevolutionary Toryism, which was also undergoing a similar abnegation of its prior courtly orientation. But several factors complicate this easy assimilation. First, it must be remembered, Anglicanism did not possess oppositional resources comparable to those Tories possessed in property, Parliament, and the institutions of local governance. Second, such moves to enshrine the independent powers of the lower clergy within the English constitution cut clean against the grain of late-seventeenth-century Anglicanism, reconstructed after the trauma of regicide and disestablishment to militate against the leveling impulses of republicanism and presbyterianism. Finally, it should be noted, country ideology has traditionally been considered bereft of any particular religious content. As John Brewer has argued, religion was a peculiar area where the precepts of country ideology simply did not apply.[14] Others, however, have suggested that country ideology, with its suspicion of unaccountable power, tends to breed anticlericalism in religious thought.[15] All of these factors would seem to render country ideology profoundly unsuitable for the conservative lower clergy of the established church. So what might have constituted its appeal?

Anglican high churchmen at the turn of the eighteenth century discerned in country ideology a remarkably pluralistic vision of the English constitution. Such a framework allowed high churchman to enshrine the Church of England with a variety of "rights, powers and privileges" (to use Francis Atterbury's phrase) with which it was to be effectively immunized from court interference. Such historically realized immunities were increasingly called upon by these churchmen to ground powers and privileges that a more reactionary strain of nonjuring Anglicanism simply considered immutably divine and not subject to constitutional abridgment or authorization. Anglican high churchmanship in this period was thus preoccupied with the squaring of divine rights with constitutional ones. Country ideology allowed high churchmen to glean some measure of ecclesiastical security and independence within the constitution reaffirmed in the Revolution of 1688–1689.

This chapter will consider one particular manifestation of country ideology among the Anglican high churchmen of the late seventeenth century. In the wake of the great Trinitarian controversy of the 1690s, high churchmen began campaigning for the restoration of convocation, the long dormant provincial assembly of the Church of England, as means to refurbish the lapsed discipline of the postrevolutionary church.[16] Their objective was to imbue the ecclesiastical assembly with the same sort of constitutional indispensability achieved by Parliament in the Revolution of 1688–1689. To do so, convocation had to be effectively inoculated from the royal prerogative and the impositions of the bishops. High churchmen thus found in the language of country ideology a means to secure a traditional organ of the English constitution from the undue interference of the court. The texts of the convocation controversy suggest that the complex of seventeenth- and eighteenth-century ideals, often referred to as "the separation of church and state," should not be considered merely the property of enlightenment liberals or sectarian religious minorities. Anglican high churchmen at the turn of the eighteenth century were most assuredly neither of these things, and yet they too sought some means of demarcating the distinct spheres of civil and ecclesial life. Country ideology, they believed, equipped them with a means of securing the church from the court without quite severing church from state.

Anglican high church disenchantment with the postrevolutionary establishment assumed many forms. Among the most prominent was the complaint of proliferating heterodoxy in the public sphere.[17] In the final decade of the seventeenth century, the Church of England was consumed by a particularly bitter and protracted controversy over the doctrine of the Trinity, which became, for many, emblematic of the religious lassitude of the new regime.[18] "There have been more innovations upon and blasphemies against the chief articles of our faith published in this kingdom," thundered the famed high church preacher Robert South from the pulpit of Westminster Abbey in 1694, "and that after a more audacious and scandalous manner within these several years last past, than have been known here for some centuries of years before."[19] There was no misunderstanding the political import of South's chronology. The Trinitarian controversy, in which he was a prominent defender of theological orthodoxy, was but a symptom of the broader religious infirmity afflicting England "these several years last past"—that is, since the Revolution of 1688–1689. The doctrinal controversy rapidly acquired unmistakable political overtones. To Anglican high churchmen like South, the Williamite regime in church and state seemed feckless or, worse, complicit in the face of ever more audacious assaults on Christian orthodoxy pouring forth from the press. The controversy culminated in South's own evisceration of the work of William Sherlock, his former friend and dean of St. Paul's, who had ventured an ingenious, albeit theologically suspect, defense of Trinitarian orthodoxy in his *A Vindication of the Doctrine of the Holy and Ever Blessed Trinity.* South accused Sherlock of "tritheism" for describing the persons of the Trinity as "three distinct and infinite minds" distinguished from one another by "self-consciousness," yet united to one another by "mutual consciousness."[20] The propagation of such blasphemies by such a prominently placed dignitary of the established church was for South indisputable evidence of the lapse of discipline wrought by the revolution. An unimpaired church, South argued, would surely have seen "all and every one of these propositions . . . publicly and solemnly condemned," and the author of them "severely dealt with for asserting them."[21]

If South and his allies could not induce the crown or bishops to take action against Sherlock, they would use whatever means at their disposal to see his propositions condemned. Thus when the young clergyman Joseph Bingham preached a sermon on the seventh verse of the first chapter of John, "there are three that bear record in heaven," at St. Peter-in-the-East in Oxford in October 1695, South seized his opportunity. Bingham's meditation on the doctrine of the Trinity, in which he spoke of "three minds or spirits in the unity of the Godhead," seemed to veer perilously close to that of Sherlock. At South's prompting, the university convened to formally condemn the notion that "*there are three infinite distinct minds and substances in the Trinity*" as "false, impious, and heretical." The printed account of the decree made perfectly clear that "the propositions above-mentioned are Dr. Sherlock's."[22] The Oxford decree, the university's second formal intervention in the Trinitarian controversy since the revolution, made manifest what had been one of the latent themes in the dispute: the question of ecclesiastical authority and its competence to adjudicate orthodoxy. When Thomas Tenison, the Williamite archbishop of Canterbury, learned of the university's proceedings, he condemned them as "a high usurpation upon his Majesty's prerogative and a manifest violation of the laws of this realm."[23]

Archbishop Tenison rapidly moved to put an end to the long-running Trinitarian controversy. In February 1696, he prevailed upon the king to issue a set of directions "for preserving the unity of the church and the purity of the Christian faith, concerning the Holy Trinity."[24] These mandated that the doctrine of the Trinity taught must be conformable to Scripture, the Thirty-Nine Articles, and the three creeds. They forbade the use of new terms in explication of the doctrine as well as any "public opposition between preachers." The directives designed to quell the Trinitarian controversy outraged high churchmen. Their royal promulgation manifestly undermined the church's (or indeed, the university's) own authority to police heterodoxy; and its blanket prohibition of "bitter invectives and scurrilous language" on the part of the clergy evinced a greater concern for politeness than for sound doctrine.[25] Clearly the king and the archbishop thought more to be gained by the restoration of order than by the refutation of error. This would set a pattern for the controversy that followed. The Williamite bishops and clergy evinced a growing confidence in the wisdom of the state to successfully superintend the church, while disaffected high churchmen believed such disciplinary authority to be dispersed amid a variety of public organs subsisting beyond the court.

The high church agitation to restore the ecclesiastical assembly of convocation stemmed directly from controversy surrounding the Oxford condemnation of Joseph Bingham in 1695. In late 1696, the London clergyman Francis Atterbury (collaborating with the lawyer Sir Bartholomew Shower, a veteran of the Bingham affair and other Tory Anglican causes) penned his epochal *Letter to a Convocation-Man,* in which he cited a "universal conspiracy . . . of deists, Socinians, latitudinarians, deniers of mysteries, and pretending explainers of them, to undermine and overthrow the Catholic faith," as grounds for the revival of the dormant assembly.[26] "In plain English, then," Atterbury pled, "I think that, if ever there was need of convocation, since Christianity was established in this kingdom, there is need of one now."[27] Picking up on a thread from the Bingham affair, the letter proceeded to examine the variety of available instruments for the suppression of heterodoxy, underscoring the liabilities of each. The jurisdiction of the bishops was confined to their respective dioceses and jealously watched since the Reformation by the secular courts for any possible infringement upon the crown and its prerogatives. The authority of the universities could not be construed to extend beyond its own members. The House of Commons was composed of "country gentlemen, merchants, or lawyers" who lacked the skill in languages and theology to "sit judges of religious doctrines and opinions."[28]

Atterbury then warmed to his theme, which was the irreducible pluralism of the English Constitution. "The constitution," he wrote, "can be no otherwise upheld, than by the several parts of it being preserved in their just rights and powers; allowed to act in their proper spheres and circumscribed within them." The jealousy with which the houses of Parliament maintained "the rights and privileges of their bodies" would ensure "they would be careful not to invade those of another." The sphere of ecclesiastical affairs was the province of the convocation, Atterbury asserted, "as much a part of the constitution as the parliament itself."[29]

The Letter to a Convocation-Man was not, as Mark Goldie has argued, simply invoking the nonjurors' cherished doctrine of the two societies, the "coterminous, yet distinct spheres" of church and state, to underscore the constitutional parallelism of convocation and Parliament.[30] On the contrary, Atterbury wished to see the liberties of each enshrined in a singular, continuous common law.[31] The convocation, he rather curiously remarked, operates "by the same law as the gentlemen receives his rent, or the member [of Parliament] enjoys his privilege."[32] Indeed, the very first article of Magna Carta, "owned by every English-man to be only a royal publication of the common law," secured the liberty of the church, "a liberty of doing all that is requisite for a Church to do, and of using all its necessary powers and jurisdiction."[33] Such were the rights reaffirmed by every monarch in their coronation oaths—that indispensable linchpin of Whig political thought; and, Atterbury pointed out, the most recent oath, "framed and established by the

Convention Parliament, 1688" was no exception.[34] Atterbury construed this liberty of the Church not as the nonjurors did, as an independence from the state, but rather as an insulation by the common law from the royal supremacy, not fundamentally different from that which preserved Parliament from the royal prerogative. "An English Christian king," he wrote, "is as much obliged by the laws and usages had and accustomed in this kingdom in regard to the Church, as the sovereign of England is with regard to the state."[35] Just as the "king's share in the sovereignty . . . is lodg'd in the Parliament, is cut out to him by law, and not left at his disposal," Atterbury reasoned, so was the royal supremacy similarly embedded in the synods of the established church.[36] Atterbury did not dispute that the formal authority of assembling the convocation "is entirely dependent on the sovereign's will," but such must be construed as an ordinary prerogative realizable within law rather than as an absolute prerogative exercised against it; "the fundamentals of our government show him, when and how, that power is to be exercised."[37] The king, therefore, had no more right to dispense with convocations than with parliaments. "The liberties of the Church do, in great measure, run parallel to those of the State; and both of them, must according to the nature and constitution of our English government, stand or fall together."[38]

Atterbury was, however, far more gifted as a stylist than as a historical thinker. Throughout the *Letter,* he could not decide whether he believed Parliament and convocation to be merely analogous or, at some level, one and the same body. He placed a not inconsiderable amount of weight on the so-called *praemunientes* or "premonitory" clause, traditionally appended to the writs that summoned the bishops to Parliament. The clause directed the bishops "to attend upon the king in Parliament" with their deans, archdeacons, and proctors from their cathedral and diocesan clergy, thus providing the institutional basis for the lower house of convocation and, indeed, implying a parliamentary foundation for its assembly. This would, of course, allow the benefits of the common law arguments on behalf of the Parliament to accrue to the convocation, as well. The *praemunientes* clause furnished Atterbury with what he conceived as an "argument of invincible strength to establish the necessity of convocations meeting as often as parliaments."[39]

William Wake's weighty treatise *The Authority of Christian Princes over Their Ecclesiastical Synods,* written at the behest of Archbishop Tenison, appeared the following year as something of a court response to the anonymous *Letter to a Convocation-Man.*[40] Wake's book was a thunderous affirmation of the royal supremacy, that "Christian princes have a right, not only to exercise authority over ecclesiastical persons, but to interpose in the ordering of ecclesiastical affairs, too"—not only within the Church of England but in all European states "ever since the empire became Christian."[41] The power to convene all ecclesiastical assemblies rested with the "free and absolute will" of the sovereign, "a will not determined by any humane law," but only reason, divine law, and "the public good and welfare of the community."[42] Wake assailed the *Letter's* slipshod historical scholarship; its author, he claimed, had confused the historical parliamentary convocation summoned by the *praemunientes* clause with the provincial synods convened by the king's writ to the two archbishops. Traditionally, the lower clergy no less than the bishops were accounted "as part of the parliament of the realm," summoned to treat "with the other estates in granting money to the king." Though this assembly "consisted of ecclesiastical persons," it was convened expressly "for a civil end, and seems rather to have been a state convention than a Church synod."[43] Therefore, Wake conceded, "the convocation was once accounted, in this a respect, a member of parliament," but their membership in that body lapsed once the clergy in 1664 ceased to assess themselves in taxation.[44] These obsolete assemblies were not to be confused with the synods of the provinces of Canterbury and York, neither of which could be said to constitute a national assembly comparable to the Parliament. The Reformation restored against papal usurpations the right of the king to convene the two provincial synods; and indeed, that right remains a part of the royal prerogative, and a viable, if somewhat extravagant, instrument for the exercise of the royal supremacy over the church. However, Wake emphatically believed that the church had no need for such extraordinary recourses. "In a well-established Church," Wake wrote, "it can hardly be supposed that there be such a frequent need of convocations." Wake could not imagine anything more ridiculous than the spectacle of clergymen assembling to reaffirm the existence of God and Revelation, the divinity of Christ, and the triune nature of the deity; or that the doctrinal controversies of the day could be attributed in any way to the failure to do so. Moreover, the state already possessed in the sanction of the law sufficient resources to curb the heterodox; "'tis ridiculous to think that all the synods in the world should able to persuade them" more effectively than the restraint of "civil authority."[45] The Protestant monarchy, restored by the Revolution, offered more security for the church than any powers that might be reckoned amongst the nebulous rights of the clergy.[46] To drive this point home, Wake supplemented his treatise the following year with a compendium of Anglican vindications of the royal supremacy, so that his critics might see "what true agreement is between the priesthood and the empire, which our laws have established."[47]

An extraordinary response came forth from the pen of the Somerset clergyman Samuel Hill. Perhaps sensing the magnitude of Wake's historical assault on the *Letter to a Convocation-Man,* Hill's *Municipium Ecclesiasticum* abandoned Atterbury's "ancient constitution" for the state of nature. In this, he was remarkably replicating a tension inherent in Whig thought between the "ancient constitution" and the "original contract"—what Martyn Thompson and Harro Höpfl have described as "constitutional contractarianism" versus "philosophical contractarianism."[48] Hill located the origins of

human sociality in religious life, what he called "consociation with God."
"The first and most fundamental society," he wrote, "is the natural society
between God and man, maintained by the offices of natural religion on our
part, and the acts of God's paternal providence on his. . . . Herein was laid the
first foundation of ecclesiastical society and communion with God, which
more formally ripened into public and canonical form."[49] From this elemen-
tal form followed the succession of natural societies in which human life is
embedded: the matrimonial society, "founded in the structure of the sexes";
the economical society of the household, "between parents and children . . .
tutors and pupils, masters and servants"; what he called the "coordinate"
societies, bound either by justice, charity, or contract: "the friendships, factories, artificial fraternities and commerces, between either men, or nations,
cities, villages, &c." Finally, civil society obtained, "entrusted with the power of the sword . . . for the preservation of those rights and liberties, which are
necessary to the good order and well-being of mankind in all its forms of
society."[50] In Hill's ingenious formulation, the state existed not to preserve
the rights of the individuals that had freely contracted at its foundation, but
rather the corporate rights of the nested societies in which the natural life of
humans was apportioned. "Civil power was therefore superinduced at last
upon all the other substrate forms of society, not to destroy and devour, but to
defend them to the common felicity." Otherwise, "we shall think it the most
unnatural monster, made to devour its parents and originals." Simply put, the
Church preceded the State, which was merely charged with the preservation
of all natural societies; it was, therefore, "exempt from all right of extinction
by civil society."[51]

Samuel Hill's grounding of Anglican ecclesiology in human sociability
represented a road not taken by high churchmen at the turn of the eighteenth
century.[52] Though his account purported to secure the inviolability of the
church from what he called the "enslaving principle of sovereignty," it did so
only by affirming a generalized right of association. According to Hill's
principles, critics charged, any organization putatively devoted to the public
good could claim a heavenly mandate. "The divine right of convocations,"
the Whig clergyman Humphrey Hody wrote, "will as much prove a divine
right of constables and churchwardens."[53] Indeed, another critic scoffed,
Hill's doctrine afforded every company of tradesmen and artisans the same
"divine, unalienable authority" as any church in Christendom. "And is the
divine right of the Church come to this at last? The divine right of synods,
and the divine right of grocers and mercers all alike?"[54] Most problematic,
however, was Hill's manifest failure to secure the establishment of the
church along with its independence. For independence from the civil power,
without the privileges attendant upon legal establishment, was no more than
might be claimed by any nonconformist sect "either in Holland or the emu-
lous England," where dissenting churches maintained "an exemption" from

the civil power, "as entire as the chapels of foreign factories or ambassadors."[55] Indeed, in a subsequent pamphlet entitled *The Rites of the Christian Church Further Defended,* Samuel Hill supplemented his original covenant between ecclesial and civil society with "the terms of the several local contracts and coalitions . . . diverse in diverse places, and mutable in all," by which the rights of prerogative and ecclesiastical liberty had been historically apportioned.[56]

Francis Atterbury's response, *The Rights, Powers, and Priviledges of an English Convocation,* did not appear until 1700, but his general framework had not altered significantly in the intervening years. If anything, the unabashed Erastianism of William Wake's polemic, "a plea for the boundless authority of sovereigns in Church-matters," only confirmed the constitutionalist thrust of his initial position.[57] Wake's discrimination between parliamentary convocations and provincial synods comprised a distinction without a difference: mere convenience had allowed the clergy to "meet parliamentarily" in fulfillment of the *praemunientes* clause, even though assembled provincially.[58] The inferior clergy, he conceded, were thus not one of three estates of Parliament, "not an intrinsic member . . . or estate of Parliament; but only an extrinsic part of it, or an estate of the realm, called with the Parliament always, and attending upon it."[59] The clergy were, "a lesser wheel in the machine of government, that is acted by the same springs and weights, and therefore moves and ceases together with the greater."[60] Their rights could not be suppressed, "without doing violence to our good old constitution."[61]

Perhaps most importantly, Atterbury's vague "country" churchmanship was now paired with a strident critique of a recognizable court interest.[62] The Williamite bishops and clergy who wrote in defense of the royal supremacy comprised a pack of "Church-Empsons and Dudleys," Atterbury wrote, invoking the notorious ministers of Henry VII, whose names had become a byword for court aggrandizement.[63] Even more outrageously, Atterbury repeatedly compared the Williamite clergy to the ultra-Erastian bishops Samuel Parker and Thomas Cartwright, who colluded with James II in "new schemes of Church government twelve years ago."[64] A new breed of court instruments afforded the crown a supremacy so exalted that it would "have an immediate tendency toward subverting liberty in general." Indeed, Atterbury warned, the laity had no less cause for concern than did the beleaguered clergy, for "if slavery be once established in the Church, it will quickly spread itself into the state."[65] Court creatures such as the Williamite bishops were incapable of defending the rights of the church. Such men "dare not say no to the state," Samuel Hill chided, "because the Leviathan is not safely to be angered."[66] This characterization of a supine episcopate colluding with an aggrandizing monarch effectively completed the fusion of an older country

ideology, in which the liberty secured by the ancient constitution was imper-
iled by the corruptions of the court, with an emergent rhetoric of "the church
in danger."[67]

This tropology rapidly spread beyond the boundaries of the convocation
controversy. Indeed, one need look no farther than Henry Sachverell's incen-
diary *The Character of a Low-Churchman,* written in 1702, to find this
rhetoric deployed in its full amplitude. "To whom does the Church owe its
weakness and impotency," asked Sacheverell, "but either to those supreme
officers that are its judges, who have stopped that power in themselves, or
[those who] have given it out of the Church . . . into the hands of the civil
power?"[68] There, and increasingly elsewhere, one can clearly find the complaints of the clergy fully integrated into a litany of more familiar country
grievances such as the national debt, the standing army, the partition treaty,
and the misapplication of public funds.[69] For a moment, at least, it was
possible to insinuate the Church of England among the panoply of traditional
institutions putatively threatened by the burgeoning post revolutionary state.

The strain of country ideology discernible in Anglican high churchmanship would by no means retain the prominence it possessed at the end of the
reign of William III. The accession of the devoutly Anglican Queen Anne in
1702 offered the prospect of a rapprochement with the court by which high
churchmen could simply revert to their default royalism. Anne's selection of
high church bishops helped to ameliorate in some measure the profound
alienation of the lower clergy under William's supremacy. Moreover, by this
point the nonjuring schism had evolved into something more than simply the
clerical wing of Jacobitism; it was now rather an intellectually vibrant revolt
against Erastianism, whose sacerdotal and sacramental principles were increasingly palatable even to the conformist clergy.[70] In other words, the
choice between Jacobitism and Whiggery faced by high churchmen at the
revolution seemed no longer quite so stark. During the reign of Queen Anne,
Anglican high churchmen could resume the posture of a court party, subsid-
ing under an increasingly Tory episcopate and railing in defense of the royal
supremacy, as Henry Sacheverell would do in his infamous 1709 sermon,
The Perils of False Brethren. And yet, they could also flirt with the high
sacerdotalism that had come to define the nonjurors, particularly after the
deaths of the last of the deprived bishops went some length toward healing
the initial schism. Moreover, more than a few prominent high churchmen
during the reign of Queen Anne, faced with the prospect of an alien Lutheran
dynasty and the concomitant Whig hegemony that would surely obtain at its
succession, even warmed to the idea of a Stuart restoration.[71] In the early
eighteenth century, it seems, there was a diminished need for opposition as
well as a far greater number of positions from which to articulate a full-
throated defense of the Church of England.

However, the impulse behind the high church adoption of country ideology persisted throughout the early eighteenth century, and provides something of map to the locations of ecclesiastical conflict throughout the period. The rapprochement between church and crown was never fully realized under Anne, who still depended on Whigs to wage the War of the Spanish Succession; ensure the credit and revenues of the state; and secure the Protestant succession of the house of Hanover. The lower clergy nursed their alienation, as evident from the long-running defense of the independence of the lower house of convocation from the bishops; the clamoring for re-impropriation of tithes; and the attempts to insulate the cathedral chapters from episcopal visitation that prompted the Whig-sponsored Cathedrals Act of 1708. All of these, proceeding under the banner of "the rights of the clergy," were indeed further attempts to gain some constitutional footing for the lower clergy against the encroachments not of the state per se, but rather of the court: the potentially dangerous confluence of episcopal and monarchical power that threatened to unbalance the constitution and overwhelm the church. This superimposition of country ideology, with its concomitant critique of the court, over the general platform of "the church in danger," continued to appeal to Anglican high churchmen. It allowed them to, in some measure, overcome the limitations on clerical dissent posed by the extreme hierarchism of Restoration ecclesiology. Opposition to what Sacheverell deemed "the state machines" of the court could perhaps retain a legitimacy traditionally disallowed to critique of either episcopal or royal governance of the established church.

Nowhere is this more evident than in the convocation itself. The high church agitation to restore convocation culminated in the recall of the assembly by William in 1701. Unfortunately, the restoration of convocation merely gave institutional form to the intractability and bitterness of the preceding pamphlet wars. The high church majority of clergy in the lower house struggled mightily but fruitlessly to achieve some form of operative independence from both the bishops in the upper house and the crown, whose patent was required for the transaction of business. The lower house formed an intransigent opposition bogged down in procedural skirmishes, and their pretensions of autonomy from the bishops and the crown prompted Whig clergymen to denounce (often with great relish) what William Sherlock warned was "the new danger of presbytery" among Anglican high churchmen.[72] This situation was not altered in any substantial way by the accession of Queen Anne, in spite of her alleged sympathy for the high church cause. Indeed, on February 25, 1706, Anne was forced to dispatch a letter to Archbishop Tenison, in which she pledged to "preserve the constitution of the Church of England as by law established," and "resolved to maintain our supremacy and the due subordination of presbyters to bishops, as fundamental parts thereof."[73] Of course, such affirmations had been a fairly routine occurrence in the lives of

Stuart monarchs, at least since the Hampton Court Conference almost exactly a century earlier. That Anne's letter was directed not toward Puritan, Covenanter, nor Whig, but toward the conservative Anglican clergy in the lower house of convocation, gives some measure of the extraordinary ideological distance already traveled by Anglican high churchmen in their long sojourn from the court.

REFERENCES

"A Letter to a Friend, offering some Reasons, why the University of Oxford could not handsomely create Mr William Nicholson (Lord Bishop of Carlisle Elect) Doctor in Divinity 29 June 1702," BL Add MS 27440 f. 21.

Atterbury, Francis. *A Letter to a Convocation-Man, Concerning the Rights, Powers and Privileges of that Body.* London, 1697.

———. *The Rights, Powers, and Priviledges of an English Convocation.* London, 1700. BL Lansdowne 1024 f. 105

Babcock, W. S. "A Changing of the Christian God: The Doctrine of the Trinity in the Seventeenth Century," *Interpretation,* 45 (April 1991).

Barclay, Andrew. "James II's 'Catholic' Court," *1650–1850: Ideas, Aesthetics, and Inquiries into the Early Modern Era,* 8 (2003).

Beddard, R. A. "Bishop Cartwright's Death-Bed." *Bodleian Library Record* 11 (1984).

———. "The Restoration Church," in J. R. Jones, ed., *The Restored Monarchy 1660–1688.* Totowa, NJ: Rowman & Littlefield, 1979.

Beiser, F. C. *The Sovereignty of Reason.* Princeton, NJ: Princeton University Press, 1996.

Bennett, G. V. "Conflict in the Church," in Geoffrey Holmes, ed., *Britain after the Glorious Revolution, 1689-1714.* London: Macmillan, 1969.

———. "King William III and the Episcopate" in G. V. Bennett and J. D. Walsh, eds., *Essays in Modern English Church History.* New York: Oxford University Press, 1966.

———. "The Seven Bishops: A Reconsideration," in *Studies in Church History,* 15 (1978).

———. *The Tory Crisis in Church and State 1688–1730: The Career of Francis Atterbury, Bishop of Rochester.* Oxford, UK: Clarendon Press, 1975.

Bodleian [Bodl] Ballard MS 9 ff. 28–29.

Brewer, John. *The Sinews of Power: War, Money and the English State, 1688–1783.* Cambridge, MA: Harvard University Press, 1988.

Brooks, Colin. "The Country Persuasion and Political Responsibility in England in the 1690s," *Parliaments, Estates and Representation,* 4 (Dec. 1984).

Burgess, Glenn. *The Politics of the Ancient Constitution: An Introduction to English Political Thought, 1603–1642.* University Park, PA: Pennsylvania State University Press, 1992.

Burtt, Shelly. *Virtue Transformed: Political Argument in England, 1688–1740.* Cambridge, UK: Cambridge University Press, 1992.

Carpenter, E. *Thomas Tenison, Archbishop of Canterbury.* London, 1948.

Chamberlain, Jeffrey S. *Accommodating High Churchmen: The Clergy of Sussex, 1700–1745.* Urbana & Chicago: University of Illinois Press, 1997.

Champion, J.A.I. "Making Authority: Belief, Conviction and Reason in the Public Sphere in Late Seventeenth-Century England," *Libertinage et philosophie au XVIIe siecle* 3 (1999).

Champion, Justin. *The Pillars of Priestcraft Shaken: The Church of England and Its Enemies, 1660–1730.* Cambridge, UK: Cambridge University Press, 1992.

Claydon, Tony. *William III and the Godly Revolution.* Cambridge, UK: Cambridge University Press, 1996.

Cornwall, Robert D. "Politics and the Lay Baptism Controversy in England, 1708–1715," in Robert D. Cornwall and William Gibson, eds., *Religion, Politics and Dissent, 1660–1832: Essays in Honour of James E. Bradley.* Farnham, UK: Ashgate, 2010.

———. *Visible and Apostolic: The Constitution of the Church in High Church Anglican and Non-Juror Thought.* Newark, DE: University of Delaware Press, 1993.

Cruickshanks, Eveline, and Howard Erskine-Hill, *The Atterbury Plot.* New York: Palgrave Macmillan, 2004.

Dickinson, H. T. *Liberty and Property: Political Ideology in Eighteenth Century Britain.* New York: Holmes and Meier, 1977.

Directions to our arch-bishops and bishops for preserving the unity of the church and the purity of the Christian faith, concerning the Holy Trinity. London, 1695.

Dixon, Philip. *Nice and Hot Disputes: The Doctrine of the Trinity in the Seventeenth Century.* London & New York: T&T Clark, 2003.

Douglass, David. *English Scholars 1660–1730,* 2nd ed. London: Eyre & Spottiswoode, 1951.

Glassey, L.K.J. "William III and the Settlement of Religion in Scotland, 1689–1690." *Records of the Scottish Church History Society,* 23 (1989).

Goldie, Mark. "John Locke and Anglican Royalism." *Political Studies,* XXXI (1983).

———. "The Nonjurors, Episcopacy, and the Origins of the Convocation Controversy," in E. Cruickshanks, ed., *Ideology and Conspiracy: Aspects of Jacobitism, 1689–1759.* Edinburgh: J. Donalds, 1982.

———. "The Political Thought of the Anglican Revolution," in Robert Beddard, ed., *The Revolutions of 1688.* Oxford, UK: Clarendon Press, 1991.

———. "Priestcraft and the Birth of Whiggism," in N. T. Phillipson and Quentin Skinner, eds., *Political Discourse in Early Modern Britain.* Cambridge, UK: Cambridge University Press, 1993.

Hampton, Stephen. *Anti-Arminians: The Anglican Reformed Tradition from Charles II to George I.* Oxford, UK: Oxford University Press, 2008.

Harris, Tim. *Revolution: The Great Crisis of the British Monarchy, 1685–1720.* Penguin Books, 2007.

Hayton, David. "The 'Country' Interest and the Party System, 1689–c.1720," in C. Jones, ed., *Party and Management in Parliament, 1660–1784.* New York: Palgrave Macmillan, 1984.

———. "Moral Reform and Country Politics in the Late Seventeenth-Century House of Commons," *Past and Present,* 128 (Aug. 1990).

Hedley, D. "Persons of Substance and the Cambridge Connection: Some Roots and Ramifications of the Trinitarian Controversy in Seventeenth-Century England," in M. Muslow and J. Rohls, eds., *Socinianism and Arminianism: Antitrinitarians, Calvinists and Cultural Exchange in Seventeenth-Century Europe.* Leiden: Brill, 2005.

Hoak, Dale, and Mordechai Fiengold (eds.). "The Act of Toleration and the Failure of Comprehension: Persecution, Nonconformity, and Religious Indifference," in *The World of William and Mary: Anglo-Dutch Perspectives on the Revolution of 1688–89.* Stanford, CA: Stanford University Press, 1996.

Hill, Samuel. *Municipium Ecclesiasticum, or, The Rights, Liberties, and Authorities of the Christian Church.* London, 1687.

———. *The Rites of the Christian Church further defended, In Answer to the Appeal of Dr. Wake.* London, 1698.

Hody, Humphrey. *Some thoughts on a Convocation, And the Notion of its Divine Right.* London, 1699.

Holmes, Geoffrey (ed.). *Britain after the Glorious Revolution, 1689–1714.* London: Macmillan, 1969.

———. *Politics, Religion and Society in England, 1679–1742.* London: Hambledon Press, 1986.

———. *The Trial of Doctor Sacheverell.* London: Eyre Methuen, 1973.

Horwitz, Henry. *Parliament, Policy and Politics in the Reign of William III* (Newark, DE: University of Delaware Press, 1977.

Kenyon, John P. *Revolution Principles: The Politics of Party 1689–1720.* Cambridge, UK: Cambridge University Press, 1977.

Kramnick, Isaac. "Augustan Politics and English Historiography: The Debate on the English Past, 1730–35," *History and Theory,* 6 (1967).

Lund, R. D. "Guilt by Association: The Atheist Cabal and the Rise of the Public Sphere in Augustan England," *Albion*, 34 (2002).

Marshall, John. *John Locke: Resistance, Religion and Responsibility*. Cambridge, UK: Cambridge University Press, 1994.

Mather, F. C. *High Church Prophet: Bishop Samuel Horsley (1733–1806) and the Caroline Tradition in the Later Georgian Church*. Oxford, UK: Oxford University Press, 1992.

Monod, Paul. "Jacobitism and Country Principles in the Reign of William III." *Historical Journal*, 30 (June 1987).

Mortimer, Sarah. *Reason and Religion in the English Revolution: The Challenge of Socinianism*. Cambridge, UK: Cambridge University Press, 2010.

Nicolson, William. *The Copy Correspondence of Bishop William Nicolson & Archbishop Wake, 1697–1725*. Victoria & Albert Museum, Forster Collection, microfilm.

Nockles, Peter B. *The Oxford Movement in Context*. Cambridge, UK: Cambridge University Press, 1994.

Overton, J. H. *The Nonjurors: Their Lives, Principles and Writings*. London: Smith, Elder, 1902.

Pincus, Steve. *1688: The First Modern Revolution*. New Haven, CT: Yale University Press, 2009.

Redwood, J. *Reason, Ridicule and Religion: The Age of Enlightenment in England, 1660–1750*. London: Thames & Hudson, 1976.

Placher, William C. *The Domestication of Transcendence*. Louisville, KY: Westminster John Knox Press, 1996.

Queen Anne to Thomas Tenison, Feb 25, 1705/6, BL Add MS 61612 f. 144.

Rose, Craig. *England in the 1690s*. Malden, MA: Blackwell, 1999.

Rose, Jacqueline. "The Ecclesiastical Polity of Samuel Parker." *The Seventeenth Century*, 25 (Oct 2010).

———. "Royal Ecclesiastical Supremacy and the Restoration Church." *Historical Research*, 209 (June 2007).

Rowell, Geoffrey (ed.). *Tradition Renewed: The Oxford Movement Conference Papers*. Allison Park, PA: Pickwick Publications, 1986.

Rupp, Gordon. *Religion in England 1688–1791*. Oxford, UK: Oxford University Press, 1987.

Sacheverell, Henry. *The Character of a Low-Churchman*. London, 1702.

Schochet, Gordon. "Between Lambeth and Leviathan: Samuel Parker on the Church of England and Political Order," in N. T. Phillipson and Quentin Skinner, eds., *Political Discourse in Early Modern Britain*. Cambridge, UK: Cambridge University Press, 1993.

———. "From Persecution to 'Toleration,'" in J. R. Jones, ed., *Liberty Secured? Britain Before and After 1688*. Stanford, CA: Stanford University Press, 1992.

———. "Samuel Parker, Religious Diversity and the Ideology of Persecution," in Roger D. Lund, ed., *The Margins of Orthodoxy: Heterodox Writing and Cultural Response 1660–1750*. Cambridge, UK: Cambridge University Press, 1995.

Sharp, Richard. "New Perspectives on High Church Tradition: Historical Background 1730–1780," in Geoffrey Rowell, ed., *Tradition Renewed: The Oxford Movement Conference Papers*. Allison Park, PA: Pickwick Publications, 1986.

Sherlock, William. *The New Danger of Presbytery, or, The Claims and Practices of some in the Lower House of Convocation very dangerous to the constitution of an Episcopal and Metropolitical Church*. London, 1703.

———. *A Vindication of the Doctrine of the Holy and Ever Blessed Trinity and the Incarnation of the Son of God, occasioned by the Brief Notes on the Creed and St, Athanasius, and the Brief History of the Unitarians, or Socinians*. London, 1690.

Sirota, Brent S. "The Trinitarian Crisis in Church and State: Religious Controversy and the Making of the Post-Revolutionary Church of England, 1687-1702," *Journal of British Studies*, forthcoming.

Smith, R. J. *The Gothic Bequest: Medieval Institutions in British Thought, 1688–1813*. Cambridge, UK: Cambridge University Press, 1987.

South, Robert. *Animadversions upon Dr. Sherlock's book, entituled A vindication of the holy and ever-blessed Trinity, &c.* London, 1693.

———. "Christianity Mysterious and the Wisdom of God in making it so prov'd in a Sermon Preached at Westminster-Abbey, April 29, 1694," in *Sermons Preached upon several occasions*, 6 vols. London, 1737.

Spurr, John. "The Church of England, Comprehension and the Toleration Act of 1689" *English Historical Review*, 413 (Oct. 1989).

Taylor, Stephen. "The Character of a Church Whig" (unpublished lecture delivered at Dr. Williams's Library, November 24, 2007).

Tension, Thomas. "Thomas Tension to Fitzherbert Adams," Dec. 24 1695, British Library [BL] Add. MS 799 ff. 149–151; Bodleian [Bodl] Ballard MS 9 ff. 28–29.

Thomas, Roger. "Comprehension and Indulgence," in Owen Chadwick and G. F. Nuttall, eds., *From Uniformity to Unity, 1662–1962.* London: SPCK, 1962.

Thompson, Martyn P., and Harro Höpfl, "The History of Contract as a Motif in Political Thought," *The American Historical Review*, 84 (Oct 1979).

Trevor-Roper, Hugh. "Toleration and Religion after 1688," in Ole Peter Grell, Jonathan I. Israel, and Nicholas Tyacke, eds, *From Persecution to Toleration: The Glorious Revolution and Religion in England.* Oxford: Clarendon Press, 1991.

Trowell, Stephen. "Unitarian and/or Anglican: The Relationship of Unitarian to the Church from 1687 to 1698," *Bulletin of the John Rylands University Library of Manchester*, 78 (1996).

Wake, William. *An appeal to all True Members of the Church of England In behalf of the King's Ecclesiastical Supremacy.* London, 1698, sig. A2r.

———. *The Authority of Christian Princes over the Ecclesiastical Synods.* London, 1697.

———. *William Wake Diary*, Lambeth Palace Library [LPL] MS 2932 f. 80.

NOTES

1. William Nicolson to William Wake, Mar. 3, 1697 f. 1 in *The Copy Correspondence of Bishop William Nicolson & Archbishop Wake, 1697–1725*, Victoria & Albert Museum, Forster Collection, microfilm. Spelling, punctuation, and capitalization in all quotations have been modernized; titles cited have been left unaltered.

2. On the "new high church party" of the postrevolutionary era, see G. V. Bennett, "Conflict in the Church" in Geoffrey Holmes, ed., *Britain after the Glorious Revolution, 1689–1714* (London: Macmillan, 1969), 165; Geoffrey Holmes, *The Trial of Doctor Sacheverell* (London: Eyre Methuen, 1973), 22–44; Gordon Rupp, *Religion in England 1688–1791* (Oxford: Oxford University Press, 1987), 53–70; for a broader perspective, see Robert D. Cornwall, *Visible and Apostolic: The Constitution of the Church in High Church Anglican and Non-Juror Thought* (Newark, DE: University of Delaware Press, 1993); Jeffrey S. Chamberlain, *Accommodating High Churchmen: The Clergy of Sussex, 1700–1745* (Urbana & Chicago: University of Illinois Press, 1997); Richard Sharp, "New Perspectives on High Church Tradition: Historical Background 1730–1780" in Geoffrey Rowell, ed., *Tradition Renewed: The Oxford Movement Conference Papers* (Allison Park, PA: Pickwick Publications, 1986), 4–23; F. C. Mather, *High Church Prophet: Bishop Samuel Horsley (1733–1806) and the Caroline Tradition in the Later Georgian Church* (Oxford, UK: Oxford University Press, 1992); Peter B. Nockles, *The Oxford Movement in Context* (Cambridge, UK: Cambridge University Press, 1994), 44–103.

3. R. A. Beddard, "The Restoration Church" in J. R. Jones, ed., *The Restored Monarchy 1660–1688* (Totowa, NJ: Rowman & Littlefield, 1979), 155–175; Mark Goldie, "John Locke and Anglican Royalism," *Political Studies* XXXI (1983), 61–85; J. P. Kenyon, *Revolution Principles: The Politics of Party 1689–1720* (Cambridge, UK: Cambridge University Press, 1977), 61–82.

4. John Spurr, *The Restoration Church of England, 1646–1689* (New Haven, CT, and London: Yale University Press, 1991), 147; Jeffrey R. Collins, "The Restoration Bishops and the Royal Supremacy, *Church History,* 68 (Sept. 1999), 549–580; Jacqueline Rose, "Royal Ecclesiastical Supremacy and the Restoration Church," *Historical Research,* 209 (June 2007), 324–345.

5. G. V. Bennett, "The Seven Bishops: A Reconsideration" in *Studies in Church History,* 15 (1978), 267–287; Mark Goldie, "The Political Thought of the Anglican Revolution," in Robert Beddard, ed., *The Revolutions of 1688* (Oxford, UK: Clarendon Press, 1991), 102–136; Tim Harris, *Revolution: The Great Crisis of the British Monarchy, 1685–1720* (Penguin Books, 2007), 239–268; for a critique of the notion of an Anglican Revolution, see Steve Pincus, *1688: The First Modern Revolution* (New Haven, CT: Yale University Press, 2009), 400–434.

6. Kenyon, *Revolution Principles,* 101.

7. This, of course, was not the case in Scotland, see L.K.J. Glassey, "William III and the Settlement of Religion in Scotland, 1689–1690," *Records of the Scottish Church History Society* 23 (1989), 317–329; Tim Harris, *Revolution,* 350–351.

8. Henry Horwitz, *Parliament, Policy and Politics in the Reign of William III* (Newark, DE: University of Delaware Press, 1977), 22–26; Craig Rose, *England in the 1690s* (Malden, MA: Blackwell, 1999), 161–171.

9. Roger Thomas, "Comprehension and Indulgence," in Owen Chadwick and G. F. Nuttall, eds., *From Uniformity to Unity, 1662–1962* (London: SPCK, 1962), 190–253; John Spurr, "The Church of England, Comprehension and the Toleration Act of 1689" *English Historical Review,* 413 (Oct. 1989), 927–946; Gordon J. Schochet, "From Persecution to 'Toleration'," in J. R. Jones, ed., *Liberty Secured? Britain Before and After 1688* (Stanford, CA: Stanford University Press, 1992), 122–157; idem., "The Act of Toleration and the Failure of Comprehension: Persecution, Nonconformity, and Religious Indifference," in Dale Hoak and Mordechai Fiengold, eds., *The World of William and Mary: Anglo-Dutch Perspectives on the Revolution of 1688–89* (Stanford, CA: Stanford University Press, 1996), 165–187; Hugh Trevor-Roper, "Toleration and Religion after 1688," in Ole Peter Grell, Jonathan I. Israel, and Nicholas Tyacke, eds., *From Persecution to Toleration: The Glorious Revolution and Religion in England* (Oxford, UK: Clarendon Press, 1991), 389–408.

10. On the nonjurors, see J. H. Overton, *The Nonjurors: Their Lives, Principles and Writings* (London: Smith, Elder, 1902).

11. On the ideological composition of the Williamite episcopate, see G. V. Bennett, "King William III and the Episcopate " in G. V. Bennett and J. D. Walsh, eds., *Essays in Modern English Church History* (1966), 104–132; Craig Rose, *England in the 1690s,* 182–183; Tony Claydon, *William III and the Godly Revolution* (Cambridge, UK: Cambridge University Press, 1996); Steve Pincus, *1688: The First Modern Revolution* (New Haven, CT: Yale University Press, 2009), 400–434.

12. Indeed, Paul Monod has argued that after 1693, Jacobitism conspicuously abandoned an older strain of high royalism and embraced a "country" program; see Paul Monod, "Jacobitism and Country Principles in the Reign of William III," *Historical Journal,* 30 (June 1987), 289–310.

13. John Brewer, *The Sinews of Power: War, Money and the English State, 1688–1783* (Cambridge, MA: Harvard University Press, 1988), 155–161; H. T. Dickinson, *Liberty and Property: Political Ideology in Eighteenth Century Britain* (New York: Holmes and Meier, 1977), 163–192; Colin Brooks, "The Country Persuasion and Political Responsibility in England in the 1690s," *Parliaments, Estates and Representation* 4 (Dec. 1984), 135–146; David Hayton, "The 'Country' Interest and the Party System, 1689–c.1720," in C. Jones, ed., *Party and Management in Parliament, 1660–1784* (New York: Palgrave Macmillan, 1984), 37–85.

14. Brewer, *Sinews of Power,* 157; although David Hayton associates "country ideology" with a politics of virtue and moral renewal that had certain affinities with Anglican churchmanship in this period, David Hayton, "Moral Reform and Country Politics in the Late Seventeenth-Century House of Commons," *Past and Present* 128 (Aug. 1990), 48–91; see also Shelly Burtt, *Virtue Transformed: Political Argument in England, 1688–1740* (Cambridge, UK: Cambridge University Press, 1992), 87–109.

15. Mark Goldie, "Priestcraft and the Birth of Whiggism" in N. T. Phillipson and Quentin Skinner, eds., *Political Discourse in Early Modern Britain* (Cambridge, UK: Cambridge University Press, 1993), 209–231; Justin Champion, *The Pillars of Priestcraft Shaken: The Church of England and Its Enemies, 1660–1730* (Cambridge, UK: Cambridge University Press, 1992).

16. Convocation had not assembled for business since 1664, when the clergy ceased to assess themselves separately for purposes of taxation. The assembly was very briefly recalled following the Revolution in 1689, but was paralyzed by ecclesiastical partisanship and dissolved by William after sitting intermittently for about four weeks.

17. R. D. Lund, "Guilt by Association: The Atheist Cabal and the Rise of the Public Sphere in Augustan England," *Albion,* 34 (2002), 391–421.

18. On the controversy, see Brent S. Sirota, "The Trinitarian Crisis in Church and State: Religious Controversy and the Making of the Post-Revolutionary Church of England, 1687–1702," *Journal of British Studies,* forthcoming. There is a substantial literature on the controversy: J. Redwood, *Reason, Ridicule and Religion: The Age of Enlightenment in England, 1660–1750* (London: Thames & Hudson, 1976), 156–172; John Marshall, *John Locke: Resistance, Religion and Responsibility* (Cambridge, UK: Cambridge University Press, 1994), 384–410; F. C. Beiser, *The Sovereignty of Reason* (Princeton, NJ: Princeton University Press, 1996), 220–265; Philip Dixon, *Nice and Hot Disputes: The Doctrine of the Trinity in the Seventeenth Century* (London & New York: T&T Clark, 2003); D. Hedley, "Persons of Substance and the Cambridge Connection: Some Roots and Ramifications of the Trinitarian Controversy in Seventeenth-Century England," in M. Muslow and J. Rohls, eds., *Socinianism and Arminianism: Antitrinitarians, Calvinists and Cultural Exchange in Seventeenth-Century Europe* (Leiden: Brill, 2005), 225–240; W. S. Babcock, "A Changing of the Christian God: The Doctrine of the Trinity in the Seventeenth Century," *Interpretation,* 45 (April 1991), 133–146; Stephen Trowell, "Unitarian and/or Anglican: The Relationship of Unitarian to the Church from 1687 to 1698," *Bulletin of the John Rylands University Library of Manchester,* 78 (1996), 77–101; William C. Placher, *The Domestication of Transcendence* (Louisville, KY: Westminster John Knox Press, 1996), 164–178; J.A.I. Champion, "Making Authority: Belief, Conviction and Reason in the Public Sphere in Late Seventeenth-Century England," *Libertinage et philosophie au XVIIe siècle,* 3 (1999), 143–190; Stephen Hampton, *Anti-Arminians: The Anglican Reformed Tradition from Charles II to George I* (Oxford, UK: Oxford University Press, 2008), 129–191; Sarah Mortimer, *Reason and Religion in the English Revolution: The Challenge of Socinianism* (Cambridge, UK: Cambridge University Press, 2010), 233–241.

19. Robert South, "Christianity Mysterious and the Wisdom of God in making it so prov'd in a Sermon Preached at Westminster-Abbey, April 29, 1694," in *Sermons Preached upon several occasions,* 6 vols. (London, 1737), III:218.

20. William Sherlock, *A Vindication of the Doctrine of the Holy and Ever Blessed Trinity and the Incarnation of the Son of God, occasioned by the Brief Notes on the Creed and St, Athanasius, and the Brief History of the Unitarians, or Socinians* (London, 1690); Robert South, *Animadversions upon Dr. Sherlock's book, entituled A vindication of the holy and ever-blessed Trinity, &c.* (London, 1693).

21. South, *Animadversions,* i-v.

22. *An account of the decree of the University of Oxford, against some heretical tenets* (London, 1695).

23. Thomas Tension to Fitzherbert Adams, Dec. 24 1695, British Library [BL] Add. MS 799 ff. 149–151; Bodleian [Bodl] Ballard MS 9 ff. 28–29.

24. BL Lansdowne 1024 f. 105; E. Carpenter, *Thomas Tenison, Archbishop of Canterbury* (London, 1948), 299–300.

25. *Directions to our arch-bishops and bishops for preserving the unity of the church and the purity of the Christian faith, concerning the Holy Trinity* (London, 1695), 5–6.

26. Francis Atterbury, *A Letter to a Convocation-Man, Concerning the Rights, Powers and Privileges of that Body* (London, 1697), 5; On Shower's involvement, see G. V. Bennett, *The Tory Crisis in Church and State 1688–1730: The Career of Francis Atterbury, Bishop of Rochester* (Clarendon Press: Oxford, 1975), 48.

27. Atterbury, *Letter,* 2.

28. Atterbury, *Letter,* 8–15.

29. Atterbury, *Letter*, 16.

30. Mark Goldie, "The Nonjurors, Episcopacy, and the Origins of the Convocation Controversy," in E. Cruickshanks, ed., *Ideology and Conspiracy: Aspects of Jacobitism, 1689–1759* (Edinburgh: J. Donalds, 1982), 15–35; their purpose was to show the inviolability of an Apostolic episcopal church from civil interference—specifically, the parliamentary deprivation of the nonjuring bishops in 1690; but their ecclesiology, predicated as it was on Cyprianic, "quasi-monarchic" theories of episcopacy would not have served Atterbury's real purpose, which was to secure the independence of the lower clergy from scepter and miter alike.

31. R. J. Smith, *The Gothic Bequest: Medieval Institutions in British Thought, 1688–1813* (Cambridge: Cambridge University Press, 1987), 28–38; Bennett, *Tory Crisis in Church and State*, 48–56; David Douglass, *English Scholars 1660–1730*, 2nd ed. (London: Eyre & Spottiswoode, 1951), 195–221; Isaac Kramnick, "Augustan Politics and English Historiography: The Debate on the English Past, 1730–35," *History and Theory*, 6 (1967), 33–56.

32. Atterbury, *Letter*, 21.

33. Atterbury, *Letter*, 59–60.

34. Atterbury, *Letter*, 22–23, 61.

35. Atterbury, *Letter*, 50–51.

36. Atterbury, *Letter*, 33.

37. Atterbury, *Letter*, 33; on the distinctions between ordinary and absolute prerogative in the common law rhetoric of the ancient constitution, see Glenn Burgess, *The Politics of the Ancient Constitution: An Introduction to English Political Thought, 1603–1642* (University Park, PA: Pennsylvania State University Press, 1992), 89, 139–167.

38. Atterbury, *Letter*, 50.

39. Atterbury, *Letter*, 38.

40. William Wake Diary, Lambeth Palace Library [LPL] MS 2932 f. 80.

41. William Wake, *The Authority of Christian Princes over the Ecclesiastical Synods* (London, 1697), 10.

42. Wake, *Authority of Christian Princes*, 141–144.

43. Wake, *Authority of Christian Princes*, 105–106.

44. Wake, *Authority of Christian Princes*, 252.

45. Wake, *Authority of Christian Princes*, 310–313.

46. On the making of what would be called "church whiggery," see Stephen Taylor, "The Character of a Church Whig" (unpublished lecture delivered at Dr. Williams's Library, November 24, 2007). I am grateful to Dr. Taylor for making a copy of his lecture available to me.

47. William Wake, *An appeal to all True Members of the Church of England In behalf of the King's Ecclesiastical Supremacy* (London, 1698), sig. A2r.

48. Martyn P. Thompson and Harro Höpfl, "The History of Contract as a Motif in Political Thought," *The American Historical Review*, 84 (Oct. 1979), 919–944.

49. Samuel Hill, *Municipium Ecclesiasticum, or, The Rights, Liberties, and Authorities of the Christian Church* (London, 1687), 17–19.

50. Hill, *Municipium Ecclesiasticum*, 19–21.

51. Hill, *Municipium Ecclesiasticum*, 22.

52. The echoes of Hugo Grotius, who similarly in *De imperio summarum potestum circa sacra* derived the right of synodal assembly from natural law, were not lost on contemporaries; see Humphrey Hody, *Some thoughts on a Convocation, And the Notion of its Divine Right* (London, 1699), 13: "Synods, therefore are to be accounted [by Grotius] in the number of those things, which being allowed of by the Law of Nature, are yet subject to human Constitutions; and may be assembled, or prohibited by them."

53. Hody, *Some thoughts on a Convocation*, 35–36.

54. *Some observations on Municipium Ecclesiasticum* (London, 1699), 10.

55. Hill, *Municipium Ecclesiasticum*, 12.

56. Samuel Hill, *The Rites of the Christian Church further defended, In Answer to the Appeal of Dr. Wake* (London, 1698), 57–58.

57. Francis Atterbury, *The Rights, Powers, and Priviledges of an English Convocation* (London, 1700), 148.

58. Atterbury, *Rights, Powers, and Priviledges*, 40–49.

59. Atterbury, *Rights, Powers, and Priviledges,* 63–64, 353–354.

60. Atterbury, *Rights, Powers, and Priviledges,* 273.

61. Atterbury, *Rights, Powers, and Priviledges,* 353.

62. See "A Letter to a Friend, offering some Reasons, why the University of Oxford could not handsomely create Mr William Nicholson (Lord Bishop of Carlisle Elect) Doctor in Divinity 29 June 1702," BL Add MS 27440 f. 21.

63. Atterbury, *Rights, Powers, and Priviledges,* sig. A6r.

64. Atterbury, *Rights, Powers, and Priviledges,* sig. A3v, 132; see Andrew Barclay, "James II's 'Catholic' Court," *1650–1850: Ideas, Aesthetics, and Inquiries into the Early Modern Era,* 8 (2003), 161–171; on the ecclesiology of Samuel Parker, see Gordon Schochet, "Samuel Parker, Religious Diversity and the Ideology of Persecution," in Roger D. Lund, ed., *The Margins of Orthodoxy: Heterodox Writing and Cultural Response 1660–1750* (Cambridge, UK: Cambridge University Press, 1995), 119–148; idem., "Between Lambeth and Leviathan: Samuel Parker on the Church of England and Political Order," in N. T. Phillipson and Quentin Skinner, eds., *Political Discourse in Early Modern Britain* (Cambridge, UK: Cambridge University Press, 1993), 189–208; J. Rose, "The Ecclesiastical Polity of Samuel Parker," *The Seventeenth Century* 25 (Oct 2010), 350–375; on Thomas Cartwright, see R. A. Beddard, "Bishop Cartwright's Death-Bed," *Bodleian Library Record,* 11 (1984), 220–230.

65. Atterbury, *Rights, Powers, and Priviledges,* sig. A5v.

66. Hill, *Municipium Ecclesiasticum,* 10.

67. On the "church in danger," see Holmes, *Trial of Doctor Sacheverell;* and idem., *Politics, Religion and Society in England, 1679–1742* (London: Hambledon Press, 1986), 217–248.

68. Henry Sacheverell, *The Character of a Low-Churchman* (London, 1702), 9.

69. Sacheverell, *Character of a Low-Churchman,* 13–14.

70. Robert D. Cornwall, "Politics and the Lay Baptism Controversy in England, 1708–1715," in Robert D. Cornwall and William Gibson, eds., *Religion, Politics and Dissent, 1660–1832: Essays in Honour of James E. Bradley* (Farnham, UK: Ashgate, 2010), 147–163.

71. Eveline Cruickshanks and Howard Erskine-Hill, *The Atterbury Plot* (New York: Palgrave Macmillan, 2004).

72. William Sherlock, *The New Danger of Presbytery, or, The Claims and Practices of some in the Lower House of Convocation very dangerous to the constitution of an Episcopal and Metropolitical Church* (London, 1703).

73. Queen Anne to Thomas Tenison, Feb 25, 1705/6, BL Add MS 61612 f. 144.

Chapter Four

The French Revolution and the Civil Constitution of the Clergy: The Unintentional Turning Point

Noah Shusterman

It is no exaggeration, but also not a particularly daring claim, to say that church-state relations went to the heart of most political questions in Old Regime France. Catholicism was France's official religion, and rates of adherence were relatively high.[1] Although the eighteenth century is often known as the Age of Enlightenment in France, the criticisms from the leading thinkers of the Enlightenment had not reached the majority of French people. Attendance at Sunday Mass, though dropping over the course of the century, was still the rule and not the exception in most of the kingdom. Whether the popularity of religious practices lay in piety or in the role that the weekly ritual played in patterns of sociability, particularly in the rural society that made up most of the French population, is impossible to say.[2] Bishops, as well as being wealthy and powerful via their positions in the church, would often hold powerful roles in the government as well. The royal authorities, meanwhile, could not hope to match the manpower that the church had, particularly the 50,000 to 60,000 parish priests who represented the church's official presence in nearly every village and neighborhood in the kingdom. The state had, indeed, been growing; Louis XIV had done much to centralize authority and to bring local powers under control.[3] During the seventeenth and eighteenth centuries, men in both the government and the church referred to the "two powers" and spent no shortage of time discussing their relationship. No one doubted that, when push came to shove, the secular powers had prominence. But there were always limits. At the village level, those were practical limits, given the relatively small size of the French state compared to the church. At the national level, though, the limits to the king's authority could look more like a game of make-believe, where both sides agreed to pretend that there were limits. The royal authorities were willing to let the church keep its tax-exempt status, for instance—as long as the church "chose" to give its "free gift" to the king.[4]

With the 1789 outbreak of the French Revolution came, among so many other changes, an end to that game of make-believe. In general, the Revolution started out difficult—but manageable—for the Catholic Church. The lead-up to 1789 had weakened the church hierarchy in favor of the parish clergy, but what hierarchy remained was that much the stronger for it. The reforms of 1789 had also broken some of the sources of power that the Old Regime Gallican Church had enjoyed, declaring something close to freedom of religion, and nationalizing much of the Church lands. But there was still a strong belief among many that the Gallican Church could play a key role in the coming years, and that a society without religion to hold it together would be unstable and ungovernable.[5] It was in 1790 that things began to change.

For the French Revolution, the summer of 1790 was both the high point of revolutionary unity and the time when conditions for destroying that unity began.

It was on July 14, the first anniversary of the fall of the Bastille, that the Festival of the Federation showed so much of French society unified, celebrating the accomplishments of that year. Many of the liberal Revolution's most enduring reforms were in place—the Declaration of the Rights of Man, an end to much of the old feudal system, and the redrawing of the political map. The king had even sanctioned these measures, and was there—along with the National Assembly, the clergy, and the people of Paris—to celebrate them at the festival.[6]

Earlier that summer, however, the National Assembly had passed a piece of legislation called the Civil Constitution of the Clergy, aimed at reforming the Catholic Church in France. On paper, most of that constitution does not look particularly radical. The new law redrew the map of French dioceses, bringing them in line with the new departmental boundaries and reducing their number from a hundred and thirty or so to eighty-three. Given the widely disparate size of the dioceses, such a reform made sense. Some, particularly in the north, had been quite large, containing hundreds of parishes; others, particularly in the south, had contained as few as twenty parishes. The existence of "enclaves" in several dioceses made the situation even more complicated, and a likely target of reform. The Civil Constitution of the Clergy also forbade "absenteeism"—the practice of clerics holding positions that they did not actually do. And, in its one radical move, it declared that parish priests and bishops would be elected.[7]

There are two somewhat contradictory things to point out about the impact of the Civil Constitution of the Clergy. First, this new law would wind up tearing France apart. Roughly half of the nation's clerics refused to endorse it, many of them taking up actual opposition, not only to the law but also to the Revolution as a whole. The Civil Constitution would give the Counter-Revolution—so weak in July 1790—a popular base that it had never had.[8] Soon, there would be a schism in the Gallican Church, between the constitutional church, which endorsed the new law, and the refractory church, which opposed it.

Second, at the time that they passed it, the revolutionaries did not realize that the law would have anything like the impact it had, nor did those who would come to oppose it. The timing shows this clearly enough—it had not prevented revolutionaries and clergy from celebrating together the following month. So, too, do the debates over the law, which provide for some surprisingly dull reading, especially in comparison to the bitter debates that would ensue after it was law. Hence, the first reason that the history of the Civil Constitution of the Clergy is in large part a history of unintended consequences.

Over the course of the six months following the law's passage, the two sides would start facing off—first in the National Assembly, then in the nation at large.

Surprisingly enough, it was not the election of the priests and bishops that led to the most complaints, but the redrawing of the diocesan map. Bishops were not happy about seeing the number of sees go from 130 to eighty-three, as it meant that more than forty of them now no longer had the lucrative positions they had earned through the arduous process of having been born into the nobility. They did not, of course, discuss the issue in that way; rather, they expressed their outrage that the National Assembly had acted so unilaterally in the matter, not consulting with the church. They did not consider it to be part of the Assembly's purview to be able to alter things that did not, in the church's view, answer only to the government. In an *Exposition of Principles* signed by thirty bishops who were also delegates to the National Assembly, they stated that "there is a jurisdiction which belongs to the Church, which is essential to it, and which Jesus-Christ gave to it." The power to alter that jurisdiction, they wrote, could be altered only by the power that first gave it.[9] Mirabeau—at the time, the most influential man in the Assembly—replied that the *Exposition* was nothing but a "ruse of an hypocrisy" which "puts in motion all sorts of trouble and sedition, while it pretends to plead the cause of God."[10] But beyond the disagreement over the bishops' motivations, for the majority of men in the Assembly, their role was to represent the general will, and the wishes of the people. With such a mandate, resistance was not acceptable.

The will of God versus the will of the people—what it boiled down to was two groups of very stubborn men refusing to budge.

Nigel Aston, in his work on religion and the French Revolution, has suggested that the leaders of the Gallican Church might have actually approved of the Civil Constitution had the leaders of the clergy been allowed to vote on it. What made them so resistant was the government's insistence that they accept the rules with no reservations, no questions asked.[11]

The Old Regime clergy did not have much of a tradition of saying no. The men in the Gallican Church—the bishops, the priests, the canons, the monks—had been educated and trained to believe that the opening line from Romans 13, "let every soul be subject unto the higher powers," was how men of the cloth should understand the relationship between their role and the secular authorities, and that "Whosoever resisteth the power, resisteth the ordinance of God."[12] But if there was little tradition of saying no, there was a long tradition of saying yes, but . . ., and letting that "yes, but . . ." drag out until it effectively did mean no. During the eighteenth century, the bitterest religious debates had concerned the rivalry between the Jansenist movement and the Jesuits. Jansenism, which aimed at making Catholicism more Augustinian and austere, had become relatively popular in France during the seventeenth century, even claiming Blaise Pascal as one of its most prominent adherents.[13] When Pope Clement XI issued the papal bull *Unigenitus* in 1713, calling for an end to the Jansenist movement, it seemed that would be the end of the matter. What followed, though, rather than being an end to Jansenism in France, was a seemingly endless succession of books and pamphlets exploring the matter, arguing, debating what the bull did or did not prohibit, and what rights the pope did or did not have. As a result, the Jansenist movement long outlived the pope who had issued the bull; the king—Louis XIV—who had solicited the bull; and even France's Jesuit movement, which Louis XV exiled in 1764.[14]

Such were the unofficial rules of the game in Old Regime France. Absolutist in theory, perhaps, kings—and popes—had to learn the art of commanding only the commandable and of working with other powerful groups in order to achieve their aims.

This art was one with which the revolutionaries had trouble. Here it is worth taking a quick glance at the quintessential document of 1789, the Declaration of the Rights of Man and of the Citizen. That declaration had guaranteed something not unlike freedom of religion, and that guarantee would be relevant in the aftermath of the Civil Constitution. But the Assembly giveth and the Assembly taketh away. "No one must be disturbed because of his opinions, even in religious matters," the Declaration declared, "*provided their expression does not trouble the public order established by law*." The people would have freedom of religion—and the Assembly would decide just how much. But, perhaps even more telling is the article establishing that men may not be arrested arbitrarily. All arrests must be for infractions of the law. But, the declaration added, "every citizen summoned or seized by virtue of the law must obey at once; he makes himself guilty by resistance."[15]

It was these conceptions of freedom—its explicitly limited nature, and the culpability of any resistance—that show the attitudes of the National Assembly, in the early part of the revolution, to any sort of willingness to compromise.

In other words, it was not only the content of the Civil Constitution of the Clergy that made it into such a turning point. It was the way in which the National Assembly attempted to impose it on an institution that was not accustomed to being so blatantly imposed upon. It was the end of the old game of make-believe—an end to the government pretending that it agreed on spiritual issues in cooperation with the Gallican Church.

By ending that game of make-believe, the government would wind up coming face to face with the practical limits of its ability to dictate to the church.

The problems would begin in the National Assembly, and the first leaders of the opposition to the Civil Constitution of the Clergy were clerics who were in the Assembly, but it was clear that they represented a large portion of the nation's clergy. The clergy in many places were dragging their feet in implementing the new rules, when they were not openly opposing them. The Assembly's response was to double down. They ruled that all clerics would be required to take an oath "to carefully watch over the faithful in the diocese (or parish) that has been given me, to be loyal to the nation, to the law and to the king, and to support with all of my power the constitution decreed by the National Assembly and accepted by the king."[16]

Again, though, behind the seemingly innocuous wording of the oath lay the Assembly's claim to be able to dictate the terms of the debate. In the Assembly itself, the matter came to a head in early January 1791, when the clerics who were also deputies in the Assembly were called on to take the oath. Some did, to the applause of their fellow deputies. Most did not.

The debates from the National Assembly do not always make the most riveting reading. The deputies spent days on details that today seem unimportant while lavishing themselves with self-praise. But the debates from January 3, and from January 4, are filled with a palpable sense of drama. The most vociferous opponent of the oath and the Civil Constitution that day was not a bishop, but the Abbé Maury, who had hoped to plead the cause of the church, as he understood it. He wound up instead arguing simply for his right to speak, as he was shouted down time and again, and was asked to stop speaking. In response, Maury yelled out, "You do not have the right to interrupt me!"—before his colleagues, at least those on the left, decided that they did not, in fact, wish to hear him and were not obliged to do so. Ironically, despite his title, Maury held no office at the time and was therefore not

required to take the oath. As for those who were required to take it, they were
called to the podium one by one and told that they would have to relinquish
their offices should they refuse. When they asked to speak, to explain themselves, they were shouted down. When one bishop asked to speak, the cries
rang out, "No speeches! Do you take the oath, yes or no?"[17] Finally, the
president of the Assembly ended the roll call, and asked simply, "Is anyone
else going to present themselves, in order to take the oath?"

After that, the minutes of the debate state simply, "There was a quarter-
hour of silence."[18] Soon after, Mirabeau would state that which must have
already seemed clear: "The fatal moment has arrived."[19] The Assembly became the bully. The deputies who had refused to take the oath began to see
themselves as martyrs. The bishops gained the respect of the other clerics,
now reluctant to abandon their superiors at the moment of crisis. It may have
been, as Aston calls it, a "contingent parting of the ways," but it was a
parting of the ways nevertheless.[20]

This parting of the ways took on a very different look at the village level.
While the showdown in the National Assembly was—as with every dispute
between deputies there—a dispute pitting one group of men against another,
at the village level, the split would often occur along gender lines. The debate
over the Civil Constitution of the Clergy would reach every village in France.
And, here, the second unintended consequence becomes apparent: in many
places, particularly where opposition to the reforms was strongest, women
would lead the opposition. Timothy Tackett notes that women's "vociferous
presence in public demonstrations frequently dominated above all others,"
and that, "To believe certain contemporaries, the battle of the oath among all
the laity often lined up as a veritable battle of the sexes, cutting across all
social lines."[21] Jean-Clément Martin, too, points to families divided between
wives who supported the refractory church, and husbands who supported the
revolution.[22] Accounts from both sides support the view that women played
key roles in the opposition to the constitutional church, even if they spin it
differently. A refractory priest named Jacques Pierre Fleury, for instance,
wrote in his memoirs of the women in his neighborhood who "armed themselves with rocks and sticks" to defend him.[23] In the accounts that the men in
the National Assembly would hear, however, those same women would be
"misled," or even "seduced," by refractory priests.[24] One of the constitutional priests in the National Assembly complained of "the gatherings of dissident devotees" of the oppositional church protesting on behalf of their
priests, along with crowds of women who were "drunk, or might as well have
been."[25] It was clear to the men in the Assembly that the revolution was
facing a crisis, and that while the crisis had begun with the dispute between
the supporters and the opponents of the Civil Constitution of the Clergy in
the Assembly itself, as that dispute had spread, their opponents were now
disproportionately female.

The Civil Constitution of the Clergy passed in 1790. By 1793, France would be in a state of civil war. The passage from one to the other was not inevitable; it depended on other events, which would radicalize the Revolution, particularly the king's attempt to flee in 1791, and the war against Austria that began in 1792. But if the development was not an inevitable one, the line from the Civil Constitution to the civil war was still a direct one: when the fighting broke out, it broke out along the dividing lines that the disputes over the Civil Constitution of the Clergy had revealed. [26]

The opposition to the Civil Constitution, as it morphed into an overall opposition to the Revolution, posed some very difficult questions for the men leading the revolution. These were men who believed, for the most part, in the ideals of the Enlightenment. They believed that the spread of reason would lead to the improvement of society. Most believed that men were inherently more reasonable than were women, but that women should play a key role in the progress of the revolution—by supporting their husbands and by bearing and raising future revolutionaries. And they also believed in *some form* of religious freedom. Indeed, the only reason that the Declaration of the Rights of Man did not include a more robust statement of the freedom of religion came from the opposition of the Catholic clerics in the National Assembly, who in 1789 had still held onto the dream that the Revolution would adopt Catholicism as the official religion of the revolution. [27]

What then to do about the opposition to the revolution that started to bubble up from western France? What to do about the stories that began to reach the National Assembly, about priests leading women astray, about the support that women were giving to priests living in opposition to the revolution? Because it was these stories that the government in Paris started hearing about, in 1791 and in 1792. [28] Priests who had refused to take an oath to the revolution were now living hidden in the countryside, hidden by the women of the parish, giving the Mass clandestinely to packed houses on Sundays, while constitutional priests celebrated the Mass in empty churches.

There were a few consequences—all of them crucial for the way that the revolution as a whole unfolded.

The first was a willingness, on the part of the legislature, to move to more and more extreme measures to combat the influence of the priests. From laws restricting their activities, to deportation and, finally, to a not insignificant number of executions, government repression of the refractory church would get harsher and harsher, from 1792 to 1794. [29] In the first seven months of 1792, the Assembly passed one law calling for refractory priests to take the oath or be considered suspects, then later another law calling for their deportation. Louis XVI, who remained king until August of that year, vetoed both of those laws; two weeks after his reign was suspended, however, the Assembly decreed that all refractory priests should leave France.

By the following fall, such measures would seem benign, as both the Terror and the de-Christianization movement spread across France. The worst violence, though, was in the Vendée, and in the repression of the oppositional forces there. Some of this was the sort of violence that could be seen in any civil war. But the *noyades* (drownings), and the "republican marriages" hold a special place in this story. Both took place in the city of Nantes, and were aimed at the refractory priests whom the revolutionaries blamed for the civil war. In the *noyades*, priests were loaded up onto boats that were brought out onto the Loire River, and then sunk.[30] The "republican marriages" would consist of a man and a woman (when possible, a priest and a nun) tied together and drowned.[31] It was, according to Martin, a "war against women," specifically against the women who attended the clandestine masses held by the refractory priests. What becomes clear, through all of these actions, is that not only were the priests considered as mortal enemies to the revolution but that the questions of religion and gender had become intertwined in the minds of many revolutionaries, to the point where any discussion of women implied religion and vice-versa. Again, the course from the Civil Constitution of the Clergy to the civil war was not an inevitable one, but depended in part on external developments. The attempt to reshape the church would wind up shaping the civil war, although in ways that the men who wrote that law could never have intended.

REFERENCES

Aston, Nigel. *Religion and Revolution in France, 1780–1804.* Washington, DC: Catholic University of America Press, 2000.

Baker, Keith Michael (ed.). *The Old Regime and the French Revolution.* Chicago: University of Chicago Press, 1987.

Beck, Robert. *Histoire du dimanche: de 1700 à nos jours.* Paris: De l' Atelier, 1997.

Beik, William. *Absolutism and Society in Seventeenth-Century France: State Power and Provincial Aristocracy in Languedoc.* Cambridge, UK: Cambridge University Press, 1997.

Bély, Lucien (ed.). *Dictionnaire de l'ancien régime.* Paris: Quadridge, 1996.

Brissot, J. P. *Rome jugée et l'autorité législative du pape anéantie.* Paris: Buisson, 1791.

de la Gorce, Pierre. *Histoire religieuse de la Révolution française.* Paris: Plon, 1916.

Doyle, William. *Jansenism: Catholic Resistance to Authority from the Reformation to the French Revolution.* New York: St. Martin's Press, 2000.

———. *The Oxford History of the French Revolution.* Oxford: Oxford University Press, 2002.

Fleury, Jacques Pierre. *Mémoires sur la Révolution, le premier empire et les premières années de la restauration.* Le Mans: Leguicheux-Gallienne, 1874.

Martin, Jean-Clément. *La Révolte brisée: femmes dans la Révolution française et l'Empire.* Paris: Armand Colin, 2008.

———. *Révolution, contre-révolution, nation.* Paris: Seuil, 1998.

McManners, John. *Church and Society in Eighteenth-Century France,* 2 vols. Oxford, UK: Oxford University Press, 1998.

Michelet, Jules. *Histoire de la Révolution française,* 2 vols. Paris: Robert Laffont, 1979.

Sutherland, Donald. *The Chouans: The Social Origins of Popular Counter-Revolution in Upper Brittany, 1770–1796.* Oxford, UK: Oxford University Press, 1982.

Tackett, Timothy. *Religion, Revolution, and Regional Culture in Eighteenth-Century France: The Ecclesiastical Oath of 1791.* Princeton, NJ: Princeton University Press, 1986.

Van Kley, Dale K. *The Religious Origins of the French Revolution.* New Haven, CT: Yale University Press, 1995.

NOTES

1. John McManners, *Church and Society in Eighteenth-Century France*, 2 vols (Oxford, UK: Oxford University Press, 1998), provides the best background for state and society relations under the Old Regime; see especially Volume 1, chapters 1 and 3. See also, Robert Beck, *Histoire du dimanche: de 1700 à nos jours* (Paris: De l' Atelier, 1997), 35.

2. As McManners notes, "There is difficulty in disentangling religion and custom, for this was a social order in which human relationships evolved and secular business was transacted within a religious cadre; often, one can only guess at the relevance of the religious reference in the minds of ordinary people." *Church and Society*, I: 104.

3. See William Beik, *Absolutism and Society in Seventeenth-Century France: State Power and Provincial Aristocracy in Languedoc* (Cambridge, UK: Cambridge University Press, 1997), 332–335.

4. See Lucien Bély, ed., *Dictionnaire de l'ancien régime* (Paris: Quadridge, 1996), 431–434.

5. For an overview, see Nigel Aston, *Religion and Revolution in France, 1780–1804* (Washington, DC: Catholic University of America Press, 2000), 112–139.

6. Jules Michelet, *Histoire de la Révolution française*, 2 vols (Paris: Robert Laffont, 1979), I:329–339.

7. Portions of the constitution are available in English in Keith Michael Baker, ed., *The Old Regime and the French Revolution* (Chicago: University of Chicago Press, 1987), 239–242.

8. See Aston, *Religion and Revolution*, 140–162; Timothy Tackett, *Religion, Revolution, and Regional Culture in Eighteenth-Century France: The Ecclesiastical Oath of 1791* (Princeton, NJ: Princeton University Press, 1986), 11–14, 27; Jean-Clément Martin, *Révolution, contre-révolution, nation* (Paris: Seuil, 1998), 87.

9. J. Mavidal and E. Laurent, eds, *Archives parlementaires de 1787 à 1860: recueil complet des débats législatifs et politiques des Chambres françaises.* First series; 1787–1799 (Paris, 1867–1896), XX:154.

10. *Archives parlementaires* XXI:10. See also, J. P. Brissot, *Rome jugée et l'autorité législative du pape anéantie* (Paris: Buisson, 1791).

11. Aston, *Religion and Revolution*, 161.

12. Romans 13:1–2.

13. See William Doyle, *Jansenism: Catholic Resistance to Authority from the Reformation to the French Revolution* (New York: St. Martin's Press, 2000), 45–58.

14. Doyle, *Jansenism*, 73; Dale K. Van Kley, *The Religious Origins of the French Revolution* (New Haven, CT: Yale University Press, 1995), 75–134.

15. Baker, *Old Regime*, 238–39.

16. *Archives parlementaires*, XXII:17.

17. *Archives Parlementaires*, XXII:16.

18. *Archives parlementaires* XXII:17.

19. *Archives parlementaires* XXII:18.

20. Aston, *Religion and Revolution*, 162.

21. Tackett, *Religion and Revolution*, 173, 175.

22. Jean-Clément Martin, *La Révolte brisée: femmes dans la Révolution française et l'Empire* (Paris: Armand Colin, 2008), 108.

23. Jacques Pierre Fleury, *Mémoires sur la Révolution, le premier empire et les premières années de la restauration* (Le Mans: Leguicheux-Gallienne, 1874), 138.

24. See, for example, *Archives parlementaires* XXXIV:141–148.

25. *Archives parlementaires* XXXIV:512. See also Aston, *Religion*, 207.

26. See, for instance, Donald Sutherland, *The Chouans: The Social Origins of Popular Counter-Revolution in Upper Brittany, 1770–1796* (Oxford, UK: Oxford University Press, 1982), 297.

27. See Michelet, *Histoire*, I:458; Martin, *La Révolte brisée*, 121–123.

28. These reports are all included in the *Archives parlementaires*, which include minutes of the meetings of the revolutionary legislatures. Such reports appear intermittently throughout much of the revolution; a good place to start is volume 34, especially 141–148. *Archives parlementaire*, XXIV: 141–148.

29. Pierre de la Gorce, *Histoire religieuse de la Révolution française* (Paris: Plon, 1916), writing as a supporter of the refractory church, gives the most thorough account of its persecution.

30. William Doyle, *The Oxford History of the French Revolution* (Oxford, UK: Oxford University Press, 2002), 256.

31. Martin, *La Révolte brisée*, 126.

Chapter Five

The Spanish Legal Solution to the Presence of Religious Symbols in the Public Sphere: A Cautious Evolution from a Catholic Denominational Past to an Effective Secularism

Rebeca Vázquez Gómez

Regarding the role of religion in the public sphere, Jürgen Habermas declares that it seems that religion has lately increased its presence in the political area within western societies, thereby strengthening political divisions. Habermas explains how these divisions could be avoided in order to achieve a true constitutional state. The constitutional state is based on the idea of a contract: an agreement on public arguments accepted by all persons, religious and secular. In principle, the matter of religious pluralism is solved by the right to religious freedom. The separation between church and state is necessary for the efficacy of religious freedom, but it is not enough. For delimiting the spheres of one's own and others' exercise of religion where controversial issues are concerned, citizens must reach agreements. The process is that of the democratic decision making. The objective is to find a solution construed in a language accessible to and understandable by all citizens. To reach this common language, Habermas proposes an ethics of citizenship based on the mutual effort that religious citizens must carry on to take secular citizens into consideration and learn from them, and vice versa. Thus it is necessary to distinguish two different political public spheres: one informal and one formal or institutional. Religion would play a different political role, depending on the sphere. The informal public sphere is that in which individuals and communities act, putting into practice their right of religious liberty. The institutional public sphere is that in which the state and its institutions move, subject to the principle of secularism that obliges the use of a common discourse, accessible to everyone, when, for example, laws are passed or administrative decisions adopted. Religious contributions, to penetrate the institutional level, must be translated into accessible language. Without this translation, a majority could impose its opinions on the minority, and government could become repressive. On the other hand, the previous process of mutual understanding is necessary for the state to achieve solutions that citizens consider reasonable, because the state may impose only such duties as the citizens find reasonable.[1]

From this initial philosophical perspective, we can proceed to a concrete view of religion in the public sphere in order to focus on the object of our study: the use of religious signs in public spaces. Through our case analysis, we will see whether the Spanish legal system tends to permit those religious expressions when they are fruits of individual religious freedom and therefore develop in the "informal" political area. Additionally, we will examine why, on the contrary, religious symbology placed by institutions of the state is not allowed in public spaces because, in this "formal" or institutional political area, the actors are subject to the principle of neutrality; therefore only a "common discourse" understandable to all, and not one of a particular religious community, can be used.

Spain has a Catholic denominational past. For more than thirty-two years, Spain has declared itself to be a nondenominational state (through its current Constitution of 1978). The behavior of the Spanish authorities toward the symbology issue reflects their efforts to produce a real and not merely formal secularism, as required to ensure the effective religious liberty of individuals.

The aim of this paper is to examine the status of evolution of church–state relations in Spain through this example and to see how the legal system has reacted to the wearing of religious signs by individuals in the public sphere and to the presence of religious symbols placed by the state in these areas. In this way we want to find out whether the Spanish state is responding to the fact of religious pluralism according to the principles of religious liberty and secularism proclaimed by its Constitution.

THE CATHOLIC DENOMINATIONAL PAST OF SPAIN

Briefly, it could be said that after the Middle Ages—during which Christians, Jews, and Muslims coexisted in Spain—the reign of the Catholic monarchs achieved political unity; they sought a religious unity as well through the expulsion of Jews and Muslims at the end of fifteenth century and the beginning of sixteenth century.

From that moment, the Catholic denominational character of Spain was a fact formally recognized by the first constitutions passed during the nineteenth century. There were only two exceptions: the Project of Constitution of the First Republic (1873–1874) and the Constitution of the Second Republic (1931–1939). This latest one declared the separation between church and state, establishing a "negative" secularism with a radical attitude against religion.

The Spanish Civil War (1936–1939) gave victory to Francisco Franco, and the new regime again declared the Catholic Church as the official religion of the state. However, Franco's dictatorship ended in 1975, and three years later, democratic forces passed the current Constitution of 1978,[2] which recognized religious freedom as a fundamental right and established that no religion shall have a state character.[3]

CHURCH–STATE RELATIONS IN SPAIN TODAY: RELIGIOUS FREEDOM AND THE SECULARISM OF COOPERATION

Today church–state relations in Spain are defined by the right to religious liberty and the principle of secularism.

The Right to Freedom of Religion

The right to freedom of religion concerns the individual. Its content and limits are regulated mainly by the Constitution (Art. 16.1),[4] the Religious Liberty Act of 1980 (Art. 3.1),[5] and the European Convention of Human Rights of 1950 (Art. 9),[6] the most important source, ratified by Spain and guaranteed by the European Court of Human Rights (ECHR).

These precepts are similar, and from them it is deduced that religious liberty is a fundamental right that protects the individual's liberty to have and express religious beliefs, with the only limits being those, prescribed by law, that are necessary to protect the "public order" (this is an indefinite legal concept that includes principally public safety, order, health, or morals) as well as the protection of the fundamental rights and public freedoms of others.

The Principle of Secularism

The principle of secularism concerns the state and its institutions and is the necessary consequence of the recognition of religious freedom.

According to the ECHR, the recognition of religious freedom imposes on states a "duty of neutrality and impartiality." They "have responsibility for ensuring, neutrally and impartially, the exercise of various religious faiths and beliefs."[7]

This principle is deduced from the Spanish Constitution in similar terms; therefore secularism involves a state's attitude of neutrality toward religion ("Spaniards are equal before the law, without religious discrimination," Art. 14 of the Constitution declares) and the separation of church and state ("No religion shall have a state character," Art. 16.3 of the Constitution proclaims), although it is about a separation that permits cooperation—that is to say, a "positive" secularism (the same Art. 16.3 says that "public authorities shall take into account the religious beliefs of Spanish society and shall consequently maintain appropriate cooperation relations with the Catholic Church and other denominations," and Art. 9.2 affirms that the public powers shall "promote conditions ensuring that freedom and equality of individuals and of the groups to which they belong are real and effective"). So when we speak about secularism in Spain, we do not mean absolute lack of relation between the state and denominations but a relation that respects equality and promotes the religious freedom of individuals and groups. It does not mean total exclusion of religion from public sphere but is a guarantee of the effective exercise of religious liberty by everybody.

Spain is a state that formally recognizes religious liberty and declares itself to be nondenominational. But in practice, is this stance effective and real? Today several marks of the denominational past persists: for example, contrary to other denominations, until 2007, a part of the national budget was assigned to the Catholic Church. The institution of canonical marriage is recognized not only in its form of celebration; the canon law rules that marriage also has civil recognition and, in consequence, forms part of the Spanish legal system, although in an indirect and almost insignificant way.

In the case of religion classes in schools, the teaching of Catholicism is effective, but this is not always the case for other religions, such as Islam or Judaism, in spite of laws that guarantee the right of these pupils to receive Muslim or Hebrew religious instruction in public schools.

As for the issue of religious symbology, we shall examine, through it as well, the evolution of religious freedom and secularism toward effective recognition.

RELIGIOUS SYMBOLOGY IN SPAIN AND SOCIETY'S RESPONSE

There are two types of religious signs in the public sphere: symbols worn by individuals ("mobile symbols") and those placed by the state in public places ("static symbols"). Below we will refer to controversial cases that achieved notoriety in newspapers or came before the courts.

Cases Relating to Mobile Symbology

The Islamic Veil

In cases regarding signs worn by individuals, the issue of the Islamic veil is undoubtedly the most important. There are more than a million Muslims in Spain, most of them having come from Morocco,[8] and the issue involving the head scarf has grown in the past few years.

Head scarves at school. As in other countries, discussions about wearing head scarves have centered almost exclusively on the public schools. In Spain, cases have focused solely on the wearing of the head scarf by pupils but not by teachers. The use of the veil is often accepted, especially in Ceuta and Melilla, cities with high concentrations of Muslims. Also, no case has come to the courts. Possible controversies have usually been resolved by agreement between the parents of the pupil and the school, many times through the renunciation of the scarf by the pupil.[9] Some cases have required the intervention of the government.

The cases that got most media attention occurred in Madrid in 2002,[10] Gerona in 2007,[11] Ceuta in 2007[12] and 2008,[13] Madrid in 2010,[14] and Coruña in 2011.[15] From analysis of these cases, we can deduce that:

- The school refused permission for the pupil to wear the head scarf, in the first two cases, arguing that the veil is a discriminatory symbol; in the later cases, it was argued that the schools' rules forbade pupils to wear accessories that did not belong with their uniforms or caps or any clothes that covered the head.
- Regarding the solution to the situation, in the first four cases education authorities ordered the school to accept the pupil, declaring that her right to education prevailed over any other reasons. In the latest two cases, of 2010 and 2011, the authorities did not order the readmission of the pupils; consequently the pupils were transferred to other schools where there were no rules about caps and clothes.

It is interesting to note that the reasons given for forbidding the veil do not seem to correspond with any of the legal limits of religious liberty that we have already mentioned (public order, health, safety, morals, or protection of rights and liberties of others). On the other hand, we observe that the authorities, in ordering the acceptance of the pupil with the veil, do not mention, generally speaking, her right to religious liberty (it looks as though they do not consider the wearing of the head scarf as constituting an exercise of that right).

On national identity cards. In Spain, the veil causes consternation in another field: regarding the required photograph for obtaining the national identity card. Although the 2005 Regulation on this matter[16] declares that the head must appear completely uncovered,[17] the Ministry of Interior had authorized police offices to accept photos with the head scarf if the physiognomic features are distinguishable. But it also required, initially, that the card carrier present certification of her religious beliefs. This caused distress: police considered that the instructions of the government forced them to violate the law, and citizens complained of the lack of uniformity in police behavior.[18]

The Jewish Kippah of a Worker in a Public Company

We will mention another case of mobile symbology different from the veil—that of a Jewish worker, a driver in a local public company in the Balearic Islands. The company disciplined the worker because his use of a cap was considered incompatible with the rules regarding uniforms and argued before the court that the worker was subject to the secularism principle because of the public character of the company. The judges found that the use of the cap during work was protected by the right of religious freedom and rejected the argument regarding secularism. The court highlighted that the defendant is a public sector company and must therefore be more committed than those in the private sector to implement constitutional values effectively.[19] This judgment is the only one on mobile symbology that has been pronounced in Spain.

Cases Regarding Static Symbology

In relation to static signs, as in other countries, most Spanish cases refer to crucifixes that hang in classrooms as a mark of the past.

The Crucifix

In public schools. Some cases regarding static symbols in classrooms have received media attention: in Madrid in 1999, in Valladolid in 2005 and 2006, in Cáceres in 2008, and in Badajoz in 2010.

Usually those asking for the removal of crucifixes from public classrooms are the parents of pupils, most often making the request through pro-secular associations or similar groups. It is interesting to note also that usually the board of governors denies the request and that the superior education administrative authorities, who have the duty to review these decisions, do not do so. They refrain from pronouncing on such matters, invoking the competence of the school.

Only the case of Valladolid of 2005 has been resolved by a court. The decision of the High Court of Castilla-León of December 2009[20] argued that the Spanish Constitution defends a "positive" secularism (not "laicism"), a secularism that involves cooperation of the state with religious groups and considers that a general removal of religious signs would involve a laicist attitude, contrary to that positive secularism. The judgment stated that the liberty of the board of governors to decide about keeping or not the crucifixes is an example of that cooperation, because the board of governors is more than a public institution; it is a group of users or, that is to say, part of society. The court recognized the particularity of a public space, such as a school, where the presence of religious symbols can sometimes make the pupils feel in some way discriminated against, because the state would seem to accept one denomination over another. In consequence, the judges concluded that when the parents of a pupil apply for the removal on this basis, the crucifixes should be removed.

In city halls. We also find cases regarding the placement of crucifixes in city halls. In some municipalities (for example, in Berga–Barcelona and in Zaragoza and Cáceres), secular associations asked for the withdrawal of religious signs from city halls. The Zaragoza case[21] is the only one that came before the courts. It began when the city council decided, by a majority vote, to preserve the crucifix, rejecting the requested removal. The court, in an April 2010 decision,[22] stated that the piece had a relevant historical and artistic value (it was a crucifix from the seventeenth century) and that the wish of the city council was for its continued preservation. The judge concluded that there was no law preventing the city council from keeping an object (although religious) of special historical and artistic relevance.

The Bible and the Crucifix at the Act of Investiture of the Nation's President and Its Ministers

Besides these cases about schools and city halls, it is interesting to refer to another case, this time in the broader public sphere—concerning the presence of a Bible and a crucifix at the act of investiture of the nation's president and its ministers.[23] This presence is not mentioned in any rule and seems to be a result of Spain's Catholic past and customs.

According to the Constitution, it is incumbent upon the king to appoint the president and members of the government,[24] and the investiture is the final formal step of that procedure. The investiture takes place at the Zarzuela Palace, the residence of the monarchs of Spain, which is sometimes used for celebrations in which the king acts as the head of state. Its objective is to swear to or promise the observation of the obligations of the office as well as to preserve the Constitution as the fundamental law of the state.[25] Because the investiture takes place at the Royal Palace, it is in the hands of the "Royal Household of HM the King,"[26] which looks after the residence and organizes the protocol of the ceremony. This agency defends the presence of Catholic elements in the investiture, arguing that they are necessary for those who choose to take the oath instead of merely promising. In this, the investiture case is similar to the city hall situation: it is about tradition.

The Image of the Virgin in the Coat of Arms of the University of Valencia

Finally, we examine other example with a highly traditional history. The controversy took place in Valencia and was resolved in1985 by the Spanish Constitutional Court, the highest judicial court in Spain. The issue concerned the power of the university senate to change the coat of arms of the University of Valencia. The court declared that the preservation of an image of the Virgin in it was not contrary to secularism, because the image has no religious meaning any more but possesses only historical and cultural value (the image had been present in the coat of arms for centuries).[27]

This decision confirms the importance of differentiating between religious signs and religious signs with historical or cultural importance.

CONCLUSION

By way of conclusion, since 1978, Spain has formally recognized the individual's right to religious freedom while establishing a positive secularism of the state. Through the examples of religious symbology in the public sphere, we have tried to observe to what extent this differentiation is applied in practice.

From the analyses, we can deduce the following:
Regarding religious signs worn by individuals:

1. The right to religious liberty plays the main role, because the one who wears the symbol has the right to religious liberty.
2. The Islamic veil is the single symbol that causes the most controversies.
3. The behavior of administrative authorities reflects their reluctance to accept non-Christian symbols.

4. The reasons given for rejecting these symbols do not seem to fit into any legal limits that can affect the exercise of religious liberty (public order, safety, health or morals, and protection of the rights and freedoms of others).

5. The only judgment pronounced on these kinds of cases recognizes the right of the individual to wear the symbol as an exercise of religious liberty.

Regarding religious signs placed by the state in public spaces, we see that:

1. The principle that comes mainly into play is that of secularism.

2. The crucifix is the symbol that causes most of the conflicts.

3. The behavior of administrative authorities shows certain difficulties with removing Christian symbols.

4. The reasons given to keep these signs, without exception, are of two types: sometimes it is argued that the historical or artistic relevance of the crucifix prevails over its religious significance, while at other times, as, for example, regarding schools, no clear reason is given.

5. The judgments passed about crucifixes at schools, at city halls, and on a coat of arms declare that symbols with a high historical or artistic value do not threaten secularism, but especially when the sign is at schools, secularism could be hurt if the exposition of the sign affects the religious liberty of an individual.

Therefore it appears that administrative powers are not ready yet to manage the reality of religious pluralism: it is easier for them to keep crucifixes in public buildings rather than to see non-Christian symbols worn by individuals in those places.

On the contrary, judicial power shows an attitude more obedient to the formally proclaimed principles of religious liberty and secularism.

Therefore we can say that Spain is nondenominational formally and makes efforts to achieve this in practice, although these efforts are encouraged more by judicial decisions than by the spontaneous behavior of administrative authorities.

It is interesting to note the differences between the situation in Spain compared to that in Italy, where church–state relations are very similar to those in Spain. Italy defends the presence of crucifixes in classrooms. The ECHR, in its decision *Lautsi v. Italy* of March 18, 2011, declares that this presence does not violate the state's duty to neutrality, because religious freedom of students is not injured by the presence of the symbols in the classrooms. The decision of the European Court takes into account, among other things, that the religions different from the Catholicism are also present in the classroom, through celebrations of special dates, for example, as well as through the acceptance of the use of Muslim veil.[28] It seems that there is a kind of sense of multiculturalism that forbids in practice that the crucifix on the wall get too much importance. In Spain, the crucifix remains in some schools as a product of the past, but the veil is not always accepted. Sometimes it is rejected (there is a negative perception of it among many Spaniards). If the Muslim girls have problems with their veil in schools, it could follow that there is no such "multicultural environment" in that school.

These general conclusions lead us to the theoretical framework drawn at the beginning of our paper. Habermas's proposal started from the idea that a constitutional state is characterized by a "civic solidarity" that unites its citizens, which are free and equal, and makes that community different from those divided into several views of the world. All the opinions, religious or secular, must have their place within the political sphere: without limits in the "informal" level where individuals move, and with restrictions in the "formal" or institutional level where the state and its agents act. In this way, for penetrating this second level, a previous translation of the religious arguments into a general or "common discourse," accessible to every person, is necessary.

The cases highlighted here show that Spain tries to achieve this model of the constitutional state, although sometimes with difficulty by administrative authorities. We have seen, for example, that individuals are not always allowed to wear a veil in a public space, such as a state school, although they are exercising their right of religious freedom (which develops at the aforementioned "informal" political level), and the government agencies fail to provide secular justifications for such action. In the same public schools, crucifixes are retained in classrooms, often without giving a secular reason comprehensible by all persons (such as, for example, that it is an item of artistic value).

But the courts show a more decisive will to achieve the model of a constitutional state, with individual freedom of religion and the state's duty to secularism. With their few decisions on the matter, they seem to push the Spanish state from its Catholic past toward an effective secularism.

REFERENCES

Corral Salvador, C. *Confesiones religiosas y Estado español. Régimen jurídico.* Madrid: Biblioteca de Autores Cristianos, 2007.
El Mundo (Section "Madrid"). April 21, 2010.
———— (Section "España"). May 25, 2008.
El País. On-line edition (section "Sociedad"). April 16, 2008.
Habermas, Jürgen. "Religion in the Public Sphere," *European Journal of Philosophy* 14, 2006.
Montesinos Sánchez, N. *La confesionalidad, pieza clave en la historia constitucional española y en el régimen franquista.* 1991. http://rua.ua.es, 1991.

Organic Law 7/1980, of July 5, 1980, of Religious Liberty. B.O.E. July 24, 1980. (*Ley Orgánica de Libertad Religiosa*). Available at http://www.religlaw.org/template.php?id=424&search_terms[0]=LIBERTY&search_terms[1]=RELIGIOUS#searchtext
Poder Judicial. http://www.poderjudicial.es, at "Consejo General del Poder Judicial," "Jurisprudencia," "Jurisprudencia del TS, AN, TSJ y Aps," "CENDOJ."
Souto Paz, J. A. *Derecho Eclesiástico del Estado,* 3rd ed. Madrid: Marcial Pons, 1995.
U.S. Department of State. *International Religious Freedom Report 2007.* Available at http://www.state.gov/g/drl/rls/irf/2007/90201.htm

NOTES

1. Jürgen Habermas, "Religion in the Public Sphere," *European Journal of Phylosophy,* 14 (2006): 1–25.
2. An English version of the Spanish Constitution, the one we have used here, approved on December 27, 1978, is available at the web page of the Congress, www.congreso.es/, in *Congreso de los Diputados,* at www.congreso.es/portal/page/portal/Congreso/Congreso/Informacion/Normas/const_espa_texto_ingles_0.pdf
3. See Salvador C. Corral, *Confesiones religiosas y Estado español. Régimen jurídico* (Madrid: Biblioteca de Autores Cristianos, 2007), 47–87; Sanchez N. Montesinos, *La confesionalidad, pieza clave en la historia constitucional española y en el régimen franquista.* http://rua.ua.es, 1991; J. A. Souto Paz, *Derecho Eclesiástico del Estado,* 3rd ed. (Madrid: Marcial Pons, 1995), 49–64.
4. Article 16.1 Spanish Constitution: "Freedom of . . ., religion, and worship of individuals and communities is guaranteed."
5. Article 3.1 of the *Organic Law 7/1980, of July 5, of Religious Liberty* (B.O.E. 24 July 1980) (*Ley Orgánica de Libertad Religiosa*) states that: "The rights deriving from the freedom of worship and religion may not be exercised to the detriment of the rights of others to practice their public freedoms and fundamental rights or of public safety, health and morality, elements which constitute the order ensured under the rule of Law in democratic societies." An English version of this act is available at the Religion and Law International Document Database, at www.religlaw.org/, at http://www.religlaw.org/template.php?id=424& search_terms[0]=LIBERTY&search_terms[1]=RELIGIOUS#searchtex
6. Article 9 of the European Convention for the Protection of Human Rights and Fundamental Freedoms of 1950 (within the framework of the Council of Europe), a treaty ratified by all the European states, in general, declares: "Freedom of thought, conscience and religion. 1. Everyone has the right to freedom of thought, conscience and religion; this right includes freedom to change his religion or belief and freedom, either alone or in community with others and in public or private, to manifest his religion or belief, in worship, teaching, practice and observance. 2. Freedom to manifest one's religion or beliefs shall be subject only to such limitations as are prescribed by law and are necessary in a democratic society in the interests of public safety, for the protection of public order, health or morals, or for the protection of the rights and freedoms of others."
7. Judgment of the ECHR on *Lautsi and others v. Italy,* March 18, 2011.
8. "Spain." *International Religious Freedom Report 2007.* U.S. Department of State. Available at http://www.state.gov/g/drl/rls/irf/2007/90201.htm.
9. According to the education authorities of Madrid, 40 percent of secondary schools prohibit covering the head; when controversy has arisen, it has been resolved through agreement with parents and removal of the head scarf. See *El Mundo* print edition (section "Madrid") of April 21, 2010.
10. Juan Herrera School (public school).
11. Annexa-Joan Puigbert School (public school).
12. Severo Ochoa School (private school receiving state subsidy).
13. San Daniel School (private school receiving state subsidy).
14. Camilo José Cela School (public school).

15. Novo School (public school).

16. Royal Decree 1553/2005, of December 23, 2005, regulating the issuance of the National Identity Document and its electronic signature (B.O.E. December 24, 2005) (Real Decreto 1553/2005, de 23 de diciembre, por el que se regula la expedición del documento nacional de identidad y sus certificados de firma electrónica).

17. ". . . and without dark lenses glasses or any other garment that can prevent or make the identification of the person difficult" (Article 5.1 b) (The translation is ours).

18. See, for example, *El Mundo* online edition (section "España") of June 20, 2006, and the print edition (section "España") of June 11 and 19, 2007.

19. Decision 457/2002 of September 9, 2002, of the High Court of Balearic Islands (*sentencia del Tribunal Superior de Justicia de Baleares*). This decision resolved an appeal against the decision of the Industrial Court no. 2 of Palma de Mallorca, of February 8, 2002. Its text is available at *Poder Judicial*, www.poderjudicial.es, at "Consejo General del Poder Judicial," "Jurisprudencia," "Jurisprudencia del TS, AN, TSJ y Aps," "CENDOJ."

20. Decision 3250/2009 of December 14, 2009, of the High Court of Castilla-León. This decision resolved an appeal against the decision of the Contentious-administrative Court no. 2 of Valladolid, of November 14, 2008. Its text is available at *Poder Judicial*, www.poderjudicial.es, at "Consejo General del Poder Judicial," "Jurisprudencia," "Jurisprudencia del TS, AN, TSJ y Aps," "CENDOJ."

21. See, for example, *ABC* online edition (section "Nacional") of April 26, 2008.

22. Decision 156/2020 of April 30, 2010, of the Contentious-administrative Court no. 3 of Zaragoza.

23. See, for example, *El País* online edition (section "Sociedad") of April 16, 2008, and *El Mundo* one (section "España") of May 25, 2008.

24. Articles 62, 99 and 100.

25. Royal Decree 707/1979, of April 5th, 1979, regulating the formula of oath in public offices and functions (Real Decreto 707/1979, de 5 de abril, por el que se establece la formula de juramento en cargos y funciones públicas).

26. See information about this organ at www.casareal.es/.

27. Decision of the Supreme Court of June 12, 1990. Its text is available at *Poder Judicial*, www.poderjudicial.es, at "Consejo General del Poder Judicial," "Jurisprudencia," "Jurisprudencia del TS, AN, TSJ y Aps," "CENDOJ."

28. Judgment of the ECHR on *Lautsi and Others v. Italy,* March 18, 2011.

Chapter Six

Church, State, and Capital Punishment in Seventeenth-Century Connecticut

Lawrence B. Goodheart

Capital punishment was not a casual or arbitrary matter for the Puritans of New England. There was scrupulous attention paid to law and procedure, which were influenced by English tradition and scriptural interpretation. The saints, God's elect, held the individual responsible for his or her actions as measured against the law, whose ultimate basis was believed to be sacred.[1] In the Connecticut and New Haven colonies, two separate plantations until the latter merged in 1665 with the former, thirty-three people were judicially executed in nonmilitary situations over the course of the seventeenth century. The ideal, as the Code of 1672 stated, was to ensure "justice and equity," an earthly reflection of the "most perfect rule" of heaven. Based largely on biblical retribution, certain crimes were capital. But who was executed and why? Were all weighed the same in the balance? What were the circumstances of guilt and innocence?

New England was a Puritan redoubt in the contentious religious wars that continued a century after the origins of the Reformation. What the dissident monk Martin Luther had wrought with his ninety-five theses posted on the church door in Wittenberg in 1517 played out with fresh urgency with the ascension of Charles I in 1625 to the throne in England. A divine right autocrat, the Stuart monarch in 1629 arrogantly suspended Parliament and instituted personal rule. Among his critics were Puritans who also hoped to purge the Anglican Church of its popish ways, encouraged by Archbishop William Laud. The royal power hounded the Puritans and harried thousands from the land in what became the Great Migration of the 1630s. The errand into the wilderness was less a retreat than a flanking movement in the Atlantic world, by which these latter-day Calvinists hoped eventually to redeem

England, if not the world. As the Cambridge-educated John Winthrop famously instructed his fellow emigrants on board the ship *Arabella* in 1630, "Wee must consider that wee shall be as a citty upon a hill, the eies of all people are upon us." Like the Hebrews, the relentless God of Israel demanded that his chosen people were "to walke in his wayes and to keepe his Commandments and his ordinance, and his lawes."[2] Winthrop, who would be a twelve-term governor of Massachusetts Bay and its 700 settlers, founded the colony with a charter from the king, who was pleased that these zealots were far away.

Among those seeking refuge from the Anglican persecution of nonconformist ministers were the influential John Cotton, Thomas Hooker, and Samuel Stone—all graduates of Cambridge University, who arrived at Boston abroad the ship *Griffin* in 1634. Hooker and his assistant Stone joined their followers in Newton (Cambridge), where they were ordained. The Newton residents were eager for farmland and hopefully looked westward toward the fertile valley of the Connecticut River. Already in 1633, the Dutch from New Netherlands, who explored the area in 1614, had established a trading post with the Indians. Pilgrims from Plymouth Colony in the same year established a base to the north at Windsor, which received additional arrivals in 1635 from a congregation in Dorchester, Massachusetts. Another Connecticut River town in 1634 was formed to the south at Wethersfield, principally by emigrants from Watertown, Massachusetts, as well as people from other locations, including directly from England. With permission from the Massachusetts General Court, Hooker and Stone in 1636 moved their congregation 100 miles overland to the Dutch settlement at Hartford. On January 14, 1639, the residents of Windsor, Wethersfield, and Hartford "in Combination and Confederation together" adopted the Fundamental Orders of Connecticut "to maintain the purity of the gospel of Lord Jesus."[3]

With his appointment in 1633 as archbishop of Canterbury, Laud escalated harassment of dissidents, demanding complete adherence to Anglican doctrine. John Davenport, a principled nonconformist, fled his London church for exile in Holland. Hooker and Cotton had earlier failed to convince Davenport to emigrate with them, but now, under threat of arrest, he was convinced that relocation to New England was imperative. Returning to England in disguise, he organized his congregation for an expedition to Massachusetts Bay Colony. These expatriates were staunch Puritans and included prominent merchants, among them Davenport's confidant Theophilus Eaton, who were eager to establish a "Bible State."[4] Governor John Winthrop welcomed their arrival in Boston in the early summer of 1637. The attraction of Quinnipiac (New Haven), with a good harbor in Long Island Sound, suitable for mercantile endeavors, spurred the original company and new arrivals to found New Haven Colony in the spring of 1638. They subsequently acquired extensive landholdings, ceded by compliant Indians, along the coast and well into the interior. In organizing their church and civil government in 1639, the colonists adopted a code of laws, "a Model of Moses his judicials compiled in an exact method," a draft of which Cotton had drawn up in 1636. The New Haven Colony had no royal charter; it was distant from Massachusetts Bay to the east and independent of Connecticut to the north. Cotton's model fit their needs nicely and in its religious rigor gave distinct rendering to the criminal justice system. The General Court for New Haven Colony in 1644 officially mandated "the judicial laws of God, as they were delivered by Moses" throughout its jurisdiction.[5]

The rationale for the death penalty was deeply embedded in the religious foundation of New England. It was the logical, albeit extreme, extension of presuppositions about human nature and civil society. "The Puritans," Perry Miller observed, "were gifted—or cursed—with an overwhelming realization of an inexorable power at work not only in nature but in themselves, which they called God."[6] These dissenters believed that humans were almost irrevocably flawed by original sin, an innate human propensity to disobey the divine will. The Puritans, however, had modified the relentless predestination of John Calvin, in which a hidden, unknowable God had eternally damned the many and elected the few. Although mindful of divine absolutism, the theology of Thomas Hooker stressed human volition, especially the hope that the righteous might gain gradual assurance of regeneration.[7] "God of an unwilling will, doth make a willing will," Hooker preached.[8] "We must sin," he acknowledged, but he demanded, "look sin in the face, and discern it to the full." And with the gift of divine grace, "*cure these inordinate and raging lusts* and thence wil follow a stil and quiet composure of mind."[9] Sin was a choice; people were accountable, particularly for criminal conduct. God proposed, but man disposed. Puritanism demanded a rigorous regime of inner discipline, self-regulation, spiritual examination, and a dedicated work ethic.[10]

Furthermore, the Bible Commonwealth was an external check on individual tendencies toward wrongdoing. In addition to theology and creed, New Englanders had an explicit political program to create a godly community. The well-being of society depended on a single religious truth. The Puritans had come to New England not for religious tolerance but, as Laud intended in England, to enforce orthodoxy (as they saw it) and punish dissent. In their small homogenous communities, the congregational church structure was well suited for the isolated, local situation. Neither Connecticut nor New Haven merged state and church in a true theocracy, but they were linked body and soul. They differed in form but not purpose.[11] The court in New Haven, for example, met in the meetinghouse. The political franchise (limited to free men with property) was dependent on church membership, which meant owning the covenant—making a persuasive public profession of faith. As Hooker preached in a Hartford election sermon in 1638, "The choice of public magistrates belongs unto the people by God's own allowance."[12] And John Davenport reiterated in 1669: "The orderly ruling of men over men, in general, is from God, in its root, though voluntary in the manner of coalescing."[13]

Popular democracy, however, was suspect. Winthrop in 1645 reminded a restive population in Higham, Massachusetts, during a disputed militia election, "If you will be satisfied to enjoy such civil and lawfull liberties, such as Christ allows you, then you will quietly and cheerfully submit unto that authority, which is set over you, in all the administration of it, for your own good."[14] It was expected that the populace accept the social covenant, as they had the spiritual compact, and defer to the most worthy saints. The rule by male elders, as Stone famously said, was "a speaking aristocracy in the face of a silent democracy."[15] The magistrates and ministers were predictably the colony's elite—the college-educated, the major landowners, and the well connected. Government was hierarchical and mirrored a stratified social order, with medieval vestiges that banned usury, set fixed prices, and observed sumptuary laws. Mindful of Stuart abuses and their own postlapsarian proclivities, New Englanders feared that liberty might degenerate into license and authority into absolutism. "It is therefore most wholsome for magistrates and officers in church and common-wealth, never to affect more liberty and authority then will do them good, and the people good," Cotton reflected. He further warned, "There is a straine in a mans heart that will sometime or other runne out to excesse, unlesse the Lord restaine it , but is not good to venture it."[16]

The search for an Aristotelian balance between extremes was rooted in rules and regulation. The Puritans were a litigious but well-ordered people who, like the Jews with whom they identified in the mutual quest for Zion, devoted great intellectual effort to exegesis of the word, scriptural and statutory. The Fundamental Orders of Connecticut boldly made no mention of the English crown or the fact that the colony had no royal charter. This constitution established two general assemblies and provided for the selection of magistrates by the legislature. Bound by oath to honor the written law, the magistrates were limited to one-year terms, while the governor was restricted to a term of one year in any two. The document declared, "Our civil affairs [are] to be guided and governed according to such laws, rules, orders, and decrees as shall be made, ordered and decreed." The magistrates had the "power to administer justice according to the laws here established, and for want thereof according to the rule of the word of God."[17] Secular and sacred law was the standard. Original sin would produce obstinacy from some, for whom correction was necessary. And if the fault was a grievous one, death was divinely mandated but subject to human implementation.

In creating a body of law, the Puritans selected applicable scriptural mandates that identified capital crimes. English statues also made frequent biblical references, but the Puritans, given their religiosity, were much more inclined to do so. The scriptural emphasis in the Connecticut and New Haven Colonies allowed for flexibility and innovation in the traditional law code. The stamp of divine approval meant that the colonists might revise English statues and make more explicit what was often vague in common law. Until the establishment of the Dominion of New England by King James II in 1686, English law did not apply if it was not mentioned in colonial law. The Puritans kept parts of the old system while incorporating what was pertinent to their New England experience, part of the Americanization experience. England and New England concurred that witches be executed. In vivo evisceration, burning alive, and being racked and broken on the wheel were practiced in Europe but were never sanctioned in New England. The Connecticut Code of 1672 stated in regard to punishment that "none shall be inflicted that are Inhumane, Barbarous or Cruel."[18] Adultery was not a capital crime in England, but the Puritans, concerned with confining sexual relations to marriage, made it a violation punishable by death. Ecclesiastical courts in England oversaw morals; civil courts in New England were the censors. The Puritans (with the notable exception of Roger Williams, whom Massachusetts Bay banished in 1635 to Rhode Island) saw a typology in the Hebrew Bible corresponding to their own momentous situation. What an omnipotent divinity had made incumbent upon the Jews with the covenant of Abraham currently applied to the Puritans. The Mosaic Code, however, was subject to interpretation. The Hebraic stoning of adulterous women was a tribal patriarchalism beyond the pale for seventeenth-century Europeans.[19]

Rather than an escape from orthodoxy in Massachusetts, Connecticut and New Haven were its western extension. Connecticut's list of capital crimes, enacted in 1642, closely copied that of Massachusetts of a year earlier (see Table 6.1).

Table 6.1 Connecticut's Capital Laws, 1642[20]

1. Idolatry	5. Killing through guile	9. Rape
2. Witchcraft	6. Bestiality	10. Man stealing
3. Blasphemy	7. Sodomy (male)	11. Perjury (to take a life)
4. Murder (killing with malice or cruelty)	8. Adultery	12. Rebellion

Only the last crime, rebellion, did not have a clear biblical imprimatur. Now that the Puritans were establishing their own fledging regimes, they knew, as did King Charles I and Archbishop Laud, that sedition and treason must be severely punished. Accommodation to worldly necessity—raison d'etat, in this case—made a breach in the spiritual fortress, one that would widen by the end of the century. Indeed, the Puritan dilemma, as Edmund Morgan pointed out in the case of Winthrop, was "the paradox that required a man to live in the world without being of it."[21] Seventeenth-century law made further compromises with Scripture. Willful intent to defame religion or deny God was necessary to demonstrate blasphemy. False witness in a capital trial applied only if the perjurer deliberately lied to convict the accused. And conviction for adultery required direct evidence of the sexual act (in flagrante delicto), not merely the presence of a man in the bed or boudoir of a married or betrothed woman who was not his wife or fiancée.

Following the revision of the Massachusetts law in 1648, Roger Ludlow, Connecticut's only formally trained lawyer, followed its lead in devising a new law code that added five new capital crimes to the original dozen (see Table 6.2).

Table 6.2 Connecticut's Capital Laws, 1650[22]

1-12 (repeated from 1642, although the sequence changed)	
13. Cursing a natural parent	16. Burglary (third offense)
14. Smiting a natural parent	17. Robbery (third offense)
15. Defiance by a rebellious son	

The founding generation found a disturbing diminution in filial piety at mid-century. In keeping with their own traditions, not the Bible, the Puritans made age sixteen the demarcation point, so that sons younger than that age were not subject to the death penalty. The authorities instructed parents to encourage literacy, so that, in part, children could read the "Capitall Lawes" and appreciate the dire consequence of not honoring their parents.[23] Because "many persons," it was thought, were engaged in robbery and burglary in homes and on highways, these common law crimes were added to the list. These property crimes were graduated, however. The first and second offenses provided for branding the letter "B" on the forehead and a severe whipping. And if the offense was on the Sabbath, the ears were cropped. For the third conviction, the incorrigible could be hanged.[24] Unlike the 1642 code, manslaughter was now distinguished from murder as justifiable homicide committed in self-defense. Trained at Oxford and the Inner Temple,

Ludlow made clear the commitment to individual rights and the rule of law: "No mans life shall be taken away . . . no mans person shall be arrested, restrained banished, dismembered nor any way punished . . . vnless it bee by the virtue or equity of some express Law of the Country warranteing the same, established by a Generall Courte, and sufficiently published, or in case of the defect of a Law in any particular case, by the word of God."[25]

New Haven in 1639 had adopted Cotton's *Judicial*, the most rigorous biblical codicil in New England, which conveniently met their high expectations. Its strict Puritanism influenced the formal law code adopted in 1656 (see Table 6.3).

Table 6.3 New Haven Capital Laws, 1656[26]

1. Idolatry	10. Fornication with very young ("unripe") female	19. Rape (death penalty not mandatory)
2. Witchcraft	11. Masturbation (male)	20. Incest
3. Blasphemy	12. Adultery	21. Burglary (third offense)
4. Murder	13. Man stealing	22. Robbery (third offense)
5. Manslaughter (involving anger or cruelty)	14. Perjury (to take a life)	23. Profaning the Sabbath (provocatively)
6. Killing through guile	15. Rebellion	
7. Bestiality	16. Cursing a natural parent	
8. Sodomy (male)	17. Smiting a natural parent	
9. Sodomy (heterosexual)	18. Defiance by a rebellious son	

Scripture underscored capital cases. Unlike its sister colonies, New Haven made provocative profanation of the Sabbath a hanging offense. A recidivist convicted of burglary for a second time on the Sabbath not only was branded and whipped but had to stand in the pillory and "wear a halter in the day time constantly and visibly about his neck, as a mark of infamy."[27] Sexual infractions most set New Haven apart. It was the only colony to adopt literally the Hebraic ban on incest, to punish heterosexual sodomy, and to outlaw male masturbation with the death penalty. The Mosaic Code, which allowed a rapist to marry his victim and pay restitution to her family, did not fit Puritan sensibilities. New Haven made rape of an unmarried woman and statutory rape of a girl under the age of ten hanging offenses. The latter was included broadly under the concept of sodomy, an unnatural sexual act. The rape of married and betrothed women fell under the category of adultery, which in this case condemned the male assailant. No provision of marital rape existed in a system of female coverture. The Code of 1656 echoed New Haven's affirmation of the rule of law and due process in death penalty cases.

The restoration of the Stuart monarchy under King Charles II in 1660 and the end of the Puritan interregnum confronted Connecticut and New Haven with a crisis. Neither colony had a royal charter. Connecticut's Governor John Winthrop, Jr., the capable eldest son of Massachusetts's founder, agreed to represent both colonies in England. He gained one, not two, charters from the king in 1662, which allowed for a remarkable amount of self-government, but only for Connecticut. New Haven was reluctant to accept its extinction. With only 2,500 settlers, it was, however, in an untenable position. Eaton died in 1658, at a time when his dynamic leadership was wanted. The colony's ultra-Puritanism might well have caused problems in gaining legal sanction from London. To the west, it was bounded by Anglican New York, and to the north blocked by Connecticut. As the uncertain situation threatened the political integrity of New England, New Haven reluctantly merged with Connecticut in 1665. [28]

In the revision of statues in 1672, Connecticut significantly avoided the provisions in the capital crimes that had made New Haven distinctive (see Table 6.4).

Table 6.4 Connecticut's Capital Laws, 1672[29]

1. Idolatry	7. Sodomy (male)	13. Arson
2. Blasphemy	8. Incest	14. Cursing a natural parent
3. Witchcraft	9. Rape	15. Smiting a natural parent
4. Murder (killing with malice or cruelty)	10. Man-stealing	16. Defiance by a rebellious son
5. Killing through guile	11. Perjury (to take a life)	17. Burglary (third offense)
6. Bestiality	12. Rebellion	18. Robbery (third offense)

Adultery was dropped as a capital crime—the first time in the colony that such a deletion had occurred. The substitution for the death penalty was whipping, branding on the forehead with the letter A, and wearing a halter around the neck while in the colony. [30] Connecticut added incest but limited the definition to parents and children, not the biblical literalism of New Haven. Both parties were to be executed unless "the Woman was forced or under fourteen years of age," at the time of discretion.[31] A case of father–daughter incest had occurred the year before in Norwich and forced the subject on the books. Arson was a serious concern in an era of wood frame structures and uncertain fire protection. The colony distinguished, however, between conflagrations that threatened property and those that endangered human life. Although manslaughter was deleted from the murder statue, unpremeditated homicide in response to sudden provocation remained a capital offense. Killing in self-defense, as the code of 1650 stipulated, was the only form of justifiable homicide. Not until 1719, when Connecticut adopted the English standard on manslaughter, was the critical distinction given greater clarity.

The statutes per se are deceptive as to what occurred in practice. The laws represented a religious ideal, a public declaration, as the Code of 1672 put it, of what was "suitable for the people of Israel."[32] The judicial system was much more lenient. The courts aspired to be scrupulous and fair. There was concern to balance individual protection with the greater good. Drawing on centuries of English tradition, the Puritans upheld civil rights, including no unreasonable search or seizure, no double jeopardy, no compulsory self-incrimination, no torture, no cruel or barbarous punishments, right to bail (except in capital cases), grand and petite juries in capital cases, speedy trial, presumption of innocence, and the right to confront accusers in open court. New Haven did not have a jury system, since there was no scriptural basis for it.[33] Attorneys did not usually function in either colony; the wise and impartial rule of the magistrates was deemed sufficient. The plaintiff managed the prosecution, called witnesses, and presented evidence. The defendant responded and called witnesses. The judges interrogated deponents and commented on the evidence; their function was to clarify the matter for the jury.

The royal charter of 1662 provided for different levels of courts. Oversight rested with the General Court. The Assistants Court (composed of the governor, deputy governor, and magistrates or assistants) was the immediate venue for all crimes punishable by banishment, dismemberment, or death. There was a reluctance to execute unless there was a confession of the accused or two eyewitnesses of "competent age, of sound understanding, and good reputation."[34] This amended biblical stipulation is an outstanding example of how scriptural compunction acted to limit executions. Another check on the rush to judgment was that a two-thirds majority was needed for a *billa vera* (true bill) or jury indictment. Otherwise, a jury might declare *ignoramus* and not arrive at a verdict. The magistrates could twice return a verdict to the jury, which usually meant reconsideration of a sentence of death.[35]

Law was a social cohesive among a contentious people. The legal system sought to resolve issues that would otherwise prove disruptive and thus to integrate the community. Justice, moral clarity, and spiritual regeneration through God's grace were the goals. Frequent resort to the death penalty, as in the Salem witch hunt of 1692, was more indicative of social pathology than of divine blessing. Benefit of clergy, a medieval Catholic contrivance that was used to escape execution, understandably never took hold among antipapists. Most capital offenses in Connecticut and New Haven during the seventeenth century did not end on the gallows, including blasphemy, burglary, fornication with a young female, heterosexual sodomy, killing through guile, man-stealing, perjury, profanation of the Sabbath, robbery, and various forms of filial disrespect.

There was a graduation of punishment available that fell short of execution. In a "high offence," Abigail Betts declared she could prove that Jesus was a bastard. A Hartford court in 1663 sentenced her to humiliation but not to hang on the gallows "to ye open view of spectators that all Israel may hear and feare."[36] In 1655, an insolent youth, Samuel Ford, injured a young boy, disobeyed his father, sassed his mother, and defied Sabbath observance. When an elder sought to correct him, "he turned up his breech and bid him kiss it." The New Haven magistrates did not enact the full force of biblical retribution. Instead, they whipped him and warned, "Take heed."[37] Abraham, an African American slave, with one name defining his racial bondage, confessed to "breaking open" several houses on the Sabbath and other robberies, as well as escaping jail in Fairfield. Rather than execution, this recidivist in 1698 was "severely whipt" and branded with a B on his forehead.[38]

Thirty-one people in criminal proceedings during the seventeenth century did not, however, escape execution in the colonies of Connecticut and New Haven. The executed fall into three broad categories: homicide (nine), sexual violations (eleven), and witchcraft (eleven). Witchcraft was confined to the period, as were some of the sexual violations.

The circumstances surrounding the nine people executed for homicide reveals the following profile. Eight men were executed, compared with one woman, who died for the gender-specific crime of neonaticide as a result of an illegitimate birth. Male violence was often directed at women, of whom six were murdered. Excluding neonanticide, intrafamily violence included two husbands who murdered their wives and one brother who killed his sister. In six of eight known cases, the perpetrators were known to the victims. All perpetrators were hanged except for two Indians, who were beheaded in the first decade of settlement. These were the only decapitations to occur and the only murderers executed in New Haven Colony. The ritual of beheading was meant to set Indians apart from whites at a time when the English sought to impose their dominance over the indigenous people. In interracial homicide, three Indians were executed for killing whites but no whites were convicted for killing Indians. A black man killed his African American wife and was hanged. Alcohol is indicated in one murder, an Indian assault on a white woman. No firearms were involved; blunt and sharp instruments, common to households of the day, predominated as the instruments of murder. A miscarriage of justice may well have occurred in the execution of Peter Abbot. A history of lunacy did not spare him from the hangman, but the jury may have found him lucid at the time of his assault on his family, which would have held to the letter of the law. A lack of documentation, however, leaves the issue moot. Four young children and infants died, including three at the hand of John Stoddard, himself a sixteen-year-old, who was hanged as a culpable adult. Beyond the scope of this study, there looms the bloody multitude that died violently in two racial wars.

Contrary to a persistent stereotype, the Puritans were not particularly prudish for their day. As antipapists, they rejected Roman Catholic ideals that equated holiness with neo-Platonic self-abnegation of the body and desire, such as celibacy, flagellation, monasticism, and mortification of the flesh. The lesson of original sin for the Puritans was that humans were flawed and had difficulty in obeying divine precepts, including carnal restraint. Puritans sought to contain sexuality within marriage, couple it with reproduction, and ensure the survival of the saints. The errand into the wilderness gave special urgency to the divine injunction to go forth and multiply. They sought to regulate, not renounce. Sexuality, rightly expressed, produced the "little commonwealth" of husbands and wives, parents and children; the family was the harmonious, organic embryo of the larger, biblical polity. Outside of marriage, sexual intercourse was banned. New Haven's sweeping prohibition that prescribed death for "carnal knowledge of another sexual vessel than God in nature appointed to become one flesh," included heterosexual sodomy, which was not mentioned in the Bible.[39] The courts generally dealt with most sexual violations, especially noncapital offenses, with moderation and graduated punishment.[40] In keeping with its law code, New Haven, with six of nine executions for sexual crimes, outpaced Connecticut. These specific cases—involving bestiality, male sodomy, adultery, incest, and rape—had, however, distinct circumstances that led to the gallows. These executions represented extremes that affirmed sexual taboos at the intersection of law, religion, and community standards.

In sum, the death penalty for sexual infractions had distinct seventeenth-century characteristics. Excluding a woman (Ruth Briggs) and an adulterer of unknown identity in 1650, nine males were hanged. The four executions for bestiality, three for sodomy, one exclusively for adultery (Briggs was convicted of adultery and infanticide), and one for incest were the last of their kind to occur in Connecticut. The delisting of adultery as a capital crime in 1672 further marked the reluctance to execute for these violations. As the spiritual fervor of the founding generation waned over time, rape remained the only sexual offense for which anyone was executed after 1672, the year that Thomas Rood was hanged for incest. Lessening religious zeal undercut the basis for biblical retribution, with the notable exception of homicide (see Genesis 9:6).

Eight of the hangings for sexual offenses occurred in New Haven, with its broad-ranging prescriptions.[41] Of the seven executions for bestiality and sodomy, six were in its jurisdiction. No one of elite standing was convicted. Nicolas Sessions, a well-to-do resident of Windsor, escaped execution, despite a long history of predatory homosexuality. There was no such toleration for John Knight, a servant in New Haven, who was convicted of sodomy for two liaisons. If fortuitous eyewitnesses to illicit acts were not forthcoming, officials sought to coerce confessions through intense interrogation. William Potter's son and wife caught him copulating with domestic animals, and a fisherman spied Walter Robinson servicing his sheep dog. Under duress from officials, the swineherd George Spencer confessed to bestiality with a sow, an act that probably never happened. Thus, the first execution of a white person in what is now Connecticut was the outcome of a coerced confession, an ominous precedent for death penalty proceedings.

Despite sophisticated adjudication and observance of the rule of law in the context of the times, justice was not always blind. Homicide cases were most straightforward and adhered most closely to universal standards. The prosecution of Indian perpetrators, however, was notably fraught with racial tension. Sexual infractions could be arbitrary and problematic. Contradictions and inequities existed, which a date with the gallows made irreparable and final.

A double standard also prevailed. The sole rapist hanged, an outsider charged in 1694 with the violent assault of two prepubescent girls, was initially granted a reprieve. But in 1699, the concealment of the death of an illegitimate baby was made presumptive evidence of homicide unless one witness could validate a stillbirth. The punishment put a grave burden on the mother and particularly on lower-status women. They did not have the connections that the better sort had to hide a bastard birth.

The most flagrant misogyny in capital punishment during the seventeenth century, however, was witchcraft. Spectral evidence was particularly nebulous and elusive, according to standards of judicial proof, no matter how functional, as anthropologists might put it, the belief in witchcraft was in the Puritan village. Some magistrates and ministers sought to harmonize the law with folk culture through the relentless coercion of confessions, which aided and abetted witch hunts. Other officials were cautious and skeptical about spectral evidence and resolved cases of witchcraft short of the death penalty, a moderation that calmed interpersonal relations and community tension. New Haven executed no one for the crime, despite some highly charged cases during the 1650s. Connecticut, after much contention, hanged the last of eleven witches in 1663, and authorities, following the New Haven precedent, blocked anyone else going to the gallows, including convictions that were overturned in 1665, 1668, and 1692. The historical challenge is to understand the cultural mandate that made witchcraft a capital crime, to explain who was identified as a witch, and why, within three decades after settlement, no one was executed.

In seventeenth-century New England, religion and mores overlapped, reinforcing and complementing one another, including on the evil of witchcraft. The Bible recounted Satan's numerous temptations and condemned witchcraft, the voluntary human alliance with the diabolical. Puritan ministers in expansive exegesis interpreted the Calvinistic relationship between a wrathful deity and a sinful humanity. Yet the federal theology, as comprehensive as it was, left the cause of many perplexing, everyday issues unresolved. New beer soured, breast milk dried up, infants sickened, livestock died, and dreams appeared portentous. Mysterious things happened; the explanation was not clear. A supernatural world, it was assumed, existed. Cunning folk probed the preternatural by astrology, casting spells, conjuring, and fortune telling. Magic might be benign but also malevolent. Personal and social relations in the close-knit Puritan village on the frontier were intense. Fear, jealousy, and animosity might, particularly after a quarrel between neighbors and heightened by broader currents of unease, set the stage for accusations of witchcraft against vulnerable residents. As John Davenport warned his New Haven congregation in 1652, a discontented mind was "a fit subject for the devil to work upon."[42]

Witch hunts during the sixteenth and seventeenth centuries in Europe claimed more than 50,000 lives.[43] As Christians regarded the Jew as the anti-Christ, the witch was the personification of sin, the negation of holiness. Scripture condemned her. She was typically an older woman of low status and humble economic means who acquired an unsavory reputation. A vulnerable woman, she was on the margins of society. At times of acrimony, villagers singled her out as the agent of malevolence. Like the Jew, she had unnatural proclivities and upset the normal balance of things. But unlike the readily identifiable Jew, the witch was a covert member of the community and had to be unmasked. The New England witch hunts were a trans-Atlantic extension of a craze concentrated in northwestern Europe.

Accused and indicted as a witch, the defendant, in the trial for life and death, as the Puritans described it, was confronted with sworn testimony affirming her *maleficium*, her devilish wickedness. Villagers and officials, especially ministers, coerced her to confess. A confession was double-edged: by admitting her guilt, she called on divine mercy to save her eternal soul but at the same time legitimated the protocol that condemned her. If she was found guilty, a special sermon solemnized the event. Villagers accompanied her to the gallows at the edge of town, a boundary between civilization and wilderness, order and chaos. She ascended a ladder to the scaffold, and the constable placed the noose around her neck. Authorities, secular and spiritual, stood nearby, endorsing the execution by their presence. Curious villagers gathered about in anticipation, looking up at the high stage. Dangling in space, killed by the weight of her suspended body, she jerked spasmodically and died grotesquely. Quickly cut down, she was presently buried, probably near the gallows, but not in a Christian cemetery. The sanctioned death with its set dramaturgy purged and purified the community of evil, or so it was hoped.

Satan, according to the lore, made unholy pacts with willing disciples, particularly women, the flawed sisters of the archetypal femme fatale, Eve. A virulent misogyny projected anxiety about sexuality and reproduction upon aged women, who were the antithesis of fecund maternity.[44] Not only did Nathaniel Hawthorne's fictional character, the misanthropic Goodman Brown, see abundant deviltry, but so did King James I and the learned Boston divines, Increase and his son Cotton Mather, who shared a passion in ferreting out the nether world. Like England and Massachusetts, Connecticut and New Haven's law codes made witchcraft a capital crime. Although backed by scriptural imprimatur not to let a witch live, the judicial standard for finding a defendant guilty was ambiguous.[45] Satan was devious and spectral events elusive. Fiendish trickery played havoc with legal rigor. "It is very certain," Cotton Mather opined, "that the devills have sometimes represented the shapes of persons not only innocent, but also very virtuous."[46] Would the innocent be executed, while the guilty escaped? Would the devil get his due?

From the perspective of Anglo-Puritan jurisprudence, murder was relatively straightforward. There were the graphic remnants of violence: a corpse, weapon, a perpetrator. The supernatural essence of witchcraft made it a legal quagmire. Like the three witches in *Macbeth*, the otherworldly was a twilight zone, a crepuscular realm that confounded empirical ways of knowing. "I'[n] the name of truth," Banquo demanded of the weird sisters, "Are ye fantastical, or that indeed Which outwardly ye show?"[47] Diabolical magic suspended Aristotelian logic at the heart of judicial inquiry. Deponents testified that defendants had flown, appeared as black animals, or sickened a child, statements whose corroboration rested on other phantasms. Cause and effect were open ended, according to the classic fallacy of post hoc ergo propter hoc. The rooster crowed; the sun arose; ergo, the rooster caused the sun to rise. In the constricted world of the Puritan village, the witch was a scapegoat for neighborly complaints, communal stress, and larger patterns of discontent. Witchcraft jurisprudence pivoted on an elusive epistemology. No other capital crime so challenged routine standards for admissible evidence.

Based on courtroom experience, in which lives hung in the balance, officials sought to make the diabolical bend to demonstrable proof. Rational minded theologians after all had bound a *deus absconditus* to various covenants, essentially contracts in which the reciprocal relationship of an omnipotent deity and sinful humanity were inextricably tied. Important as they were, ministers and magistrates were not exclusive historical agents. Nor were the accusers. The condemned, who refused to confess, even as they stood on the gallows with their eternal souls in the balance, were heroically challenging the verdict. And husbands who filed suits of slander against the defamers of their wives, and others who defended the accused, sought to derail the juggernaut. In the broad scheme of things, the dissenters, especially the maligned women who refused to quietly accept their fate, were without conscious intent subverting the capital code.

The prime evidence of guilt was a "voluntary confession." An open admission confirmed the reality of witchcraft. Connecticut and New Haven by statue banned torture of defendants. In contrast, grim-minded European inquisitors justified the rack and thumb screw in order to save the immortal soul of the witch. For New Englanders, physical abuse not only rendered the truthfulness of statements suspect, but also degraded the rule of law and the sanctity of the biblical commonwealth. The putative admission of guilt was further subject to evaluation by magistrates and ministers as to its truthfulness. Much as the U.S. Supreme Court recognized in *Miranda v. Arizona* (1966), people charged with crimes and under a state of emotional duress might confess to authorities actions that they did not commit, even without direct corporal mistreatment. Through oversight, Puritan officials had the obligation to forestall a miscarriage of justice. Nonetheless, at the local level, defendants were subject to overwhelming community pressure to confess. Delegations of citizens and ministers repeatedly visited the defendants in jail and demanded that they confess. Several women did so and were hanged.

A second standard for conviction was "the good and honest report" of two witnesses under oath before a magistrate, verifying the practice of witchcraft. Such testimony might demonstrate three points of evidence: the accused had made a pact with the devil; the accused had entertained a "familiar," the devil in the form of cat, mouse, or other "visible" creature; and the accused had performed various examples of diabolical enchantments. The rub was the devil acted covertly, and his machinations were "difficult things to prove." Judicial rigor cautioned "jurors, etc. not to condemne suspected psons on bare prsumtions without good and sufficient proofes."[48]

After a disruptive witch panic during the early 1660s, key magistrates and ministers in Connecticut sought to rationalize an often capricious procedure. Eleven people had been executed since 1647 and dozens suspected. All manner of spectral evidence was offered in court. Some zealous ministers and inquisitorial citizens badgered defendants to confess and to implicate others, which escalated tension. Remarkably, after 1663, juries convicted only three defendants, magistrates overturned the convictions, and no one was subsequently executed for witchcraft in Connecticut. Officials had not set out to debunk witchcraft, but close attention to the rule of law rendered this capital

crime a dead letter. Precedents in New Haven Colony and a cautious Govern-
or John Winthrop Jr. in Connecticut Colony checked the rush to judgment
and barred the way to the gallows. Defiant defendants, the women who
refused to confess, and their allies spurred conscientious officials to adopt a
systematic standard that rendered execution problematic. As the legal culture
changed, so did the social structure and religious mandate that had fueled the
misogyny of witchcraft. The years 1692–1693 were the finale of this capital
crime in New England.[49]

To look ahead briefly, there was a pivotal transformation of the legal
culture from divine terms to a secular ethic, and the evolution from Puritan to
Yankee that affected the capital laws and who was executed.[50] Expanding
population and extensive commerce increased opportunities for advance-
ment. New markets and bustling towns enticed farmers, manufacturers, and
merchants with the promise of profits. The possibility of worldly advance-
ment in eighteenth-century New England that had earlier been the lot of a
fortunate few now seemed available for the many.[51] Small storekeepers
sought wealth; frugal farmers engaged in land speculation. As the North
America colonies prospered, the British ministry had compelling reasons to
regulate its far-flung empire and centralize its administration. During the
seventeenth century, Connecticut was largely autonomous under the Fundamental Orders of 1639 and Charter of 1662. The Board of Trade and Plantations after 1700 sought an end to benign neglect and to integrate its once
insignificant colony into a global network. Commercial entrepreneurship
within an imperial framework altered the legal landscape from a Puritan
emphasis on morality and orthodoxy to one emphasizing commercial law,
property crime, and religious toleration. In addition, the Great Awakening
that swept intensely over Connecticut during the 1740s radically challenged
the Congregational order. Itinerant preachers impugned the settled clergy,
communal churches were rent, and the individualistic logic of Protestantism
was emphasized as never before. With traditional religion shattered and people loosened from ancient bonds, Connecticut enacted the most substantial
modification to date in its capital laws since the settlement of southern New
England over a century earlier. The Code of 1750 dropped entirely any
biblical citation to justify capital punishment, a mark of significant secularization of criminal justice.

REFERENCES

Bailyn, Bernard. "The Apologia of Robert Keayne." *William and Mary Quarterly,* 7 (1950).
Briggs, Robin. *Witches and Neighbors: The Social and Cultural Context of European Witchcraft.* New York: Viking, 1996.

Bushman, Richard L. *From Puritan to Yankee: Character and the Social Order in Connecticut, 1690-1765.* New York: Norton, 1967.

Calder, Isabel M. "John Cotton and the New Haven Colony." *New England Quarterly,* 3 (1930).

Clark, Stuart. *Thinking with Demons: The Idea of Witchcraft in Early Modern Europe.* New York: Oxford University Press, 1997.

The Code of 1650, Being a Compilation of the Earliest Laws and Orders of the General Court of Connecticut. Hartford, CT: S. Andrus and Son, 1821.

Cohn, Norman. *Inner Demons: An Enquiry Inspired by the Great Witch-Hunt.* New York: Basic Books, 1975.

———. *Pursuit of the Millennium.* London: Secker and Warburg, 1957.

———. *Warrant for Genocide.* New York: Harper and Row, 1967.

Cotton, John. "Limitation of Government," in David Dutkanicz, ed., *John Winthrop's Sinners.* Mineola, NY: Dover, 2005.

Cushing, John D. (ed.). *The Earliest Laws of the New Haven and Connecticut Colonies 1639–1673.* Wilmington, DE: Michael Glazier, 1977.

Demos, John. *A Little Commonwealth: Family Life in Plymouth Colony.* New York: Oxford University Press, 1970.

Dexter, Franklin. *Ancient Town Records, I.* New Haven, CT: New Haven Colony Historical Society, 1917.

Fundamental Orders of Connecticut. January 14, 1639. The full document is available at www.bartleby.com/43/7.htlm.

Ginzburg, Carlo. *The Night Battles: Witchcraft and Agrarian Cults in the Sixteenth and Seventeenth Centuries.* Baltimore: Johns Hopkins University Press, 1983.

Goodwin, Everett C. *The Magistracy Rediscovered: Connecticut, 1636–1818.* Ann Arbor, MI: University of Michigan Research Press, 1979.

Grasso, Christopher. *A Speaking Aristocracy: Transforming Public Discourse in Eighteenth-Century Connecticut.* Chapel Hill, NC: University of North Carolina, 1999.

Greene, M. Louise. *The Development of Religious Liberty in Connecticut.* Freeport, NY: Books for Libraries Press, 1970; original, 1905.

Greenhouse, Linda. "The Justices Consider Religious Displays." *New York Times,* March 3, 2005.

Hall, David, John M. Murrin, and Thad W. Tate, eds., *Saints and Revolutionaries: Essays in Early America.* New York: Norton, 1984.

Hoadley, Charles J. *Records of the Colony or Jurisdiction of New Haven from May, 1653, to the Union.* Hartford, CT: Case, Lockwood., 1858.

Hooker, Thomas. "Hartford Election Sermon," in David Dutkanicz, ed., *John Winthrop's Sinners.* Mineola, NY: Dover, 2005.

———. "A True Sight of Sin, Meditation, Wandering Thoughts, Repentant Sinner and Their Ministers," in David Dutkanicz, ed., *John Winthrop's Sinners.* Mineola, NY: Dover, 2005.

"Islamists in Somalia Say They Plan to Execute 5 Rapists by Stoning." *New York Times,* June 27, 2006.

Jones, Mary J. A. *Congregational Commonwealth: Connecticut, 1636-1662.* Middletown, CT: Wesleyan University Press, 1968.

Karlsen, Carol F. *The Devil in the Shape of a Woman: Witchcraft in Colonial New England.* New York: Norton, 1986.

Lacy, Norbert B. *The Records of the Court of Assistants of Connecticut, 1665–1701,* 2 vols. Master's thesis. New Haven, CT: Yale University, 1937.

Levack, Brian. *The Witch-Hunt in Early Modern Europe.* New York: Longman, 1995.

Konig, Dave Thomas. *Law and Society in Puritan Massachusetts: Essex County, 1629–1692.* Chapel Hill, NC: University of North Carolina Press, 1979.

Larner, Christina. *Enemeies of God: The Witch-Hunt in Scotland.* Baltimore: Johns Hopkins University Press, 1981.

Marcus, Gail Sussman. "'Due Execution of the Generall Rules of Righteousness': Criminal Procedure in New Have Town and Colony, 1638–1658," in David D. Hall, John M. Murrin, Thad W. Tate, eds., *Saints and Revolutionaries: Essays in Early America.* New York: Norton, 1984.

McManus, Edgar J. *Law and Liberty in New England.* Amherst, MA: University of Massachusetts Press, 1993.

Midelfort, H. C. Erik. *Witch-Hunting in Southwestern Germany, 1582–1684.* Stanford, CT: Stanford University Press, 1972.

Miller, Perry. *The New England Mind: Colony to Providence.* Cambridge, MA: Harvard University Press, 1953.

———. *The New England Mind: The Seventeenth Century.* NY: Macmillan, 1939.

Morgan, Edmund S. *The Puritan Dilemma: The Story of John Winthrop.* Boston, MA: Little, Brown, 1958.

———. "The Puritans and Sex." *New England Quarterly,* 15 (1942).

Murrin, John M. "Magistrates, Sinners, and a Precarious Liberty: Trial by Jury in Seventeenth-Century New England," in Hall, Murrin, Tate, eds., *Saints and Revolutionaries.*

Perkins, William. *A Discourse of the Damned Art of Witchcraft.* London: Printer to the University of Cambridge, 1608.

Pettit, Norman. "Hooker's Doctrine of Assurance: A Critical Phase in New England Spiritual Thought." *New England Quarterly,* 47 (1974).

Records of the Particular Court of Connecticut, 1639–1663.

Reis, Elizabeth. "The Devil, the Body, and the Feminine Soul in Puritan New England." *Journal of American History,* 82 (1995).

———. *Damned Women: Sinners and Witches in Puritan New England.* Ithaca, NY: Cornell University Press, 1997.

Roper, Lyndal. *Witch Craze: Terror and Fantasy in Baroque Germany.* New Haven, CT: Yale University Press, 2006.

Shakespeare, William. *Macbeth.*

Sharpe, James. *Instruments of Darkness: Witchcraft in England, 1550–1750.* London: Hamish Hamilton, 1996.

Taylor, John M. *The Witchcraft Delusion in Colonial Connecticut (1647–1697).* New York: Grafton Press, 1908.

Thomas, Keith. *Religion and the Decline of Magic.* London: Weidenfeld and Nicholson, 1971.

Tomlinson, R. G. *Witchcraft Trials of Connecticut.* Hartford, CT: Bond Press, 1978.

Trevor-Roper, H. R. *The European Witch-Craze of the Sixteenth and Seventeenth Centuries, and Other Essays.* New York: Harper, 1967.

Trumbull, J. Hammond. *The Public Records of the Colony of Connecticut, Prior to the Union with New Haven Colony, May, 1665,* Vol. I. Hartford, CT: Brown and Parsons, 1850.

Van Dusen, Albert E. *Connecticut.* NY: Random House, 1961.

Walzer, Michael. *Revolution of the Saints: A Study in the Origins of Radical Politics.* Cambridge, MA: Harvard University Press, 1965.

Weber, Max. *The Protestant Ethic and the Spirit of Capitalism,* Talcott Parsons, trans. London: Allen and Unwin, 1930.

———. *The Protestant Ethic and the Spirit of Capitalism,* Talcott Parsons, trans. New York: Scribner, 1958.

Weir, David A. *New England: A Covenanted Society.* Grand Rapids, MI: Eerdmans, 2005.

Winthrop, John. "A Modell of Christian Charity," in David Dutkanicz, ed., *Sinners in the Hands of an Angry God and Other Puritan Sermons.* Mineola, NY: Dover, 2005.

NOTES

1. In a discussion before the Supreme Court on the constitutionality of a monument of the Ten Commandments in a park surrounding the Texas Capitol, Justice Antonin Scalia commented that the Decalogue is "a symbol of the fact that government derives its authority from God." The Puritans would have concurred. Linda Greenhouse, "The Justices Consider Religious Displays." *New York Times*, March 3, 2005, A18.

2. John Winthrop, "A Modell of Christian Charity," in David Dutkanicz, ed., *Sinners in the Hands of an Angry God and Other Puritan Sermons* (Mineola, NY: Dover, 2005), 64–65. See David A. Weir, *New England: A Covenanted Society* (Grand Rapids, MI: Eerdmans, 2005).

3. "Fundamental Orders of Connecticut." The full document is at www.bartleby.com/43/7.htlm.

4. Albert E. Van Dusen, *Connecticut* (New York: Random House, 1961), 49.

5. Isabel M. Calder, "John Cotton and the New Haven Colony," *New England Quarterly*, 3 (1930), 93.

6. Miller, *The New England Mind*, 489.

7. Norman Pettit, "Hooker's Doctrine of Assurance: A Critical Phase in New England Spiritual Thought," *New England Quarterly*, 47 (1974), 518–534.

8. Perry Miller, *The New England Mind: The Seventeenth Century* (New York: Macmillan, 1939), 22. Increase Mather similarly commented, "Altho'it is true, (as has been shewed) that sinners cannot convert themselves, their *Cannot* is a willful *Cannot*." "Predestination and Human Exertions," in John Winthrop, *Sinners*, 99.

9. Thomas Hooker, "A True Sight of Sin, Meditation, Wandering Thoughts, Repentant Sinner and Their Ministers," in John Winthrop, *Sinners*, 32, 45.

10. Puritan thought represented a transition between the organicism of medieval society and the individualism of Lockean liberalism. See Max Weber, *The Protestant Ethic and the Spirit of Capitalism*, Talcott Parsons, trans. (London: Allen and Unwin, 1930); and Michael Walzer, *Revolution of the Saints: A Study in the Origins of Radical Politics* (Cambridge, MA: Harvard University Press, 1965).

11. See Everett C. Goodwin, *The Magistracy Rediscovered: Connecticut, 1636–1818* (Ann Arbor, MI: University of Michigan Research Press, 1979).

12. Thomas Hooker, "Hartford Election Sermon," in David Dutkanicz, ed., *Sinners*, 31.

13. Davenport quoted in Miller, *The New England Mind*, 421.

14. Winthrop quoted in Miller, *The New England Mind*, 427. In New England, the source of Puritan civil authority was legitimized by *Romans* 13:1–2. 1. "Let every person be subject to the governing authorities. For there is no authority except from God, and those that exist have been instituted by God." 2. "Therefore he who resists the authorities resists what God has appointed, and those who resist will incur judgment."

15. Stone quoted in M. Louise Greene, *The Development of Religious Liberty in Connecticut* (Freeport, NY: Books for Libraries Press, 1970; original 1905), 92 note b. See Christopher Grasso, *A Speaking Aristocracy: Transforming Public Discourse in Eighteenth-Century Connecticut* (Chapel Hill, NC: University of North Carolina, 1999).

16. John Cotton, "Limitation of Government," Dutkanicz, ed., *Sinners*, 3–4.

17. The full document is available at www.bartleby.com/43/7.htlm.

18. John D. Cushing, ed., *The Earliest Laws of the New Haven and Connecticut Colonies 1639–1673* (Wilmington, DE: Michael Glazier, 1977), 132.

19. See Dave Thomas Konig, *Law and Society in Puritan Massachusetts: Essex County, 1629–1692* (Chapel Hill, NC: University of North Carolina Press, 1979); and Edgar J. McManus, *Law and Liberty in New England* (Amherst, MA: University of Massachusetts Press, 1993). For a modern example of stoning, see "Islamists in Somalia Say They Plan to Execute 5 Rapists by Stoning." *New York Times*, June 27, 2006, A9.

20. J. Hammond Trumbull, *The Public Records of the Colony of Connecticut, Prior to the Union with New Haven Colony, May, 1665*, vol. 1 (Hartford, CT: Brown and Parsons, 1850), 77–78; and McManus, *Law and Liberty*, 189. I have used McManus's classification.

21. Edmund S. Morgan, *The Puritan Dilemma: The Story of John Winthrop* (Boston, MA: Little, Brown, 1958), 31.

22. Trumbull, *Public Records*, I, 515; and McManus, *Law and Liberty*, 190. I have used McManus's classification.

23. Quoted in Van Dusen, *Connecticut*, 66.

24. *The Code of 1650, Being a Compilation of the Earliest Laws and Orders of the General Court of Connecticut* (Hartford, CT: Andrus and Son, 1821), 26.

25. Cushing, *The Earliest Laws*, I, 509.

26. Cushing, *The Earliest Laws*, 18; and McManus, *Law and Liberty*, 190. I have used McManus's classification.

27. Cushing, *The Earliest Laws*, 17.

28. Cushing, *The Earliest Laws*, viii.

29. Cushing, *The Earliest Laws*, 9–10, and McManus, *Law and Liberty*, 190. I have used McManus's classification.

30. Cushing, *The Earliest Laws*, 2–3, 77.

31. Cushing, *The Earliest Laws*, 9.

32. Cushing, *The Earliest Laws*, 73.

33. See Gail Sussman Marcus, "'Due Execution of the Generall Rules of Righteousness': Criminal Procedure in New Have Town and Colony, 1638–1658," David D. Hall, John M. Murrin, Thad W. Tate, eds., *Saints and Revolutionaries: Essays in Early America* (New York: Norton, 1984), 99–137.

34. Cushing, *The Earliest Laws*, 14, 69, 143. The two eyewitness rule applied in New Haven and Connecticut.

35. Mary J. A. Jones, *Congregational Commonwealth: Connecticut, 1636*-1662 (Middletown, CT: Wesleyan University Press, 1968), 99–137; John M. Murrin, "Magistrates, Sinners, and a Precarious Liberty: Trial by Jury in Seventeenth-Century New England," Hall, Murrin, Tate, eds., *Saints and Revolutionaries*, 152–206; and McManus, *Law and Liberty*, 90–93.

36. *Records of the Particular Court of Connecticut, 1639–1663*, 268.

37. Franklin Dexter, *Ancient Town Records*, I, 238–240.

38. Norbert B. Lacy, *The Records of the Court of Assistants of Connecticut, 1665–1701*, 2 vols. (Master's thesis: Yale University, 1937), I, 279.

39. Charles J. Hoadley, *Records of the Colony or Jurisdiction of New Haven from May, 1653, to the Union* (Hartford: Case, Lockwood, 1858) [There is no volume number, since the dates serve to define the coverage], 577.

40. See Edmund Morgan, "The Puritans and Sex." *New England Quarterly* 15 (1942), 591–607; and John Demos, *A Little Commonwealth: Family Life in Plymouth Colony* (New York: Oxford University Press, 1970).

41. Briggs's execution for adultery and infanticide occurred in New Haven in 1668. The date is shortly after the merger of the New Haven and Connecticut colonies.

42. Davenport quoted in McManus, *Law and Liberty*, 142.

43. See Norman Cohn, *Pursuit of the Millennium* (London: Secker and Warburg, 1957); Cohn, *Warrant for Genocide* (New York: Harper and Row, 1967); H. R. Trevor-Roper, *The European Witch-Craze of the Sixteenth and Seventeenth Centuries, and Other Essays* (New York: Harper, 1967); Keith Thomas, *Religion and the Decline of Magic* (London: Weidenfeld and Nicholson, 1971); H. C. Erik Midelfort, *Witch-Hunting in Southwestern Germany, 1582–1684* (Stanford, CT: Stanford University Press, 1972); Cohn, *Inner Demons: An Enquiry Inspired by the Great Witch-Hunt* (New York: Basic Books, 1975); Christina Larner, *Enemies of God: The Witch-Hunt in Scotland* (Baltimore: Johns Hopkins University Press, 1981); Carlo Ginzburg, *The Night Battles: Witchcraft and Agrarian Cults in the Sixteenth and Seventeenth Centuries* (Baltimore: Johns Hopkins University Press, 1983); Brian Levack, *The Witch-Hunt in Early Modern Europe* (New York: Longman, 1995); Robin Briggs, *Witches and Neighbors: The Social and Cultural Context of European Witchcraft* (New York: Viking, 1996); James Sharpe, *Instruments of Darkness: Witchcraft in England, 1550–1750* (London: Hamish Hamilton, 1996); Stuart Clark, *Thinking with Demons: The Idea of Witchcraft in Early Modern Europe* (New York: Oxford University Press, 1997); and Lyndal Roper, *Witch Craze: Terror and Fantasy in Baroque Germany* (New Haven, CT: Yale University Press, 2006).

44. See Carol F. Karlsen, *The Devil in the Shape of a Woman: Witchcraft in Colonial New England* (New York: Norton, 1986); Elizabeth Reis, "The Devil, the Body, and the Feminine Soul in Puritan New England." *Journal of American History* 82 (1995), 15–36; and Reis, *Damned Women: Sinners and Witches in Puritan New England* (Ithaca, NY: Cornell University Press, 1997).

45. See Exodus 22:18, Leviticus 20:27, and Deuteronomy 18:10, 11.

46. Mather quoted in Perry Miller, *The New England Mind: Colony to Providence* (Cambridge, MA: Harvard University Press, 1953), 184. William Perkins, *A Discourse of the Damned Art of Witchcraft* (London: Printer to the University of Cambridge, 1608) was a representative text that New England divines consulted on the subject.

47. William Shakespeare, *Macbeth*, I: iii, 51-54. Shakespeare wrote the play in 1606, contemporaneously with the Puritan experience in England.

48. Taylor, *The Witchcraft Delusion*, 42.

49. In Connecticut, there were several other accusations worth noting. In 1692, Winifred Benham of Wallingford and Hugh Croasia of Stratford were accused in separate incidents of witchcraft. Grand juries, however, dismissed the charges. Then, in 1697, the same accusers charged Winifred and her thirteen-year-old daughter of witchcraft, a pairing of parent and offspring only seen in Connecticut in the case of the Harveys in 1692. The case was heard by a special court in New Haven, which found no *billa vera* and released the defendants. The family, nonetheless, found it prudent to move to New York and escape what was a bitter local quarrel. Joseph Benham at one point threatened to shoot antagonists of his wife and daughter. The Benham trial was the last of its kind in Connecticut. See Lucy, *Records,* I, 263; and Taylor, *The Witchcraft Delusion*, 64–65, on the Benhams. See *Crimes and Misdemeanors*, Vol. 1, Part 1 (1663–1706), 43–44, 186–187, Connecticut State Library; Lucy, *Records,* I, 193; and Taylor, *The Witchcraft Delusion*, 117–119; and Tomlinson, *Witchcraft Trials*, 64.

50. See Max Weber, *The Protestant Ethic and the Spirit of Capitalism*, Talcott Parsons, trans. (New York, NY: Scribner, 1958); and Richard L. Bushman, *From Puritan to Yankee: Character and the social Order in Connecticut, 1690–1765* (New York: Norton, 1967).

51. See Bernard Bailyn, "The Apologia of Robert Keayne." *William and Mary Quarterly* 7 (1950), 568–587. Keayne's guilt over his sharp business practices in seventeenth-century Boston is a foreshadowing from an individual example to the anxiety of the many a century later during a period of economic expansion.

Chapter Seven

Roger Williams, English Law and Religious Tolerance: The Jewish Experience in the Southern New England Colonies, 1677–1798

Holly Snyder

When the Rhode Island Superior Court of Judicature met at Newport to open its spring term on March 11, 1762, its docket comprised some 49 cases. The majority of these were the usual appeals from debt judgments awarded in the recent session of the Court of Common Pleas, but the Superior Court's business also included several actions for trespass, the appointment of a guardian for the two minor children of a decedent, and an appeal of the Overseers of the Poor in South Kingstown of a judgment in favor of the Town Council of Little Compton over the removal of an impoverished widow from the town's charge. The most significant cases on the docket, however, were the four bunched together a quarter of the way through the proceedings: two capital trials, a case of perjury, and the Petition for Naturalization of two Jews who had resided in Newport for more than a decade. [1]

Among those in the audience at this session of the court was one of Newport's two Congregational ministers, the Reverend Ezra Stiles. An erudite man and an acute observer of all matters concerning the welfare of his town, Stiles made careful note of the proceedings he would observe this day. He had little concern with the majority of these lawsuits and made no record of the court's proceedings in the first eleven cases on the docket. His attention was piqued, however, when the court reached the first of the capital trials. Following the presentation of the evidence and the jury's verdict, the sentence of death by hanging was pronounced on mariner John Shearman, a notorious thief, for breaking and entering the house of shopkeeper Sarah

Rumreil and stealing money from a desk found there. Then William Lawton of Middletown, who had falsely alleged an account against Benjamin Fish of Portsmouth in a debt action in the Court of Common Pleas, was sentenced to one month's confinement in gaol, a heavy fine, and an hour in the pillory for having committed "wilful and corrupt perjury" in court. Next, Fortune, a Negro laborer belonging to blacksmith Simeon Price, pled guilty to arson, having set fire to the warehouse of merchant Thomas Hazard at the end of Long Wharf on February 19—an act that destroyed not only Hazard's property but also three adjoining warehouses. With property damages of £5,000 and the threat of fire to the entire town having resulted from his deeds, the court was not inclined to show mercy to Fortune. He, like Shearman, was sentenced to hang.[2]

Following closely on the heels of these dramatic criminal trials came the case in which Stiles was most interested, the Petition for Naturalization of the two Jewish merchants, Aaron Lopez and Isaac Elizer. Lopez and Elizer, both "born out of the Ligeance of his Majesty the King of Great Britain," had originally filed their petition for hearing by the Superior Court during its previous term. Since each had been living in Rhode Island for "upwards of Seven Years—without being Absent at any one Time Two Months,"[3] they considered that they met the chief requirement for naturalization set out in the 1740 Act of Parliament entitled "An Act for naturalizing such foreign Protestants, and others therein mentioned, as are settled or shall settle, in any of his Majesty's Colonies in America," which expressly provided for the naturalization of Jews as well as foreign-born Protestants in Britain's American colonies.[4] Notwithstanding their having met the statutory requirements, however, the Superior Court had previously declined to act on their petition, ruling that only Rhode Island's General Assembly had the power to naturalize "Foreigners who have desired to be admitted to the Enjoyment of the Liberties and Privileges . . . in this Colony," and that it would violate the 1663 Charter for the Court to take action on the petition without specific direction from the General Assembly.[5] Lopez and Elizer then dutifully brought the matter before the General Assembly, where the Lower House voted that they might indeed be naturalized by appearing before the Superior Court to take the oaths specified under the Parliamentary Act.[6] Thus the petition that came before the court on March 11, 1762, was neither new nor unanticipated. The court certainly had had sufficient time, in the intervening six months, to consider the statutes and the legal issues involved and to consult with members of the General Assembly, local lawyers, and even Crown officials on the matter. Yet despite Rhode Island's self-professed strict adherence to English law and the precedents already established for the naturalization of Jews in other British American colonies, the court rejected outright the Lopez and Elizer petition after only a brief hearing, arguing that the request was "absolutely inconsistent with the first Principles upon which the Colony was founded"—by which, they said, they meant "Christianity," for the Charter itself defined Rhode Island as a colony devoted to the true "Christian faith and worship of God."[7] After giving a week's consideration to all he had witnessed on March 11, Ezra Stiles found it most remarkable that the two Jewish merchants were "called up to hear their almost equally mortifying sentence" on the Petition for Naturalization during the same session as the three felony cases, although "[w]hether this was designedly, or accidental in proceeding upon the Business of Court," he wrote, "I dont learn."

Even a cursory examination of the extant historiography finds that the Lopez-Elizer naturalization case has long been disregarded in discussions of Roger Williams and the practice of Liberty of Conscience in Rhode Island. Most historians who have studied the issue declare that, in the words of Jacob Rader Marcus, Roger Williams "deserves to be recognized as extraordinary" for the degree of tolerance he purportedly extended to Jews in the earliest phase of Rhode Island's history as an English colony;[8] the Lopez-Elizer case, if it is mentioned at all, is viewed as an unrelated aberration. Some Jewish scholars have even discounted Stiles as a partisan observer whose self-interest, as a Christian minister, led him to take a measure of satisfaction from the trials and tribulations routinely meted out to nonbelievers. Nevertheless, the Stiles commentary provides a useful window for examining the legacy of Roger Williams and the boundaries of liberty of conscience in the public life of Rhode Island, as it was lived and experienced by ordinary Rhode Islanders, both Christian and, as with Aaron Lopez and Isaac Elizer, otherwise.

The Lopez-Elizer case is not the only evidence of a disjuncture between rhetoric and reality in early Rhode Island. A critical examination of both seventeenth- and eighteenth-century Rhode Island records shows significant reason to question assertions by later generations concerning the extent to which "liberty of conscience," as articulated by Roger Williams, was put into practice at the inception of the colony. It is true that, both in his private correspondence and in the first public statement to articulate the "design" for the new colony of Rhode Island following his break with the Puritan hegemony of Massachusetts Bay, Williams made use of repeated references to Jews. In *The Bloudy Tenent of Persecution,* which he published in London in 1644 while in England to obtain a Parliamentary patent for the colony, Williams laid out his vision of a Christian commonwealth in which variant religious persuasions were given liberty to function as they chose in the ecclesiastical realm, while civil authority rested separately—not in any one group, but in the hands of secular magistrates acting according to the dictates of their individual consciences. According to Williams, such a commonwealth could tolerate infinite varieties of "conscience," even Jews or Muslims.[9] Yet most historians have since read this polemic as if it were a factual representation of early Rhode Island, without making close examination of the colony's records to see whether that assumption bears weight under scrutiny of the facts on the ground.

In fact, court records indicate that by 1684, two Jews (Simon Mendes and David Brown) had cause to petition the Assembly of Rhode Island for legal protection.[10] Although they did so without naming their persecutor, subsequent court pleadings revealed that it was Major William Dyre, who then served as controller and surveyor general of rates and duties for the colony. This William Dyre was the son of the Quaker Mary Dyre, who had been hanged in Boston in 1660 as a martyr to her religious profession, and one might imagine that her son—who had, indeed, interceded with Massachusetts authorities for his mother's release from prison in 1659—might have had some sympathy for religious outsiders. But Major William Dyre was enamored of power. He had been arrested and transferred, in chains, to England for prosecution in 1681 as a result of his abusive (some would have said malicious) enforcement of customs regulations under the Navigation Acts in New York and Connecticut. None of his Rhode Island contemporaries, therefore, could have been surprised when, just three years later, he filed suit against Mordecai Campanal, Moses Pacheco, and six other "fforeigne borne" Jewish merchants at Newport for conducting trade as "Enemy Aliens." On Dyre's application, the governor had ordered their property seized so as to compel their appearance at the next meeting of the General Court. Although the petition of Mendes and Brown to the Assembly appears to have been readily granted, the case against the eight Jews remained on the General Court's schedule for trial. But when Dyre did not appear in court to press his claim as the case was brought to trial in March 1685, the jury found for the defendants and their property was ordered returned to them.[11] This prosecution was instructive, despite the case having been dismissed, since Dyre's entire cause of action, as supported by the governor's warrant, appears to have been merely that the Jews were "fforeigne born" and "Alien," circumventing the evidence that most or all had resided in Newport since at least 1677.[12] It is notable that although both the court and the Assembly ultimately supported the position of the Jews in this case, the Assembly promised only "as good protection *as any Strangers being not of our Nation*" (emphasis added).[13]

If these proceedings ultimately failed to meet Dyre's apparent expectation for the expulsion of Jews from the colony, they nevertheless suggest that the perception of Jews as separate from and somehow unequal to colonists of Christian extraction was so broadly held among Rhode Islanders as to carry weight with those who governed the colony. A second court case some sixty years later lends further support to this suggestion. In May 1743, suit was brought on a charge of trespass in the Newport Court of Common Pleas by three Jewish merchants following the confiscation of some of their goods by a second (and distantly related) William Dyre. In this case, Dyre did not deny the seizures but protested that in so doing he had acted in his official capacity as constable for the town of Newport, under the authority of the town council, to collect delinquent taxes assessed on each of the merchants as "foreigners" who had come from New York. Here, too, the court ultimately rejected the younger Dyre's argument, even though he produced as evidence orders from Justice of the Peace William Coddington, Jr., authorizing the Newport town sheriff to make the seizures. Indeed, Dyre had not acted alone; the machinations that resulted in the seizure of property belonging to the three merchants were set in motion (before Dyre himself was drawn into the matter) by a bevy of town tax assessors, the town tax collector, and a justice of the peace acting under the aegis of a 1738 Act of the Rhode Island General Assembly designed to tax foreigners trading in Rhode Island.[14] Evidently, while the views of these two separate William Dyres were ultimately deemed extreme by Rhode Island policy makers, they did reflect some commonly held reservations with respect to Jews and their inclusion within the larger community. In fact, these distinctions continued to be a feature of Rhode Island's public life well after the American Revolution. The Charter of 1663, with its provision for liberty to protect Rhode Island against the "enemies of Christianity," remained as the founding instrument of Rhode Island statehood—a posture that would not be finally and irrevocably abandoned until the adoption of a state constitution in the 1840s. Although the Federal Constitution of the new United States was completed in 1787, Rhode Island was the very last of the thirteen states to give it effect through ratification. In the intervening period, Rhode Island Jews were limited by those "privileges" allotted them under state law. The distinction had been underscored in 1783, when the General Assembly (ostensibly in gratitude to the French forces who had helped to liberate Newport from British occupation in 1779) amended a putative law that prohibited voting and officeholding by non-Protestants, revising the language to prohibit these activities only to non-Christians. By this means, civil rights were thus extended to Catholics, while the prohibitions against Jews, as earlier articulated by the Superior Court in the Lopez-Elizer case, were left in place.[15]

When George Washington visited Newport in August 1790, following Rhode Island's belated ratification of the Constitution, Moses Seixas took the opportunity to put his sentiments about these distinctions into writing. The letter that he presented to Washington on behalf of Congregation Jeshuat Israel expressed overt satisfaction at the inclusion of American Jews as citizens under the new Constitution, along with an understated cognizance of the precarious political status Jews had occupied under British rule and in fact continued to occupy under Rhode Island law, in stating, "Deprived as we have hitherto been of the invaluable rights of free citizens, we now . . . behold . . . a Government which to bigotry gives no sanction, to persecution

no assistance—but generously affording to All . . . immunities of citizenship—deeming every one, of whatever nation, tongue, or language equal
parts of the great governmental machine."[16]

Although the letter does not openly denigrate Rhode Island, extolling the
benefits of the new federal government allowed Seixas to make coded references to the unequal treatment meted out to Jews under Rhode Island law, for
Rhode Island—unlike the United States—gave to bigotry a sanction, and
assisted persecution, as it did not offer Jews what both Seixas and Washington extolled as the "immunities of citizenship" or strive in any way to include
Jews in "the great governmental machine" in 1790. Indeed, Seixas's employment of the phrase "deprived as we have hitherto been of the invaluable
rights of free citizens" was a direct reference to the exclusion of Jews from
voting rights in Rhode Island. To his mortification, Seixas found that the
ratification process did little to change local attitudes with respect to the
extension of civil rights to Jews. Whereas he and other Jews were now
enabled to vote in federal elections, they were still barred from the polls for
purposes of state elections.[17] Only in 1798, eight years after Rhode Island
became part of the federal Union under the aegis of the Constitution, would
the General Assembly adopt a statement of principle concerning religious
freedom—at last removing all disabilities imposed on the grounds of religious conviction, and allowing Rhode Island Jews to make their first appearance at state elections as voters.[18]

From our standpoint in the twenty-first century, schooled as we are in the
tenets of the Bill of Rights to the U.S. Constitution, the evidence of a practical distinction between the application of English law to Rhode Island Jews
and to Rhode Island Christians sounds a discordant note with our understanding of the basic principle of liberty of conscience. How could Rhode Islanders claim to be an extraordinary exception to religious intolerance, when in
fact they discriminated in—what seems to our sensibilities—such an obvious
manner? If the charter of 1663 guaranteed "liberty of conscience," shouldn't
Jews be free to conduct their business affairs and related economic activities
in the same way as Christians, and not just to worship as they chose?
Shouldn't they have had a voice in selecting those who served in local
government, to which they contributed their taxes—the very principle for
which the war against Britain had been waged?

Perhaps if we examine the conditions encountered by Jews who attempted to establish themselves in the neighboring Puritan colonies of Connecticut and Massachusetts, the rationale of the distinctions made in Rhode
Island courts will become clearer. In Massachusetts, the 1639 Body of Liberties, the colony's first legal code, stated that the religious freedom extended
to "familists, antinomians, Anabaptists and other Enthusiasts" was designed
for the principal purpose of having them "keep away from us."[19] These were
not idle principles, as the stories of the religious outcasts who established

Rhode Island—from Anne Hutchinson and Roger Williams to John Clarke—attest.[20] Yet, examining how these principles were applied to Jews may be instructive. In the case of Connecticut, we know of two Jews who settled in early Hartford as itinerant traders. Hartford town records indicate that one, named David, was residing there by the fall of 1659, when he was fined for entering households to trade when the master of the house was not home, as well as for trading with local children to obtain provisions. Hartford records in 1661 referred to residence by "the Jewes" in the house of one townsman and money held on their behalf in the hands of another without ever naming or identifying the Jews involved. One "Jacob the Jew" appears on a listing of those exporting horses from town during March of 1667–1668. During the winter of 1669–1670, the two Jewish traders were still nominated only as "David Jew" and "Jacob Jew" on a town census—that is to say, they were noted by their religious and ethnic identity and denied the dignity of a surname, much as was the local custom with Indians and slaves; thus they were clearly identified as outsiders to the Puritan community.[21] Although the incorporation of two itinerants in this census might appear at first blush to be an inclusive gesture—particularly in light of the well-documented persecution meted out to professing Quakers and Baptists in Puritan colonies—it should be noted that the purpose of the census was to determine where stores of grain might be found in Connecticut Colony and who held them. The way in which David and Jacob were listed for this utilitarian purpose documents their ongoing marginalization, even after a decade of residence and trading in the town.[22]

There is a somewhat more substantial record of the treatment Jews encountered in seventeenth-century Massachusetts, where Jewish traders of substance appeared frequently enough. Rowland Gideon, for example (known in the Jewish world as Rohiel Abudiente), though granted a surname, was nevertheless recorded in the 1674 Boston tax list with the epithet "ye Jew" after his name, despite having been born in London of substantial Sephardic lineage and high-born social connections. Although he maintained an honorable reputation in local trade, Gideon was so cognizant of his precarious legal status that he felt called to remind the Massachusetts Court of Assistants, in which he prosecuted an appeal of a suit for debt in 1675, of the Old Testament provision that "God Commands our Fathers that the Same Law should bee for the Stranger & Sowjournner" as for the ancient Israelites with whom Massachusetts Puritans publicly identified themselves.[23] Still, Massachusetts Puritans followed their brethren in Connecticut by ignoring Jews whenever they could and reducing the significance of their social encounters with believing Jews through the employment of the generic ethnic reference ("Jew") rather than using the proper names of Jewish men and women.

Indeed, even this limited form of tolerance espoused by New England's Puritans was extended only for the purpose of persuading Jews to forsake Judaism for the embrace of Christianity. This goal was nowhere more evident than in Puritan Massachusetts. The theology espoused by English millenarians and their Puritan brethren in seventeenth-century New England was little concerned with Jews except as potential converts. Jews who wished to remain Jews had no place in the millenarian world, for the individual Jew could never hope to absolve himself of the collective guilt for the death of Christ as long as he continued to adhere to traditional Judaism. Increase Mather best expressed this point in a 1669 sermon, in which he preached that Jewish conversion opened the way to salvation for *all* sinners: "such is the infinite grace of God, that . . . if the *Jews* shall be converted, then there is grace enough with God to convert and save the greatest sinners upon earth. For what guilt can there be greater, than the guilt which lyeth upon the miserable Nation of the *Jews?*"[24]

Many Puritans followed firmly the dictates of millenarian theology. References to Jewish conversion were not infrequent in Massachusetts sermons and other forms of theological discourse: Samuel Sewell noted in his diary that such discussions were instigated by different Boston ministers in February 1685–1686, January 1686–1687, and September 1722. Cotton Mather, the son of Increase, recorded over and over his deep desire for the conversion of Jews, both individually and as a group. One Saturday in July 1696, a day he set apart for yet another "secret Fast before the Lord," the 33-year-old Mather prostrated himself on the floor of his study and prayed desperately, "For the Conversion of the *Jewish Nation*, and for my own having the Happiness...to baptize a *Jew*, that should by my Ministry . . . bee brought home unto the Lord." Three years later, in April 1699, he had the inspiration to pen a catechism "of the whole Christian Religion," intending that it would "mightily convince, and confound the *Jewish* Nation." He had it printed under the title *The Faith of the Fathers*, and was gratified a few months later to hear from Carolina that a Jew there had embraced Christianity "and my little Book . . . therein a special Instrument of good unto him." Yet closer to home, his conversionary efforts were stymied, much as he tried to convince himself otherwise. For nearly twenty years, he worked mightily on Samuel Frazao, a Jewish merchant who then resided in Boston with his two brothers and with whom Mather had some occasional discourse. But Frazao could not be moved to abandon Judaism despite Mather's prayers and pleading. In May 1699, Mather wrote Frazao a letter enclosing his newly printed *Faith of the Fathers*, but as he did not record Frazao's response in his diary, we can safely assume it was not the one Mather had hoped for. Indeed, a pamphlet written by Samuel Sewell and published anonymously eight years later refers to Mather's "*Pretended Vision*," a method by which Mather plainly hoped to persuade Frazao, at long last, of the superiority of Christianity. However, in

Sewell's view, Mather's performance was executed so poorly that Frazao, who had been raised a *converso*, easily detected it as a forgery and forced Mather to confess his duplicity. One can only imagine Mather's frustration when, in September 1702, his fellow divine Simon Bradstreet celebrated the public conversion of a Jew in nearby Charlestown. In the end, both 1711 and 1713 found Mather renewing his periodic supplications for Frazao's conversion, which he dutifully recorded in his diary, along with notes referencing the number of years he had expended on this fruitless trial.[25]

The case of Judah Monis, who converted to Christianity in 1722 and then became the first instructor in Hebrew at Harvard College, is perhaps the exception that proves the general rule for what it meant to be a Jew in colonial Massachusetts. Monis had studied rabbinics in Leghorn and Amsterdam and called himself a rabbi, though it is unclear whether he was ever ordained. He seems to have arrived in Boston in 1720 with the expectation that he might remain a Jew; but if so, he was quickly disabused of this notion when he applied to Increase Mather, then president of Harvard College, for a teaching position. Within two years, Mather had successfully persuaded Monis to become a Christian, and his conversion was celebrated by Rev. Benjamin Colman in a public baptism at which Monis himself gave a sermon entitled *The Truth*, which acknowledged Jesus as the true Messiah. Just a month after his conversion, Mather awarded him the coveted position at Harvard, which Monis held for nearly forty years. Yet though he lived as a Christian for the rest of his life, even taking a Christian woman as his wife, Monis found that, in the minds of his new friends and neighbors, he could not escape the stigma that came from having once been a believing Jew. Within a few months of his baptism, he had issued two supplemental discourses, titled successively *The Whole Truth* and *Nothing But the Truth*, in an attempt to persuade a skeptical audience that his commitment to Christianity was indeed sincere. Yet while he was termed a "valuable proselyte" by the ministers who presided at his baptism, he nevertheless found the epithet "the converted Jew" consistently attached to his name in subsequent records of both the church he had joined and the college where he was employed. His gravestone conveys a sense of his dual and ambiguous existence as both Jew and Christian, recording his claim to be a rabbi and stating that "He was by Birth and Religion a Jew but embraced the Christian Faith & was publickly baptized."[26]

These vignettes help to highlight the boundaries to the promise of liberty of conscience in Rhode Island. As Dwight Bozeman has argued, the key to Williams's plan for Rhode Island was the establishment of civil order in a colony composed of various dissenting groups. This was in large part a response to English fears that permitting various Christian dissenters to cohabit in the same place would result in the kind of civil anarchy that had devastated the German city of Münster during the sixteenth century, when devout Anabaptists questioned the imposition of religious uniformity. Williams was, thus, addressing a picture of Christendom as a whole in which Jews did not figure except as a rhetorical device denoting the extremes of the religious "otherness" that Christian sects had imposed on each other.[27] In this respect Williams was typical of the English Protestant theologians and Hebraists of his time. Even the Protestant millenarians who argued for Jewish readmission to England during the 1650s desired, as David Katz has noted, to have "Judaism without Jews"—that is, to know the Israelites of the Old Testament without experiencing the rabbinical Judaism of their Jewish contemporaries in early modern Europe.[28]

Taking Roger Williams and his rhetoric concerning religious liberty at face value, we assume that of any colony, Rhode Island would have been the place where Jews could find themselves welcomed. But the language of the 1663 Charter allowed for ambiguities, specifically empowering Rhode Islanders "to defend themselves, in their just rights and liberties, against all the enemies of *the Christian faith*, and others, in all respects."[29] So the question of Jewish presence in Rhode Island could easily be conditioned on whether Jews might be defined as foreign, alien, or indeed as "enemies of the Christian faith." Roger Williams bragged about the exceptional nature of the colony's charter in a letter to friends in Connecticut in June 1670, proclaiming:

> The Kings Ma[jes]tie wincks at Barbadoes where Jews and all sorts of Christians and Antichristian perswasions are free, but our Graunt . . . is Crowned with the Kings extraordinary favour to this Colony. . . . In w[hi]ch his Ma[jes]tie declar'd himselfe that he would experim[e]nt whether Civill Govrm[e]nt Could consist with such a Libertie of Conscience.[30]

But just two years after making this boast, confronted with the reality of a strong Quaker presence during George Fox's visit to Newport, Williams asked in print, "Is it not enough that the most High Potter made us Men and Women and *not Serpents and Toads, &c., not Pagans, Turks, Iews, Papists &c. but* English Protestants &c?"[31] Thus, Williams found within himself some bifurcation between liberty of conscience in theory and liberty of conscience in practice. Although Williams argued that in theory Jews—as well as Moslems, Catholics, and pagans—possessed religious "*conscience*" (which he defined as "a *perswasion* fixed in the minde and heart of a man"),[32] there is nothing explicit in his writings about the prospective inclusion of actual Jews within Rhode Island Colony under the practice of "Libertie of Conscience." As in the *Bloudy Tenent*, Jews represented a simple rhetorical device that served Williams in making a larger point about the divisions within Christianity and in setting out a scheme for how different Christian sects might be able to live together in an orderly (if not entirely harmonious) manner while preserving to each person the "soul liberty" in which Williams so deeply believed.[33] The true tenor of the argument was that if even Jews (or Muslims) might, theoretically, be encompassed in such a Christian commonwealth as Williams had envisioned, certainly any Christian would be welcome there.

Close examination of the Jewish experience in early Rhode Island makes manifest that the design envisioned by Roger Williams could be, and in point of fact often was, interpreted in ways that spoke to Christian anxieties about the possibility that Jews might take advantage of their privileges and assume authority over Christians. In keeping with their understanding and commitment to the basic principles of liberty of conscience, early Rhode Island Christians tolerated a Jewish presence and allowed Jews the same freedom to worship that they expected for themselves, giving tacit encouragement to the contributions of Jewish merchants in the local economy. But when it came to governance, they consistently drew lines that professing Jews could not cross. So when Lopez and Elizer put their claim to naturalization under the 1740 Act of Parliament before the General Assembly, the Assembly noted that they could not expect "the full freedom of this Colony." Once naturalized, Lopez and Elizer would "have leave to purchase Lands within this Colony" and to pass such property to their heirs. However, they were warned, "Inasmuch as the said Aaron Lopez hath declared himself to be by Religion a Jew, . . . the said Aaron Lopez nor any other of that Religion is not Liable to be chosen into any office in this Colony nor allowed to give a Vote as a Freeman in Choosing others."[34] To underscore the point, another former Portuguese "new Christian" who continued to live publicly as a Christian in Rhode Island was at the same time readily naturalized.[35] And though both Jews were eventually naturalized in other colonies—Lopez, ironically, in Massachusetts (after obtaining legal advice from a Boston lawyer) and Elizer in New York—their naturalization papers did not change the political status of either man in Rhode Island. They were still prohibited from voting or holding office.

In 1762, the disappointment of two Rhode Island Jews in failing to obtain the legal recognition and protections afforded by British naturalization seemed to Ezra Stiles logically of a piece with history, both ancient and modern. "Providence Seemd to make every Thing to work for Mortification to the Jews," he wrote, "& to prevent their incorporating into any Nation; that thus they may continue a distinct people." With a sense of foreboding, he opined "that the Jews will never become incorporated with the people of America, any more than in Europe, Asia & Africa."[36] Lopez, who became by 1772 the single largest taxpayer in the town of Newport, remained utterly excluded from the policy-making circles, just like every other Rhode Island Jew. The marginalization of Rhode Island's Jews became something of a self-fulfilling prophecy at the moment of the revolution, when it came to choosing sides, leaving Newport's Jews vulnerable to charges of Toryism and complicity with the British. This point was underscored by Moses Michael Hays when he found his professed loyalty to the patriot cause under scrutiny in 1776. Refusing a demand to sign the test oath, Hays protested, "I am an Israelite and am not allowed the liberty of a vote or voice in common with the rest of the voters." Neither Congress nor the Rhode Island General Assembly, he noted, had ever acknowledged "the society of Israelites to which I belong" as citizens.[37] Many Jews, like Lopez, simply left town for the duration of the war. Rhode Islanders had indeed, as the Superior Court articulated that March day in 1762, defined Rhode Island as a colony by Christians and for Christians, in which non-Christians might reside but where only Christians could fully participate. Until 1798, a Jew was only a sojourner in Rhode Island, entitled, as Roger Williams put it, to the "*Perswasions* of Conscience"—but not to an equal vote in his Christian commonwealth.

REFERENCES

"A List of Persons that have intitled themselves to the Benefit of the Act (13th Geo. 2d)," 1740–1761, handwritten transcription located at Manuscripts Division of The Library of Congress.

Adelman, David C. "Strangers: Civil Rights of Jews in the Colony of Rhode Island," *Rhode Island Jewish Historical Notes,* 1, no. 2 (1954).

"An Act relative to religious Freedom, and the Maintenance of Ministers," *The Public Laws of the State of Rhode-Island and Providence Plantations, As revised by a Committee, and finally enacted by the Honourable GENERAL ASSEMBLY, at their Session in January, 1798. To Which are Prefixed the Charter, Declaration of Independence, Articles of Confederation, Constitution of the United States, and President Washington's Address of September, 1796.* Providence: Carter and Wilkinson, 1798.

Appellate case files for *Jacob Isaacks v. William Dyre, Abraham Hart v. William Dyre,* and *Issachar Polock v. William Dyre,* Newport Superior Court of Judicature, September 1743, Collections of the Rhode Island Supreme Court Judicial Record Center.

Arnold, Samuel Greene. *History of the State of Rhode Island and Providence Plantations.* (New York: Appleton, 1859–1860), vol. 1.

Austin, John Osborne. *The Genealogical Dictionary of Rhode Island; Comprising Three Generations of Settlers Who Came Before 1690.* Albany: Joel Munsell's Sons, 1887.

Bartlett, John Russell (ed.). *Records of the Colony of Rhode Island,* Vol. III, 160; Rhode Island General Court of Trial, March 13, 1685, Record Book A, f. 73, Collections of the Rhode Island Supreme Court Judicial Records Center.

———. *Records of the Colony of Rhode Island,* vol. VI (1757–1769).

———. *Records of the Colony of Rhode Island and Providence Plantations in New England.* Providence: A. Crawford Greene, State Printer, , vol. VII (1856–1865).

Bishop, George. *New England judged. The second part. Being, a relation of the cruel and bloody sufferings of the people called Quakers. . . .* London, 1667.

Bozeman, Theodore D. *The Precisianist Strain: Disciplinary Religion and Antinomian Backlash in Puritanism to 1638.* Chapel Hill, NC: University of North Carolina, 2004.

———. "Religious Liberty and the Problem of Order in Early Rhode Island," *The New England Quarterly,* 45 (March 1972).

Callendar, John. *An Historical Discourse, on the Civil and Religious Affairs of the Colony of Rhode-Island,* Collections of the Rhode Island Historical Society series, vol. IV. Providence, RI: Knowles, Vose, 1838.

"Charter of 1663," in Callendar, *An Historical Discourse*, Appendix XXI.

Clarke, John. *Ill Newes from New-England*. London, 1652.

Collections of the Connecticut Historical Society. Hartford, CT: Connecticut Historical Society, 1897, vol. VI.

Conley, Patrick T. *The Bill of Rights and Rhode Island*. Madison, WI: Madison House, 1991 (reprinted from Patrick T. Conley and John P. Kaminski [eds], *The Bill of Rights and the States: The Colonial and Revolutionary Origins of American Liberties*. Madison, WI: Madison House, 1991).

Dalin, David G., and Jonathan Rosenbaum, *Making a Life, Building a Community: A History of the Jews of Hartford*. New York: Holmes & Meier, 1997.

de Sola Pool, Rabbi David. "Introduction," in Morris A. Gutstein, ed., *The Story of the Jews of Newport: Two and a Half Centuries of Judaism, 1658–1908* (New York: Bloch Publishing Co., 1936).

Deed of Nathaniel Dickins to Mordicay Campanall and Moses Pacheckoe, February 28, 1677/8, facsimile in *Publications of the American Jewish Historical Society* 27 (The Lyons Collection, vol. II).

Dexter, Franklin Bowditch (ed.). *Extracts from the Itineraries and Other Miscellanies of Ezra Stiles, D.D., LL.D., 1755–1794, With a Selection from his Correspondence*. New Haven, CT: Yale University Press, 1916.

Friedman, Lee M. "Early Jewish Residents in Massachusetts," *Publications of the American Jewish Historical Society*, 23 (1915).

———. *Jewish Pioneers and Patriots*. Philadelphia: Jewish Publication Society of America, 1943.

———. "Judah Monis, First Instructor in Hebrew at Harvard College," *Publications of the American Jewish Historical Society*, 22 (1914).

———. *Pilgrims in a New Land*. Philadelphia: Jewish Publication Society of America, 1948.

Goldman, Shalom. "Christians, Jews, and the Hebrew Language in Rhode Island History," *Rhode Island Jewish Historical Notes*, 11, no. 3 (November 1993).

Gradwohl, David Mayer. "Judah Monis's Puzzling Gravestone as a Reflection of his Enigmatic Identity," *Markers*, 21 (2004).

Greene, Jack P. *The Quest for Power: The Lower Houses of Assembly in the Southern Royal Colonies, 1689–1776*. New York: Norton, for the Institute of Early American History and Culture, 1963.

Gutstein, Morris A. *The Story of the Jews of Newport: Two and a Half Centuries of Judaism, 1658–1908*. New York: Bloch, 1936.

Hühner, Leon. "The Jews of New England (Other Than Rhode Island) Prior to 1800," *Publications of the American Jewish Historical Society*, 11 (1903).

———. "Naturalization of Jews in New York Under the Act of 1740, *Publications of the American Jewish Historical Society*, 13 (1905).

Kagan, Richard L., and Philip D. Morgan (eds). *Atlantic Diasporas: Jews, Conversos, and Crypto-Jews in the Age of Mercantilism, 1500–1800*. Baltimore: Johns Hopkins University Press, 2009.

Katz, David S. *Philosemitism and the Readmission of the Jews to England, 1603–1655*. Oxford, UK: Clarendon Press, 1982.

LaFantasie, Glenn W., and Bradford F. Swan, *The Correspondence of Roger Williams, 1629–1682*. Hanover, NH: Brown University Press/University Press of New England, for The Rhode Island Historical Society, 1988, vols. I and II.

Lopez, Aaron. "Petition for Naturalization, September 9, 1761," in *Papers of Aaron Lopez*, Box 2, Folder 2, Collections of the American Jewish Archives, printed in Lee M. Friedman, *Pilgrims in a New Land*. Philadelphia: Jewish Publication Society of America, 1948.

Lutz, Donald S., and Jack D. Warren, *A Covenanted People: The Religious Tradition and the Origins of American Constitutionalism*. Providence, RI: John Carter Brown Library, 1987.

Marcus, Jacob Rader. *American Jewry—Documents—Eighteenth Century*. Cincinnati, OH: Hebrew Union College, 1959.

———. *The Colonial American Jew*. Detroit: Wayne State University Press, 1970, vol. I.

Mather, Cotton. *Diary of Cotton Mather, 1681-1708*, Massachusetts Historical Society Collections, 7th Series, vols. VII and VIII. Boston: Massachusetts Historical Society, 1911 and 1912.

Mather, Increase. *The Mystery of Israel's Salvation, Explained and Applyed, or, A Discourse Concerning the General Conversion of the Israelitish Nation*. London: John Allen, 1669.

Minutes of the Newport Town Meeting, 1795-1802, vol. 2059, Collections of the Newport Historical Society, unpaginated.

"Petition of Aaron Lopez and Isaac Elizer, August 1761 Term," *Record Book E of the Newport Superior Court of Judicature*, f. 171, Rhode Island Supreme Court Judicial Records Center.

"Petition of Aaron Lopez, October 30, 1761," *Petitions to the Rhode Island General Assembly*, Collections of the Rhode Island State Archives.

"Petition of James Lucena, February 26, 1761," *Petitions to the General Assembly*, Vol. 10, f. 147.

Public Records of the Colony of Connecticut [1636-1776] . . . transcribed and published, (in accordance with a resolution of the general assembly). Hartford: Brown & Parsons, 1850–1890, vols. I and II (1664–1678).

Record Book E for the Newport Superior Court of Judicature, March Term 1762, ff. 180–190, Rhode Island Supreme Court Judicial Records Center.

Record Book E for the Newport Superior Court of Judicature, March Term 1762, ff. 182–184, Rhode Island Supreme Court Judicial Records Center.

Record Book E of the Newport Superior Court of Judicature, f. 184, Rhode Island Supreme Court Judicial Records Center.

Rhode Island Supreme Court Judicial Records Center, *General Court of Trials [Superior Judicial Court] Record Book A (1671–1724)*.

Rider, Sidney S. *An Inquiry Concerning the Origin of the Clause in the Laws of Rhode Island (1719-1783) Disfranchising Roman Catholics*, Rhode Island Historical Tracts, Second Series, No. 1. Providence: Sidney S. Rider, 1889.

Sarna, Jonathan D., and Ellen Smith (eds). *The Jews of Boston*. Boston: Combined Jewish Philanthropies of Greater Boston, 1995.

Schappes, Morris U. (ed.). *A Documentary History of the Jews in the United States, 1654–1875*, 3rd ed. New York: Schocken Books, 1971.

Sewall, Samuel. *Diary of Samuel Sewall, 1674-1729*, Massachusetts Historical Society Collections, 5th Series, vols. V, VI, and VII. Boston: Massachusetts Historical Society, 1878, 1879, and 1882.

Silverman, Morris, *Hartford Jews, 1659–1970*. Hartford: Connecticut Historical Society, 1970.

Smith, Ellen. "Strangers and Sojourners: The Jews of Colonial Boston," in Jonathan D. Sarna and Ellen Smith, eds., *The Jews of Boston*. Boston: Combined Jewish Philanthropies of Greater Boston, 1995.

Snyder, Holly. "English Markets, Jewish Merchants and Atlantic Endeavors: Jews and the Making of British Transatlantic Commercial Culture, 1650–1800," in Richard L. Kagan and Philip D. Morgan, eds., *Atlantic Diasporas: Jews, Conversos, and Crypto-Jews in the Age of Mercantilism, 1500–1800*. Baltimore: Johns Hopkins University Press, 2009.

Statutes At Large, of England and of Great-Britain: From Magna Carta to the Union of the Kingdoms of Great Britain and Ireland, 20 volumes (London, 1811), vol. V [12 Charles II 1660 – 7&8 William III 1696].

William Dyre v. Jacob Isaacks, Newport Court of Common Pleas, May 1743, CCP Record Book C.

William Dyre v. Jacob Isaacks, William Dyre v. Issachar Polock, William Dyre v. Abraham Hart, Nos. 11–13, Rhode Island Court of Equity, December 1743, Collections of the Rhode Island State Archives.

Williams, Roger. *The Bloudy Tenent, of Persecution, For cause of Conscience, discussed, in A Conference betweene Trvth and Peace*. London, 1644.

———. *George Foxx Digg'd Out of His Burrovves, Or An Offer Of Disputation on Fourteen Proposalls Made This Last Summer 1672 (So Call'd) Unto G. Fox Then Present On Rode-Island in New-England*. Boston: John Foster, 1676.

NOTES

1. *Record Book E for the Newport Superior Court of Judicature, March Term 1762*, ff. 180–190, Rhode Island Supreme Court Judicial Records Center.

2. *Record Book E for the Newport Superior Court of Judicature, March Term 1762*, ff. 182–184, Rhode Island Supreme Court Judicial Records Center; Franklin Bowditch Dexter (ed.), *Extracts from the Itineraries and Other Miscellanies of Ezra Stiles, D.D., LL.D., 1755–1794, With a Selection from his Correspondence* (New Haven: Yale University Press, 1916), 52–53. The order of the cases as given here conforms to that found in the Record Book for the Newport Superior Court of Judicature. In his notations, Stiles reversed the order of two of the cases, listing Fortune's sentence ahead of that of William Lawton, possibly because Fortune had received the same capital sentence as Shearman.

3. Petition for Naturalization by Aaron Lopez, September 9, 1761, Papers of Aaron Lopez, Box 2, Folder 2, Collections of the American Jewish Archives (photostat of original in Petitions to the General Assembly, October 1761, Rhode Island State Archives), printed in Lee M. Friedman, *Pilgrims in a New Land* (Philadelphia: Jewish Publication Society of America, 1948), 34–36.

4. Act of 13 Geo II c. 7 (1740). The text of the act is reprinted in Morris U. Schappes, ed., *A Documentary History of the Jews in the United States, 1654–1875*, 3rd ed. (New York: Schocken Books, 1971), No. 22, 26–30. Section III of the act provides for the naturalization of Jews and amends the Oath of Abjuration for Jews by removing the phrase "upon the true Faith of a Christian." Under §IV of the act, persons were eligible to be considered for naturalization after "having resided and inhabited for the Space of seven Years or more . . . within the said Colonies," Ibid., 28–29.

5. Petition of Aaron Lopez and Isaac Elizer, August 1761 Term, *Record Book E of the Newport Superior Court of Judicature*, f. 171, Rhode Island Supreme Court Judicial Records Center.

6. Petition of Aaron Lopez, October 30, 1761, Petitions to the Rhode Island General Assembly, Collections of the Rhode Island State Archives; photostat in Papers of Aaron Lopez, Box 14, Folder 39, Collections of the American Jewish Historical Society. The vote of the Assembly on the Lopez and Elizer petitions was not concurred in by the Upper House, and thus did not take effect. Lopez and Elizer later sought legal advice from Boston attorney Samuel Fitch about the possibility of being naturalized in Massachusetts. See Samuel Fitch to Aaron Lopez and Isaac Elizer, September 13, 1762, Papers of Aaron Lopez, Letterbook 621, Collections of the Newport Historical Society. Lopez was finally naturalized by the Superior Court of Judicature in Massachusetts in October 1762. See Docket nos. 83444 [Petition] and 24980 [Oaths of Allegiance], Suffolk Files Collection, Massachusetts Archives. Elizer appears on a list of those naturalized in New York during 1763. See "A List of Persons that have intitled themselves to the Benefit of the Act (13th Geo. 2d) intituled 'An Act for naturalizing such foreign Protestants and others therein mentioned as are settled or that shall settle in any of His Majesty's Colonies in America,'" 1740–1761 , Plantations General, C .O. 324 /55 and 324/56, Public Record Office of Great Britain, handwritten transcription located at Manuscripts Division of The Library of Congress; Leon Hühner, "Naturalization of Jews in New York Under the Act of 1740, *Publications of the American Jewish Historical Society*, 13 (1905), 5–6. As Hühner notes, Elizer's "temporal profession" and "place of abode" are given in this record as "Rhode Island. Merchant." See also, further discussion of the case in Friedman, *Pilgrims in a New Land*, 31–46.

The issue of Jewish naturalization had not arisen in Rhode Island prior to the initial application of Lopez and Elizer in 1761, as the majority of Jewish merchants who had established themselves in Newport had already been naturalized in other locations prior to their arrival. Moses Levy, Moses Lopez, and Jacob Rodriguez Rivera and his father, Abraham Rodriguez Rivera, had all been naturalized in New York during the 1740s, after the Act of 13 George II, c. 7 (1740) first went into effect. See "A List of Persons that have intitled themselves to the Benefit of the Act (13th Geo. 2d)," 1740–1761, handwritten transcription located at Manuscripts Division of The Library of Congress; J. H. Hollander, "The Naturalization of Jews in the American Colonies Under the Act of 1740," *Publications of the American Jewish Histor-ical Society* 5 (1897), 116, 117; Hühner, "Naturalization of Jews in New York," 6. It should also be noted that a number of Jews residing in Newport during this period never sought naturalization anywhere, while others (notably Jacob and Moses Isaacks) had been born in the British colonies and therefore did not require naturalization to obtain the protections afforded by British law.

7. *Record Book E of the Newport Superior Court of Judicature*, f. 184, Rhode Island Supreme Court Judicial Records Center. The Lopez–Elizer case was the only naturalization case to have received this kind of treatment by the Rhode Island Assembly, not to mention by its courts. Another Portuguese *converso* with close links to the Jewish community, James Lucena, was naturalized without incident in March 1761 when he took the prescribed oaths "on the true faith of a Christian." Petition of James Lucena, February 26, 1761, Petitions to the General Assembly, Vol. 10, f. 147; see, also, John Russell Bartlett (ed.), *Records of the Colony of Rhode Island and Providence Plantations in New England* (Providence: A. Crawford Greene, State Printer, 1856–1865), Vol. VII, 261–262 (referencing "an Act to naturalize James Lucena, formerly of Portugal," passed in December 1760).

8. Jacob Rader Marcus, *The Colonial American Jew* (Detroit: Wayne State University Press, 1970), Volume I, 428–430; for similar statements, see also, the Introduction by Rabbi David de Sola Pool in Morris A. Gutstein, *The Story of the Jews of Newport: Two and a Half Centuries of Judaism, 1658–1908* (New York: Bloch Publishing Co., 1936), 13; and Shalom Goldman, "Christians, Jews, and the Hebrew Language in Rhode Island History," *Rhode Island Jewish Historical Notes* 11, no. 3 (November 1993), 344. Samuel Greene Arnold, one of the earliest historians of Rhode Island, was similarly effusive in his praise of Roger Williams, lauding his firmness, generosity, charity, forgiving spirit, consistency, and love of truth and emphasizing Williams's devotion to "the principles of universal toleration in the constitution of a State." Samuel Greene Arnold, *History of the State of Rhode Island and Providence Planta-tions* (New York: Appleton, 1859–1860), Vol. 1, 474–477.

9. Roger Williams, *The Bloudy Tenent, of Persecution, For cause of Conscience, dis-cussed, in A Conference betweene Trvth and Peace* ([London], 1644), 139, 150–152.

10. Bartlett, *Records of the Colony of Rhode Island*, Vol. III (1678–1706), 160.

11. *General Court of Trials [Superior Judicial Court] Record Book A (1671–1724)*, Rhode Island Supreme Court Judicial Records Center, 73. The Jews charged in this case were: Mordi-chai Campanel, Daniel Campanel, David Campanel, Abraham Campanel, Saul Brown, Rachel Mendes (widow of Simon Mendes), Abraham Burgos, and Aaron Verse (or Verde). Gutstein suggests that the majority of the group came from Speightstown, Barbados. Morris A. Gutstein, *The Story of the Jews of Newport: Two and a Half Centuries of Judaism, 1658-1908* (New York: Bloch Publishing Co., 1936), 28–31. Dyre (also spelled, interchangeably, as Dyer) was one of 24 prominent colonists (including Roger Williams and Baptist leader John Clarke) whose petition to Charles II resulted in the Charter of 1663. See Charter of 1663 in John Callendar, *An Historical Discourse, on the Civil and Religious Affairs of the Colony of Rhode-Island*, Collections of the Rhode Island Historical Society series, Volume IV (Providence: Knowles, Vose, 1838), Appendix XXI, 241, 244.

12. Deed of Nathaniel Dickins to Mordicay Campanall and Moses Pacheckoe, February 28, 1677/8, facsimile in *Publications of the American Jewish Historical Society* 27 (The Lyons Collection, vol. II), 174–175. See also David C. Adelman, "Strangers: Civil Rights of Jews in the Colony of Rhode Island," *Rhode Island Jewish Historical Notes* 1, no. 2 (1954), 106–109; Gutstein, *The Story of the Jews of Newport*, 44–45. Some historians have suggested a different interpretation of this court case, arguing that the case affirmed Jewish religious freedom in Rhode Island, as against the prejudices of a single individual using the Navigation Acts of the 1650s as a lever. But if this was indeed so, why would the governor have issued a warrant for the seizure of the property of the Jews? Why would the case have remained on the court docket and been brought to trial many months after the General Assembly had affirmed that Jews might expect equal protection under the laws of the colony? And why did the Jews, within a matter of a few years, largely disperse to other locations? Clearly, the issues at stake in this case were not as clear-cut as these writers have frequently portrayed them.

13. Bartlett, John, ed. *Records of the Colony of Rhode Island*, Vol. III, 160; Rhode Island General Court of Trial, March 13, 1685, Record Book A, f. 73, Collections of the Rhode Island Supreme Court Judicial Records Center (*emphasis added*); John Osborne Austin, *The Genealogical Dictionary of Rhode Island; Comprising Three Generations of Settlers Who Came Before 1690* (Albany: Joel Munsell's Sons, 1887), 290–293; Marcus, *The Colonial American Jew*, vol. I, 433–434.

14. The rulings of the Court of Common Pleas in the three cases hinged upon the application of the Act of 3 & 4 of William and Mary, c. 11, §6, which specified that "any Person, who shall come to inhabit in any Town or Parish" that either served in public office or "shall be charged with and pay his Share towards the publick Taxes or Levies" would be deemed a legal resident of that town or parish without the benefit of "Notice in Writing." *Statutes At Large, of England and of Great-Britain: From Magna Carta to the Union of the Kingdoms of Great Britain and Ireland*, 20 volumes (London, 1811), vol/ V [12 Charles II 1660—7&8 William III 1696], 583–584. The jury determined that if this statute had full force and effect in Rhode Island, each of the plaintiffs should prevail. When the court held that the statute did in fact apply, the jury's verdict was entered in favor of the three plaintiffs. One of the plaintiffs, Issachar Polock, introduced as evidence his receipt for the tax paid by him as a foreigner for 1741, the year immediately prior to the one for which his goods were seized. See *William Dyre v. Jacob Isaacks*, Newport Court of Common Pleas, May 1743, CCP Record Book C, . 155; see also, appellate case files for *Jacob Isaacks v. William Dyre, Abraham Hart v. William Dyre*, and *Issachar Polock v. William Dyre*, Newport Superior Court of Judicature, September 1743, Collections of the Rhode Island Supreme Court Judicial Record Center. The appellate case files contain transcriptions of the proceedings at the lower court level. See also, Adelman, "Strangers," 116. Dyre eventually prevailed on his appeal to the Court of Equity, which "reversed and declared Null & Void" the judgments of the Superior Court in favor of the three Jews, and ruled that Dyre recover his costs from them. See *William Dyre v. Jacob Isaacks, William Dyre v. Issachar Polock, William Dyre v. Abraham Hart*, nos. 11–13, Rhode Island Court of Equity, December 1743, Collections of the Rhode Island State Archives.

15. The freemanship statute which the law of 1783 repealed as to Catholic eligibility and which was also relied upon by the Superior Court in the Lopez-Elizer case had been codified prior to 1730, decades prior to the Lopez-Elizer case. This statute, which restricted freemanship to non-Catholic Christians, first appeared in the Rhode Island Digest of Laws in 1719 and referenced an alleged prior enactment of the General Assembly in March 1663, both events having occurred at times when there were no Jews residing in the colony. See Sidney S. Rider, *An Inquiry Concerning the Origin of the Clause in the Laws of Rhode Island (1719–1783) Disfranchising Roman Catholics*, Rhode Island Historical Tracts, Second Series, No. 1 (Providence: Sidney S. Rider, 1889), 14–16. Although Rider's historical research in the late nineteenth century has raised questions about whether the 1719 freemanship statute was ever legally enacted, the Superior Court in 1762 would have had no reason to doubt its legitimacy. Thus, the Superior Court's reading of the 1663 Charter and the subsequent statute law was not misplaced; the March 1762 verdict was indeed in compliance with the existing law of the colony of Rhode Island.

Given these facts, there is simply no evidence to conclude that the Superior Court based its 1763 decision on other grounds than those plainly stated in its decision—namely, that it found Lopez and Elizer ineligible for citizenship in the colony precisely because they were professing Jews. Although this decision was not in compliance with the specific provisions of the Act of George II, c. 7 (1740) for naturalizing Jews, the Superior Court evidently found in these legal precedents compelling reasons to chart a different course for Rhode Island. By the 1760s, similar decisions reflecting the authority of colonial decision makers to reject instructions adopted by Parliament and the Crown were being made in all the colonies both by legislators and by judges appointed by colonial legislators. On this point, see Jack P. Greene, *The Quest for Power: The Lower Houses of Assembly in the Southern Royal Colonies, 1689–1776* (New York: Norton, for the Institute of Early American History and Culture, 1963), 330–332, 357–361, 399.

16. Moses Seixas to George Washington, August 17, 1790, in Schappes, *A Documentary History of the Jews in the United States*, 79–80.

17.   See, e.g., *Minutes of the Newport Town Meeting, 1795-1802, vol. 2059*, Collections of the Newport Historical Society, unpaginated, which shows Moses Seixas on the proxy list only for elections involving federal issues in 1795, 1796 and 1797, while Seixas and other Jews appear on the proxy lists for all elections from 1798 forward.

18.   "An Act relative to religious Freedom, and the Maintenance of Ministers," *The Public Laws of the State of Rhode-Island and Providence Plantations, As revised by a Committee, and finally enacted by the Honourable GENERAL ASSEMBLY, at their Session in January, 1798. To Which are Prefixed the Charter, Declaration of Independence, Articles of Confederation, Constitution of the United States, and President Washington's Address of September, 1796* (Providence: Carter and Wilkinson, 1798), 82–83. The guarantee of political freedoms under the 1798 statute was neither supported nor secured by the Charter—a point which was not lost on reform-minded Rhode Islanders, and one which many Rhode Islanders had begun to recognize by the 1830s. Although the preamble to this legislative enactment asserted that "our civil rights have no dependence on our religious opinions" and spoke eloquently of the natural rights of citizenship and the "dangerous fallacy" of permitting "the civil magistrate to intrude his powers into the field of [religious] opinion," it did not specifically repeal the disabilities imposed on non-Christians in the purported Act of 1719 regarding freemanship. These disabilities had initially included Catholics beneath their rubric, although the application of the law to Catholics had been specifically repealed in 1783, in gratitude to the French Catholics who had helped to liberate the state under the leadership of Rochambeau. But the disabilities applied to Jews under the 1719 Act remained in force. Moreover, the volume of Rhode Island public laws in which the 1798 enactment appeared reinforced the preeminence of the Charter by including it within the volume (in fact, the Charter is the first item in the volume after the title page), along with the founding documents of the federal government, as the basis for Rhode Island's legislative authority. As long as the Charter remained in force, the putative exercise of the franchise by Jews necessarily remained a privilege subject to rescission rather than an inalienable right. Bartlett, *Records of the State of Rhode Island*, Vol. IX, 674–675; Patrick T. Conley, *The Bill of Rights and Rhode Island* (Madison, WI: Madison House, 1991) [*reprinted from* Patrick T. Conley and John P. Kaminski, eds., *The Bill of Rights and the States: The Colonial and Revolutionary Origins of American Liberties* (Madison, WI: Madison House, 1991)], 31–33.

19.   Donald S. Lutz and Jack D. Warren, *A Covenanted People: The Religious Tradition and the Origins of American Constitutionalism* (Providence, RI: John Carter Brown Library, 1987), 29–30.

20.   In addition to Williams's *Bloudy Tenent of Persecution* (London, 1644), see Clarke's *Ill Newes from New England* (London, 1653) and George Bishop's *New England judged: The second part. Being, a relation of the cruel and bloody sufferings of the people called Quakers . . .* (London, 1667).

21.   *The Public Records of the Colony of Connecticut [1636–1776] . . . transcribed and published, (in accordance with a resolution of the general assembly)* (Hartford, CT: Brown & Parsons, 1850–1890), vol. I (1636–1665), 343, Vol. II (1664–1678), 144, 154; *Collections of the Connecticut Historical Society* (Hartford, CT: Connecticut Historical Society, 1897), vol. VI, 133, 135; Morris Silverman, *Hartford Jews, 1659–1970* (Hartford, CT: Connecticut Historical Society, 1970), 4–6 (*note*: a facsimile of the original manuscript entries in the record book is included at p. 4); David G. Dalin and Jonathan Rosenbaum, *Making a Life, Building a Community: A History of the Jews of Hartford* (New York: Holmes & Meier, 1997), 8–9. "Jacob Jew" is most likely identified as Jacob Lucena, who was trading in the Hudson Valley in the 1670s. See Holly Snyder, "English Markets, Jewish Merchants and Atlantic Endeavors: Jews and the Making of British Transatlantic Commercial Culture, 1650–1800," in Richard L. Kagan and Philip D. Morgan, eds., *Atlantic Diasporas: Jews, Conversos, and Crypto-Jews in the Age of Mercantilism, 1500–1800* (Baltimore: Johns Hopkins University Press, 2009), 61–62. The identity of the man noted as "David Jew" is more difficult to determine.

22.   *The Public Records of the Colony of Connecticut*, vol. II, 144, 154; Leon Hühner, "The Jews of New England (Other Than Rhode Island) Prior to 1800," *Publications of the American Jewish Historical Society* 11 (1903), 86–87. Given the fact that Lucena's punishment was twice

ameliorated, with the court remarking that they "see cause, considering he is a Jew, to shew him what favoure they may," Hühner made the credible suggestion that Lucena's crime consisted of breaking the Christian Sabbath.

23. Ellen Smith, "Strangers and Sojourners: The Jews of Colonial Boston," in Jonathan D. Sarna and Ellen Smith, eds., *The Jews of Boston* (Boston: Combined Jewish Philanthropies of Greater Boston, 1995), 25–26; Lee M. Friedman, "Early Jewish Residents in Massachusetts," *Publications of the American Jewish Historical Society* 23 (1915), 80–81; Lee M. Friedman, *Jewish Pioneers and Patriots* (Philadelphia: Jewish Publication Society of America, 1943), 281–291.

24. Increase Mather, *The Mystery of Israel's Salvation, Explained and Applyed, or, A Discourse Concerning the General Conversion of the Israelitish Nation* (London: John Allen, 1669), 171–177.

25. *Diary of Cotton Mather, 1681-1708*, Massachusetts Historical Society Collections, 7th Series, vol. VII (Boston: Massachusetts Historical Society, 1911), 199–200, 298–300, 302, 315 and vol. VIII (Boston: Massachusetts Historical Society, 1912), 41, 62, 218–219, 233, 469, 500, 741; *Diary of Samuel Sewall, 1674-1729*, Massachusetts Historical Society Collections, 5th Series, vol. V (Boston: Massachusetts Historical Society, 1878), 80 (reprinting the text of a pamphlet that Sewall published anonymously in 1707, which does not appear in other editions of the diary), 85, 95, vol. VI (Boston: Massachusetts Historical Society, 1879), 121, 165, and vol. VII (Boston: Massachusetts Historical Society, 1882), 308. See also Friedman, *Jewish Pioneers and Patriots*, 95–106.

26. David Mayer Gradwohl, "Judah Monis's Puzzling Gravestone as a Reflection of his Enigmatic Identity," *Markers* 21 (2004), 66–97; Lee M. Friedman, "Judah Monis, First Instructor in Hebrew at Harvard College," *Publications of the American Jewish Historical Society* 22 (1914), 1–24. Ambiguities of the gravestone notwithstanding, Monis was a generous donor to various Congregational parishes, and left small bequests to the ministers of nine different Massachusetts parishes in his will, which made no mention at all of any Jewish attachments. Friedman, "Judah Monis," 22–24. As Hühner notes, Monis was not alone in being unable to escape his prior status as a Jew despite his ongoing commitment to Christianity; records that mention the convert Simon Barns, whom Simon Bradstreet baptized at the First Church of Charlestown in 1702, attach the Latin reference "*quondam judaeus*"—that is, "formerly a Jew"—to his name. Hühner, "Jews of New England (Other than Rhode Island)," 79–80.

27. Theodore D. Bozeman, "Religious Liberty and the Problem of Order in Early Rhode Island," *The New England Quarterly,* 45 (March 1972), 53, 56, 60–62.

28. David S. Katz, *Philosemitism and the Readmission of the Jews to England, 1603–1655* (Oxford, UK: Clarendon Press, 1982).

29. "Charter of 1663," in Callendar, *An Historical Discourse*, Appendix XXI, 244 (*emphasis added*).

30. Roger Williams to Maj. John Mason and Gov. Thomas Prence, June 22, 1670, in Glenn W. LaFantasie and Bradford F. Swan, *The Correspondence of Roger Williams, 1629–1682* (Hanover, NH: Brown University Press/University Press of New England, for The Rhode Island Historical Society, 1988), vol. II, 616–617.

31. Roger Williams, *George Foxx Digg'd Out of His Burrovves, Or An Offer Of Disputation on Fourteen Proposalls Made This Last Summer 1672 (So Call'd) Unto G. Fox Then Present On Rode-Island in New-England* (Boston: John Foster, 1676), 48 (*emphasis added*). In this tract intended to discredit the theology of the Society of Friends, Williams equated Quaker beliefs with Judaism, Catholicism, and even atheism. As Williams wrote in the appendix: "It is a mistery which neither Jews nor Turks, Atheists or Papists, or Quakers know, viz. how the Seed of all grace may be in the new born, and yet the Seed also of all sin. . . . But the Papists and Quakers are so perfect and Superperfect, that though they be full of pride, Ambition, Unbelief, Unthankfulness, Intemperancy, Covetousness, full of rash Anger, bitter Railings and dreadful Blasphemies against Heaven, yet they can with the Whore wipe their mouths, and say they are pure from all uncleanness." Ibid., 96.

32. Roger Williams to Gov. John Endicott, circa August or September 1651, in LaFantasie and Swan, *The Correspondence of Roger Williams*, vol. I, 337–351.

33. Bozeman, "Religious Liberty," 52–55. The same point was eloquently made by Dr. John Clarke, founder of the Baptist congregation at Newport, in his *Ill Newes from New-England* (London, 1652). Ibid., 55–56.

34. Petitions to the Rhode Island General Assembly, vol. 11, folio. 37. As previously detailed in footnote 6, above, the vote of the Assembly never took effect, and after the Superior Court's decision Lopez and Elizer left the state to be naturalized elsewhere.

35. Bartlett, *Records of the Colony of Rhode Island*, vol. VI (*1757-1769*), 261–262; the oaths of naturalization to which Lucena swore (which included the oath of abjuration of papal authority and the oath of allegiance to the British Crown, but not an attestation of the juror's own Christianity) have been reproduced in Jacob Rader Marcus, *American Jewry—Documents—Eighteenth Century* (Cincinnati: Hebrew Union College, 1959) as no. 77, 208–210.

36. Dexter, *Extracts from the Itineraries of Ezra Stiles*, 52–53.

37. Statement of Moses Michael Hays, July 12, 1776, in Jacob Rader Marcus, ed., "Jews and the American Revolution: A Bicentennial Documentary," *American Jewish Archives*, vol. 27, no. 2 (November 1975), 121. The original of this document is found in the records of the General Assembly at the Rhode Island Colony Archives, where it is part of a volume in which actions pertaining to "suspected persons" during the Revolutionary War were recorded.

Chapter Eight

Oaths and Christian Belief in the New Nation: 1776–1789

Tara Thompson Strauch

In the *Pennsylvania Evening Post* on September 26, 1776, an editorial signed by "A Follower of Christ" lamented the lack of religion in Pennsylvania's proposed constitution by asserting that Pennsylvanians were falling away from the behavior not just of other Christian countries but of Jews and Muslims, as well. "The Jew swears upon the Thorah," he noted, "the Mahomedan the Alcoran, the Protestants in Germany by the Holy Trinity, the English kiss the New Testament, the Roman Catholics the holy cross. But the Pennsylvanians swear by nothing. What oaths may we expect, if all religious awe is removed?"[1] This concerned citizen observed many truths about eighteenth-century oaths. First, he understood that oaths had an important religious aspect which gave them power; a "religious awe." Second, he recognized that various religious groups, even Muslims, had specific oath rituals that used religiously powerful symbols, such as the Koran, to bind oath-takers to the truth. Finally, this writer recognized that governments were attached to particular religious beliefs; Catholic countries took oaths on the holy cross, while Anglican England kissed the New Testament. Without a particular dominant religious persuasion and without any need for religious belief, Pennsylvania's oath looked and sounded remarkably different from its European and even its Muslim counterparts.

Pennsylvanians were not alone in their concerns about oaths in the new nation. Citizens throughout this young republic worried that the oaths of office, allegiance, and religious tests were either so inclusive that no religious belief was necessary for citizenship or so restrictive that pious men would be excluded from participation in the government. As "A Follower of Christ" also demonstrates, the specter of Muslims and Jews becoming important participants in the new state governments was not only a piece of inflammatory rhetoric. Many citizens feared that removing oaths and oath rituals would create an environment where there was no political difference between the oaths of Christians and Muslims. In the debates over the state constitutions, the primacy of Christianity was carefully guarded through test oaths and religious requirements for officeholders. This assurance that Christianity would remain the religion associated with America allowed citizens to consider changes to oath rituals that would lead to religious freedom.

As a site for governmental control over religious belief, debates over oaths demonstrated the concern Americans had with developing a virtuous, Christian society and the limits they desired to place on religious freedom. While all colonies debated whether they should promote an established church, most colonies also pondered whether there should be limits placed on freedom of conscience in the form of oaths of office and restrictive oath rituals, such as kneeling and kissing the Gospels, which were frowned upon by many Calvinist-leaning churches. State constitutions most often established a minimal baseline of religious belief, such as a belief in a Supreme Being, and outlined specific matters of conscience (such as the right to raise a hand toward God rather than kiss the Gospels) in legislative acts. The overall trend in these religious clauses within the state constitutions was not unlimited religious freedom but rather cautious limitations on religious belief. Although it was true that people of questionable faith or even no faith could live in most colonies without penalty, that did not mean that they could participate in the government. Oaths and test acts were used to prevent such people from being anything but marginal members of society. As the debates over oaths and religious tests in Pennsylvania and New Jersey as well as those within American religious sects such as the Mennonite Church show, religious test clauses were far from being unimportant vestiges of political tradition. The clauses in the state constitutions enabled Americans to contemplate a federal government free of religious obligation.

The eighteenth-century insistence on oaths of allegiance, naturalization, and witness testimony can seem today like bureaucratic checks on behavior, a way of policing a citizen's actions on earth. If this is the only reason we accept for the prolific giving and taking of oaths in the seventeenth and eighteenth centuries, these oaths can seem meaningless and the colonial debates over an oath's wording downright banal. An oath, however, was much more than a routine political occurrence; it invited God to witness an earthly promise, with the understanding that God would punish oath breakers at the Final Judgment. In the early modern world, where political loyalties and religious doctrine were unsettled as never before, oaths could testify to a citizen's loyalty or prevent those with questionable religious beliefs from participating in the political process. The early modern European world was full of oaths, oath ceremonies, and oath controversies; in fact, Jesuit casuists spent a great deal of time and ink explaining oaths and how they could be broken.[2] England barred Catholics from office through the use of oaths and expelled the French Huguenots from Acadia in 1755 because of their refusal to take a loyalty oath. Oaths would also play an important role in the French Revolution, where the revolutionary government used loyalty oaths to ostracize the Catholic clergy and other nonjurors during the Terror.[3]

The wording and ritual of an oath had implications for who could participate in the American governments as well. For example, several religious sects refused to swear an oath but would happily "affirm" their belief, which was a solemn promise backed by their record of piety. If an oath forbade certain sects from affirming, then Quakers, German sectarians, and some groups of Baptists were blocked from full citizenship.[4] Likewise if there was no requirement that a citizen believe in Jesus Christ, then in theory a Jew or a Muslim could actively engage in the government. For the devout, more immediately alarming was the fear that the important distinction between "swearing" and "professing" would be lost: swearing invoked God's presence as a witness, whereas professing simply meant asserting a belief or event without any outside motivations toward truthfulness. If an oath was degraded to the point that God was not invoked, there could be no assurance of honesty in this world and no promise of divine retribution in the next. It was with this understanding of oaths that the American colonies set about creating new state constitutions. Yet this belief that religion could protect the temporal government was challenged in America by the plurality of Christian denominations. Unlike European countries that restricted citizenship to those of a certain religious confession, this fledgling nation needed the participation of as many patriotic citizens as possible, and in the process of accommodating scrupulous citizens, American states often redefined their understanding of oaths and test acts.

One of the most vigorous debates over religious tests occurred in Pennsylvania, which had always had a contentious religious milieu. Because William Penn had established the colony with the intention of extending religious toleration to Quakers, among others, oath taking had been a particularly fraught notion. In Pennsylvania, Quakers and other scrupulous religious sects had the right to affirm rather than swear their oaths—a right not offered in many European lands. This right was so important in the colony that oaths in general were rare. In fact, in Pennsylvania's first Frame of Government, given May 2, 1682, no oath was required, even for witness testimony. A witness by "solemnly promising to tell the truth, the whole truth, and nothing but the truth" would assure the government of his or her honesty.[5] In 1772, the colony's General Assembly passed an act for "the relief of such persons, as conscientiously scruple the taking of an Oath in the common form." This act expanded the options for oath takers concerning how an oath was sworn. Rather than kneeling and kissing the Bible, as had been the custom in England, a citizen who found this practice too reminiscent of Catholicism could choose to raise his or her right hand toward God before swearing "by Almighty God, the searcher of all hearts."[6] The General Assembly noted that because of their concerns, certain citizens had been imprisoned or banned from testifying in court. Both situations limited the effectiveness of good citizens who, as the act also noted, were still required to profess a belief in "GOD the Father, and in JESUS CHRIST, his only Son, and in the HOLY SPIRIT," as well as in the divine inspiration of the Bible in order to hold any office.[7] Whereas in Europe both the wording and ritual of an oath had been deeply contested, the colonies were often willing to accommodate varying rituals as long as the oath and religious tests attached to it were kept intact. In the years leading up to the American Revolution, Pennsylvania had taken steps to ensure that good Christian citizens could continue to participate in the political process despite beliefs that were not in line with most established confessions. Even before the American Revolution, Pennsylvania had begun to define good citizens as Christian citizens who should be free to express their religious beliefs without political implications.

As the eighteenth century progressed, the demographics of Pennsylvania shifted, with Germans and Anglicans making up a larger part of the population. This changing population led to conflict between the Quakers and the Anglican Church, which saw Pennsylvania's patchwork of religious groups as a sign of lapsed religious belief. Nowhere was this tension more evident than in the drafting of Pennsylvania's proposed constitution in 1776. All of the delegates to the convention swore their allegiance and also gave a profession of faith, yet their opinions on the role of religion in the new state were diverse, to say the least. The constitution was rife with statements of religious belief and requirements of faith. The document's "bill of rights" stated that all citizens should enjoy their natural rights and "other blessings which the Author of existence has bestowed upon man."[8] Also in the Declaration of Rights, the convention specified that all citizens had the right to worship freely as long as they believed in God. Section Ten of the constitution required all legislative representatives to profess, but distinctly not swear, to a belief in God, a future system of rewards and punishments, and the divine inspiration of the scriptures.

After the proposed constitution was published in the newspapers, citizens reacted both in favor of and against Pennsylvania's oath requirements. Some commentators applauded the frame of government, while other citizens, such as "A Follower of Christ," strongly objected to the lack of oaths in the new constitution. "A Follower of Christ" noted that while the legislators were required to swear their allegiance to the state, they needed only to declare their belief in God. This citizen was concerned that not requiring an oath of religious belief would allow blasphemers, atheists, and perhaps even Muslims to become lawmakers in the state. In the ongoing dialogue between

"Orator Puff and Peter Easy," published in the *Pennsylvania Ledger* in the fall of 1776, Orator Puff makes an exaggerated argument that this new frame of government made Deism the established religion of the colony. Orator Puff notes that the new constitution did away with the profession of faith that legislators had been required to take under the previous Frame of Government and replaced it with what the orator considered a vague declaration of belief in a Supreme Being. In shock, Peter exclaims, "How can we ask or expect success, while we thus deliberately, in the face of the whole world, are undermining the religion graciously delivered to us by heaven with such amazing circumstances of mercy?"[9] This mock dialogue lampooned both the constitution and its opponents but reflected a real concern for the lack of limits placed on religious freedom in the new Pennsylvanian Constitution. When Peter questions whether the new constitution would in reality change the religious beliefs of the nation, since most citizens were Christian, Orator Puff makes one further argument about the lack of religion in the constitution. This lack of religion, he argues, may make the citizens in years to come less respectful towards Christianity because, as sinful creatures, they need to be reminded of their religious obligations.

Other citizens shared these concerns. The *Philadelphia Post* published the resolutions of a group of concerned citizens on October 22, 1776. Among these resolutions was the assertion that "in the Constitution formed by the said Convention, the CHRISTIAN religion is not treated with the proper respect."[10] They also resolved that members of the assembly should not subscribe to the oath and religious test required by the constitution, but instead should take a different oath, which required that the legislator believe not only in God, as per the constitution, but in "God the father, and in Jesus Christ his eternal son, and in the Holy Spirit, one God blessed forever more."[11] These resolutions outlined the concern that many Pennsylvanians had about the new constitution: that the baseline of Christian belief was set so low that atheists, Jews, or Muslims could participate in the political system.[12] This group recognized that the legislators were required to declare their belief in God, but since they were not required to swear to their beliefs, any atheist could lie in order to take their legislative seat.[13] Moreover, these citizens recognized that a belief in a Supreme Being did not restrict conscientious Jews or Muslims from the government. By requiring a belief in the Trinity, however, this group hoped to limit the freedoms of conscience for government officials in order to protect both the morality of the government and the supremacy of Christianity in America.

The German Lutheran minister Henry Melchior Muhlenberg and other clergy in Philadelphia were equally wary of the state's new constitution. When the Anglican clergy visited Muhlenberg in October 1776 and shared their concerns over the new constitution with him, Muhlenberg was concerned enough to speak out against the constitution not only in German to his

parishioners but also in English to various powerful politicians within the
city, something the German-born pastor rarely did. Muhlenberg viewed the
religious test in the new constitution as deplorably lax because it lacked any
requirement of a belief in the Trinity. But, rather than seeing this omission as
simply a lack of Christian sentiment within the provincial assembly, Muhlenberg thought that:

> There are clever puppets behind the scenes who are acting according to the
> maxim, *divide et imperabis* (divide and conquer). The courage of many a
> Christian-minded soul has fallen, for it has been observed how the beast with
> horns has been working in the background and cast the Christian religion out
> of the new form of government, in spite of the fact that, in the old constitution,
> Christianity was deemed by respectable and genuine Christians as precious
> and valuable as a pearl. [14]

Muhlenberg saw the looser religious tests as a conspiracy meant to drive
apart citizens who had come to the New World seeking religious freedom. As
a clergyman, Muhlenberg was predisposed to see a world of lapsed belief.
Yet clearly Muhlenberg was not alone in his fears about the constitution. The
active debate over the constitution and its religious obligations was typical of
the ethnically and religiously diverse colony, but Pennsylvanians were not
alone in questioning whether there should be a limit on religious freedom.

Like Pennsylvania, New Jersey had become increasingly heterogeneous
in the years before the revolution. In eastern New Jersey, Dutch and Swedish
immigrants had established communities that remained tied to their mother
countries through their Reformed and Lutheran ministers. In western New
Jersey, German sectarians and Quakers had moved in from Pennsylvania and
brought with them the experience of living under a religiously diverse
government. This variety of religious belief was only augmented by the
growing importance of the Presbyterian College of New Jersey (now Princeton University) and the devout Calvinists who sent their sons to the school
for education. Along with this plurality of religious belief, by 1776 New
Jersey was embroiled in war and was plagued with questions about the loyalty of its citizens.

The constitution of New Jersey, unlike that of Pennsylvania, was not
hotly contested by its citizens. Like most states, New Jersey required officeholders to have certain Christian beliefs. In this case, the constitution stipulated that they be Protestant but did not specify any particular beliefs (such as
the divine inspiration of the Gospels) that these men were required to hold. In
fact, New Jersey's constitution seemed to move farther from a restrictive
oath than Pennsylvania had because the oath of office was in reality not an
oath. The constitution only asked members of the assembly to "solemnly
declare" their allegiance to the state without any reference to God. [15] This
was not merely a case of semantics; in ordinances that regulated oaths of

allegiance and election procedures during the war, the provincial congress was careful to specify that the form of the oath was "I, do swear (or affirm)" rather than the religiously void "I solemnly declare."[16] Although the assembly clearly envisioned a Protestant Christian society because they required officials to be "Protestant," despite any definition of which sects this included, this declaration was vague enough to allow all Christians (and atheists, Jews, and Muslims) to participate in the government.

New Jersey's liberal constitution still did not remove all religious concerns about oaths. Shortly after the constitution was approved, Governor William Livingston received a petition similar to the 1772 Pennsylvania legislation about the ritual actions of oaths. The New Jersey General Assembly responded by writing an act titled "An Act for the Ease and Relief of Such Persons as Are Scrupulous of Taking an Oath with the Ceremony of Touching and Kissing the Book of the Gospels, by Allowing That of Holding up the Hand in Lieu Thereof."[17] The act noted that until this time "no other [manner] was deemed and admitted legal," indicating that the colonial government had only allowed the kneeling ritual for oath-taking rather than raising the right hand.[18] Governor Livingston had encouraged the assembly to pass this act in his communication with the legislature. He noted that it was not the wording but the "*English* Ceremony of kissing the Book" which the petitioners found objectionable, and that these citizens should be released from their concern, asking "can it be consistent with sound Policy, or the generous Spirit of our Constitution, to debar an honest Man, for a religious Scruple, from the Privileges of Society, which the most profligate and abandoned are permitted to enjoy in the fullest Latitude?"[19] After all, Livingston concluded, this change in ritual was "beyond Question altogether formal, and in no Respect essential to its Nature or Solemnity."[20] Yet, the change did demonstrate that citizens took their oaths and their oath rituals seriously. The need for new constitutions allowed Americans the chance to evaluate the relationship between church and state as well as the judiciousness of their religious rituals. As the petitioners in New Jersey demonstrate, when citizens found this relationship lacking, they sought solutions.

Often, scholars have assumed that the only objections to oath taking came from the Quakers or smaller religious sects.[21] In this case, however, the concern was less about the oath than about its ritual. Those who had petitioned the General Assembly appeared not to have been adherents of an obscure religious sect but rather the Congregationalists and Presbyterians affiliated with Princeton who had moved into the state in increasing numbers in the mid-eighteenth century. Unlike the requests made in other states to allow an affirmation rather than an oath or to relieve the scrupulous sects, there is no mention made of a specific religious denomination that was oppressed by this ritual. Typically, those requests mentioned the Quakers, Mennonites, or Dunkers, who were adamantly against oaths. The act in New

Jersey mentioned only that "certain well disposed persons" were jeopardized by the law. While the German presence in British America was generally tolerated, the scrupulous German sects were rarely well thought of or considered "well disposed." More likely to be considered such were Congregationalists, who had taken oaths by raising their hands toward God in Massachusetts for generations.

Although legislators dealt with the issue of the oath ritual, Governor William Livingston brought the discussion about religion in the state constitutions to the people at large. In January and February 1778, Livingston wrote a series of letters to the *New Jersey Gazette* about the role religion should play in this new democratic society. Like many colonists, Livingston attended a variety of churches. He was nominally Presbyterian, although he probably most identified with the Dutch Reformed Church, since his mother was Dutch, but attended church in Congregational, Presbyterian, Dutch Reformed, and other houses of worship. In his addresses to the General Assembly and in his newspaper editorials, Livingston elaborated a theory of religious freedom that would strengthen religion without sacrificing the virtue of the new democracy.

Cato's (Livingston's penname) solution to the problem—separating Church and State without sacrificing the virtue commanded by Christianity—required both men's hearts and bodies to be free from any religious obligations by the government. He offered a strikingly individual definition of religion which emphasized the "inward habitual reverence for, and devotedness to, the Deity" rather than a communal experience.[22] England, he said, did not restrict men's hearts, but it punished their bodies for not participating in certain common rituals. According to this argument, if a Muslim became the head of the English government, then Islam would be the state church and England would punish men's bodies for their disobedience to the Koran. In New Jersey, however, since there was no state church, Christianity's unfailing truth would always make it the dominant religion of the people. Freedom of religion, Cato suggested, would lead to a more perfect expression of Christianity because it would not simply be another state institution. He argued that the New Jersey Constitution did this perfectly by allowing freedom of religion and that this freedom could not be denied because the legislature swore not to change this section of the document.[23] This essay appeared in February 1778, just a few months after he had requested that the legislature change the oath ritual and it seems likely that this was on his mind as he extolled the virtues of New Jersey. Yet, Livingston was not advocating a society of atheists, nor did the New Jersey Constitution allow atheists to hold office, because lawmakers and judges still had to belong to a Protestant sect and peaceably attend to their religious obligations. What Livingston believed, and what the state of New Jersey enacted, was that true Christian citizens could exist only in a state that did not require a certain denominational affiliation.

Already in 1776, New Jersey's government had turned away from seeing the state as responsible for establishing religion. The constitution identified a minimal level of Christianity necessary for participation in the political process but left church funding and attendance to the citizens themselves. At the same time the General Assembly required a loyalty oath that wove traditional English rituals with a new American oath of allegiance. When Governor Livingston realized that certain trustworthy citizens were being punished because of their religious objection to the oath ritual, he pushed the legislature to protect the beliefs of these citizens because their belief that one should not endow an inanimate object with religious power did not impinge on the religious qualifications for participation in the government. In many respects, New Jersey pushed the limits of Christian belief farther than many states because it did not require an acceptance of the Trinity or of a future state of rewards and punishments. New Jersey, with an ideology championed by its governor, began to transform the concept of citizen from one who must follow certain Christian rituals and profess particular Protestant beliefs to one who simply claimed the title of Christian.

Oaths were a concern not only to those who sought to defend the government from immorality. Oaths required during the American Revolution also shaped the religious sects themselves. One of the most striking examples of this is the schism created in the Mennonite Church during the war. Most Mennonites had migrated to Pennsylvania, Maryland, or New Jersey, where they lived in heterogeneous communities of German sectarians, German high-churchgoers, and English Anglicans and Presbyterians. Despite these diverse communities, Mennonites maintained their religious beliefs, such as adult baptism, pacifism, and strict church discipline. The American Revolution presented many challenges to this religious sect; for example, the church's belief in pacifism made its members frequent targets of mob violence. One of the greatest challenges the war presented, however, was to the Mennonite resistance to oath taking. Although many Mennonites remained steadfast in their refusal to swear an oath, a significant number of them chose to take the oath of allegiance to the new nation—an act that then predisposed them to take other oaths, including the oaths of office prescribed by the new state constitutions.[24]

One of the more virulent schisms within the Mennonite Church occurred in the Franconia conference in Lancaster, Pennsylvania. Christian Funk, a young Mennonite bishop who had been born in America, and a group of his followers were banned from the church for taking the loyalty oath to the American government. Whereas many politicians saw this oath as a religious check on political behavior, Mennonites saw something more sinister. These individuals saw the oath as an attempt to regulate their religious beliefs, especially in Pennsylvania, where it was tied to paying a military tax.[25] The Mennonite community had been enticed to come to Pennsylvania precisely because the colony offered a level of religious freedom unheard of in Europe. Mennonite beliefs were tolerated in Pennsylvania, and many members of the sect saw the revolutionary government's calls for oaths and military service as a changed attitude toward smaller religious groups.

In his memoir *A Mirror for All People*, Funk wrote about his attempts to convince his fellow Mennonites that they could and should take the oath of allegiance and pay military taxes. Funk and other, younger Mennonites who had been born in the colony saw more danger to their religion and more government intrusion into religious belief in the British Empire than in the American government. These men saw the oaths and military taxes that the new government required as necessary to ensure the safety of the new American citizens. Furthermore, they saw the oath as a requirement for citizenship rather than as a religious test. Funk preached this belief throughout the Mennonite churches in Lancaster and immediately created discord within the church. His fellow Mennonite preachers refused to take communion with him because they were not "at peace" with Funk.[26] The main allegation against Funk and his fellow believers was that they had taken the oath of allegiance and had encouraged others to do the same. According to Funk, the ministers decided that, "He who is on the side of Congress has no word here. . . . He who even leans toward the side of the Congress has no word here."[27] For the Mennonites, these oaths were not mere formalities or meaningless assertions but a matter of deep religious concern.

The disagreement between Christian Funk and the other Mennonite leaders was not resolved peacefully. In fact, the Franconia conference shunned and banned Funk and his followers. The ban, or complete removal from the religious community, was rarely practiced by American Mennonites, although it was a hallmark of the followers of Joseph Amman—the Amish, who had not yet fully broken with the Mennonite Church. Funk claimed that the ban had not been used by American Mennonites in more than thirty years.[28] Yet, the Funkites, as they were called, were expelled from the Mennonite Church. This group continued to worship as Mennonites and active American citizens well into the nineteenth century. The sole difference between Funk's church and the proper Mennonite Church was that Funk's congregants had accepted the American government's definition of citizenship during the Revolution. This issue continued to prevent the Funkites from rejoining the Mennonites even after the war, because Mennonites who had maintained their religious identity and refused to take the oath of allegiance had often suffered for this decision by being imprisoned, fined, or ostracized. Many other Mennonites moved to Canada with the staunch British loyalists, because even after the war these religious adherents refused to take an oath to the new government. The members of the church who had maintained their restriction on oaths refused to allow Funk's followers to rejoin them because the Funkites refused to accept that they had broken any precepts of the religion. Thus, oaths, their religious obligations, and their political ramifications defined Mennonite belief throughout the American Revolution and well into the early Republic.

Sectarian groups such as the Mennonites had fled to America precisely because it offered a chance to escape from confining government requirements of religious belief. The nation that began to develop out of the American Revolution sought, in their opinion, to impose restrictions on individual conscience. Many smaller sects experienced instability and change as members left to join less restrictive religious sects or married outside the group; pacifist confessions like the Quakers lost many members to active participation in the war; very small sects such as the Ephrata Cloister struggled to maintain numbers in the face of upheaval and change; and scrupulous sects faced extraordinary pressure either to continue living as British subjects (which many Mennonites did by moving to Canada) because of their original naturalization oaths or to conform as oath-taking American citizens.[29] As members of these sects argued for their religious beliefs to be encompassed in America's liberal toleration, these smaller religious groups helped push the states and the nation toward a broader vision of American Christianity.

Although this essay has focused on the middle Atlantic states, all colonies had to establish whether Christian belief was necessary for citizenship. As in Pennsylvania and New Jersey, these debates were contentious and had real ramifications for individuals within these colonies. In North Carolina, for example, the constitution specified that those who "shall deny the being of God or the truth of the Protestant religion, or the divine authority of the Old and New Testaments, or who shall hold religious principles incompatible with the freedom and safety of the state" were ineligible to hold office.[30] The North Carolina Constitution did not put limits on the religious beliefs of its citizens at large, but this was not a foregone conclusion. In the original charter of Carolina enacted in 1669, the Anglican Church was established in the new colony and all citizens were required to belong to a church. Other churches had the right to be recognized as long as they espoused a belief in God and established as an oath ritual kneeling and kissing of the Gospels. The relationship between these churches and the state linked religious practice with citizenship in a way that North Carolina's state constitution did not. South Carolina's 1776 Constitution required oath takers to swear, "so help me God" but did not place any other religious restrictions on its citizens. Yet when it revised the document in 1778, the state increased religious restrictions on citizens by requiring all electors to believe in God and in a future system of rewards and punishments. Officeholders now needed to be Protestant and all inhabitants (not just electors) needed to profess a belief in God.

These debates suggest three correctives to our understanding of the relationship between church and state in the eighteenth century. First, these contested constitutions and petitions for religious considerations demonstrate that eighteenth-century Americans believed that oaths necessitated religious belief and recognized oaths as both religious and civic obligations. Oaths were not mere formalities or long-held European traditions. Second, both office holders and citizens at large felt that the government should require a certain level of Christian belief within society. The Christian religion ensured a virtuous community whose oaths held meaning on earth and in heaven. Third, these oaths and the religious tests found in most state constitutions had ramifications for devout citizens. For many devout Anglicans, Lutherans, and members of European state churches, oaths allowed them to feel secure that active citizens had the moral guidance of Christian belief and the knowledge that their earthly crimes would be punished in the future. For citizens in smaller religious sects as well as devout Baptists, Methodists, and even Congregationalists, oaths and religious tests demonstrated that the religious tolerance guaranteed by many constitutions did not allow all citizens freedom of conscience. It is surprising to realize that at least some eighteenth-century Americans saw in these revered documents religious limits on political participation while others saw them as dangerously permissive. Religious freedom in America was not a forgone conclusion once the country declared independence from Great Britain. It took the objections of a variety of Christian denominations and the general agreement that America was and would indefinitely remain rooted in Christianity for Americans to accept a government free of religious obligations.

REFERENCES

"A Follower of Christ." *Pennsylvania Evening Post*, September 26, 1776.
Constitution of New Jersey, 1776, section XXIII. Text available at http://avalon.law.yale.edu/18th_century/nj15.asp.
Constitution of Pennsylvania 1776. Text available at http://avalon.law.yale.edu/18th_century/pa08.asp.
Fagan, Patrick. *Divided Loyalties: The Question of the Oath for Irish Catholics in the Eighteenth Century*. Dublin, Ireland: Four Courts Press, 1997.
"Federal and State constitutions, colonial charters, and other organic laws of the state[s], territories, and colonies now or heretofore forming the United States of America /compiled and edited under the Act of Congress of June 30, 1906," Text, December 18, 1998. Available at http://avalon.law.yale.edu/18th_century/nc07.asp.
Funk, Christian. "A Mirror for All People," trans. John C. Wenger. *Mennonite Quarterly Review*, 59 (January 1985).
Gordon, Sarah Barringer. "Blasphemy and the Law of Religious Liberty in Nineteenth-Century America." *American Quarterly* 52, no. 4 (December 1, 2000).
Hunter, Michael. "The Problem of 'Atheism' in Early Modern England." *Transactions of the Royal Historical Society* 35, Fifth Series (January 1, 1985).

Hyman, Harold Melvin. *To Try Men's Souls: Loyalty Tests in American History.* Berkeley, CA: University of California Press, 1960.

Johnston, A.J.B. "Borderland Worries: Loyalty Oaths in Acadie/Nova Scotia, 1654–1755." *French Colonial History,* 4 (2003).

Jones, David Martin. *Conscience and Allegiance in Seventeenth Century England: The Political Significance of Oaths and Engagements.* Rochester, NY: University of Rochester Press, 1999.

Leites, Edmund. *Conscience and Casuistry in Early Modern Europe.* Cambridge, UK: Cambridge University Press, 1988.

Livingston, William (aka Cato). *The Papers of William Livingston.* February 18, 1778, in *The Papers of William Livingston.* Trenton, NJ: New Jersey Historical Commission, 1980.

MacMaster, Richard, et al. *Conscience in Crisis: Mennonites and Other Peace Churches in America, 1739–1789: Interpretation and Documents.* Scottdale, PA: Herald Press, 1979.

Muhlenberg, Henry Melchior. *The Journals of Henry Melchior Muhlenberg.* Philadelphia: Evangelical Lutheran Ministerium of Pennsylvania and Adjacent States, 1942, 2:751, October 23, 1776.

New Jersey Gazette. "An Act for the ease and relief of such persons as are scrupulous of taking an oath with the ceremony of touching and kissing the Book of the Gospels, by allowing that of holding up the hand in lieu thereof." October 7, 1778.

"Ordinance for Regulating the Ensuing Election," *Minutes of the Provincial Congress and the Council of Safety of the State of New Jersey [1775–1776].* Trenton, NJ: Naar, Day & Naar, 1879.

Penn, William. *Frame of Government,* May 2, 1682.

Pennsylvania Evening Post, October 22, 1776.

Pennsylvania Ledger. "Orator Puff and Peter Easy." October 12, 1776.

Pennsylvania Packet. May 8, 1772.

Tackett, Timothy. *Religion, Revolution, and Regional Culture in Eighteenth-Century France: The Ecclesiastical Oath of 1791.* Princeton, NJ: Princeton University Press, 1986.

Vallance, Edward. *Revolutionary England and the National Covenant: State Oaths, Protestantism, and the Political Nation, 1553–1682.* Woodbridge, UK: Boydell Press, 2005.

NOTES

1. "A Follower of Christ," *Pennsylvania Evening Post* (Philadelphia), September 26, 1776.

2. See Edmund Leites, *Conscience and Casuistry in Early Modern Europe* (Cambridge, UK: Cambridge University Press, 1988).

3. For English test oaths; David Martin Jones, *Conscience and Allegiance in Seventeenth Century England: The Political Significance of Oaths and Engagements* (Rochester, NY: University of Rochester Press, 1999); Patrick Fagan, *Divided Loyalties: The Question of the Oath for Irish Catholics in the Eighteenth Century* (Dublin, Ireland: Four Courts Press, 1997); and Edward Vallance, *Revolutionary England and the National Covenant: State Oaths, Protestantism, and the Political Nation, 1553–1682* (Woodbridge, UK: Boydell Press, 2005). For the story of the Acadians: A.J.B. (Andrew John Bayly) Johnston, "Borderland Worries: Loyalty Oaths in Acadie/Nova Scotia, 1654–1755," *French Colonial History* 4 (2003): 31–48. The French Revolution oaths are particularly interesting, since the Revolutionaries were generally against oath-abiding Catholic priests; Timothy Tackett, *Religion, Revolution, and Regional Culture in Eighteenth-Century France: The Ecclesiastical Oath of 1791* (Princeton, NJ: Princeton University Press, 1986).

4. These groups took the biblical injunction in Matthew 5:34–37 and James 5:12 that a Christian should not swear at all, but merely say "yea or nea" as truth. Other Christians, meanwhile, stressed other verses, such as 2 Corinthians 1:23, which have good Christians

swearing oaths with God as a witness. Religious sects such as Anglicans, Presbyterians, Reformed, and Catholics assert that God simply does not want careless oaths made by human guarantors.

5. William Penn, *Frame of Government*, May 2, 1682.

6. *Pennsylvania Packet* (Philadelphia), May 8, 1772.

7. Ibid.

8. *Constitution of Pennsylvania 1776*, "The Federal and State constitutions, colonial charters, and other organic laws of the state[s], territories, and colonies now or heretofore forming the United States of America/compiled and edited under the Act of Congress of June 30, 1906." Text, December 18, 1998. Available at http://avalon.law.yale.edu/18th_century/pa08.asp

9. "Orator Puff and Peter Easy." *Pennsylvania Ledger*, October 12, 1776.

10. "Philadelphia, October 22nd." *Pennsylvania Evening Post*, October 22, 1776.

11. Ibid.

12. Atheism meant something different in the early modern world than it does in modern use. An eighteenth-century atheist was not necessarily aggressively antireligion. Instead, the word indicated someone who did not believe in the existence in a deity, although he or she might have a use for religion generally. For a discussion on the development of atheism, see: Michael Hunter, "The Problem of 'Atheism' in Early Modern England," *Transactions of the Royal Historical Society* 35, Fifth Series (January 1, 1985): 135–157. Nineteenth-century America still had definite laws against atheistic expression. See, Sarah Barringer Gordon, "Blasphemy and the Law of Religious Liberty in Nineteenth-Century America," *American Quarterly* 52, no. 4 (December 1, 2000): 682–719.

13. Clearly an atheist could lie under a sworn oath as well, but the implications are different. If an atheist lied under oath, God would punish him at the Judgment Day harshly for falsely swearing before God. When these tests did not require the officeholder to swear, God was not a witness at the event and the sin would be treated as any other lie, not as a particular affront to God.

14. Henry Melchior Muhlenberg, *The Journals of Henry Melchior Muhlenberg* (Philadelphia: Evangelical Lutheran Ministerium of Pennsylvania and Adjacent States, 1942), 2:751, October 23, 1776.

15. *Constitution of New Jersey*, 1776, section XXIII, "The Federal and State constitutions, colonial charters, and other organic laws of the state[s], territories, and colonies now or heretofore forming the United States of America /compiled and edited under the Act of Congress of June 30, 1906." Text, December 18, 1998. Available at http://avalon.law.yale.edu/18th_century/nj15.asp

16. "Ordinance for Regulating the Ensuing Election," *Minutes of the Provincial Congress and the Council of Safety of the state of New Jersey [1775-1776]* (Trenton, NJ: Naar, Day & Naar, 1879), 560.

17. State of New Jersey, "An Act for the ease and relief of such persons as are scrupulous of taking an oath with the ceremony of touching and kissing the Book of the Gospels, by allowing that of holding up the hand in lieu thereof," *New Jersey Gazette*, October 7, 1778.

18. Ibid.

19. Livingston to the Assembly, *The Papers of William Livingston* (Trenton, NJ: New Jersey Historical Commission, 1980), 2: 147, May 29, 1778.

20. Ibid.

21. Almost all works on oath and conscientious objectors deal with these sects. See, for example: Harold Melvin Hyman, *To Try Men's Souls: Loyalty Tests in American History* (Berkeley: University of California Press, 1960). There has been far less attention paid to how more mainstream denominations understood oaths and oath rituals.

22. Livingston (aka Cato), *The Papers of William Livingston*. 2: 234–238, February 18, 1778.

23. The legislature swore a true oath and also allowed the option of affirming this declaration. The affirmation, in particular, demonstrated that the assembly viewed this oath as religious, because religiously scrupulous individuals could refrain from swearing.

24. The best work on Mennonites in eighteenth-century America is Richard MacMaster et al., *Conscience in Crisis: Mennonites and Other Peace Churches in America, 1739–1789: Interpretation and Documents* (Scottdale, PA: Herald Press, 1979).

25. It is important to note that the oath discussed here is not a test oath of religious belief, but a more general oath of allegiance. The oath-taker is still required to swear in God's presence, but the point is not to determine a person's religious beliefs. Instead, the goal is to use religion to certify a person's word. For Mennonites, not even an oath such as this was acceptable, because their confession dictated that people should not swear at all. Younger, American-born Mennonites, however, seemed to accept that this was not an attempt to regulate religion, but to regulate politics, and were willing to sacrifice their religious principles for the American cause.

26. Although some ministers may have been sympathetic to Funk's cause, Mennonite communion required complete agreement or no communion at all. Because some ministers were unhappy with Funk, he was not eligible to take communion.

27. Christian Funk, "A Mirror for All People," trans. John C. Wenger. *Mennonite Quarterly Review* 59 (January 1985): 42–66.

28. Ibid, 50.

29. The naturalization oath was given to immigrants before they debarked into American ports. Most German immigrants spoke no English upon their arrival and in 1755 the Mennonites petitioned that these oaths not be considered binding because they had not understood they had been repeating an oath.

30. "The Federal and State constitutions, colonial charters, and other organic laws of the state[s], territories, and colonies now or heretofore forming the United States of America/ compiled and edited under the Act of Congress of June 30, 1906," Text, December 18, 1998. Available at http://avalon.law.yale.edu/18th_century/nc07.asp.

Chapter Nine

Education, Religion, and the State in Postrevolutionary America

Keith Pacholl

In 1799, the editor of the Philadelphia magazine *The Dessert to the True American* published a letter from a reader who entitled himself "Philoctetes." The core of his letter examined the growing importance of periodicals in the fledgling United States. Philoctetes argued that periodical print played a central role in the development of the new republic. Since an increasing number of people were turning to such literature for instruction, he declared that periodicals should meet the needs of the nation by publishing articles based upon "religion and sound morals." By inculcating virtue in the reading public, the United States could avert the moral disaster witnessed in Europe, where print was incorrectly used to advance "scepticism, infidelity, and irreligion."[1] Philoctetes recognized the growing influence of periodicals in society, and he and others like him advocated using newspapers and magazines to educate the population. By the end of the eighteenth century, many considered periodical literature to be the bastion of American liberty. Americans utilized this print medium to convey political sentiments to the public. Their message emphasized the necessity of creating a virtuous citizenry who would uphold the republican values of the young nation.

This chapter explores the relationship between education, religion, and the state following the American Revolution by focusing on the messages conveyed by American periodicals to the public. I argue that newspapers and magazines offered a public forum to discuss the survival of the American republic. An examination of periodicals in this context reveals three key themes emphasized by the writers.[2] The first theme underscored the significance of education in the new nation. If the republic was going to survive, both men and women needed to be educated. Second, periodicals accentuated the moral formation of the nation's citizens. Only through moral behavior could the United States hope to succeed. Finally, periodicals explored the relationship between religion and education and outlined the nature of this religious education, which included three main components: virtue, reason, and science. Ultimately, Americans turned to periodicals in the belief that they could reach a mass audience. The wide circulation of periodicals in postrevolutionary America offered the public a new venue where ideas could be disseminated and the fate of the United States secured.

Recent scholarship has revealed how influential periodicals became in over the course of the eighteenth century. Charles Hoffer, for example, points out how Americans like Benjamin Franklin and George Whitefield "understood the power of printed words." In particular, periodicals, like newspapers and magazines, "transmitted ideas" that reflected the cultural values of the time. He and others have recognized just how hard printers worked to turn the fledgling periodical industry into a lucrative pursuit, one that had the capability to influence many Americans.[3] The rapid demise of many periodicals suggests that it was a hard course to navigate, but overall, a growing number of printers entered into the business as the century progressed. In the year 1700, not a single newspaper or magazine was published in North America. By 1800, that changed dramatically, with more than 200 periodicals circulating throughout the various states.[4] A surge in reader demand drove this rapidly growing industry. According to one estimate, approximately 15 percent of all adult white males subscribed to some form of periodical by the end of the century, creating a higher per capita readership of periodicals than anywhere else in the Atlantic world.[5]

Individuals also had access to periodicals beyond subscribing to them. Merchants and booksellers occasionally stocked periodicals on their shelves and, in a few cities, newspapers were actually sold on the street. Circulating libraries offered single and bound editions of periodicals to their readers. More commonly, people found access to periodicals through informal exchange and by visiting drinking establishments that stocked them. Those who owned a copy of a newspaper or magazine would often pass it on to another family member or business acquaintance once they were finished with it. Taverns and coffeehouses also provided an opportunity to read the public prints, and owners often advertised that their establishments included not only drinks but also current issues of newspapers and magazines. For example, the owner of the popular City Tavern in Philadelphia announced in 1786 that "Daily and Weekly Papers" would be available for the "perusal of his customers" at the tavern. By the end of the eighteenth century, most Americans living in cities and even those in rural areas would have some sort of access to periodical literature if they so desired.[6]

It was important to reach such a broad audience because eighteenth-century newspapers and magazines claimed to protect freedom and liberty by keeping the public informed and providing them with useful knowledge encompassing a wide range of issues. Dr. David Ramsay, the noted physician and historian from South Carolina, declared in a 1794 oration on the anniversary of the Declaration of Independence that the "freedom of the press" was one of the key ingredients that gave Americans "superiority" over any other European nation.[7] Many recognized the growing access that Americans had to periodical literature. The printers of *The United States Magazine* were explicit in their prospectus regarding their desire to target a broader readership. In their opinion, most people had limited resources and could not afford the kinds of books that filled the libraries of wealthier individuals. Instead, periodicals proved useful by spreading knowledge to all ranks of life. The printers declared that this lack of resources meant that information must "be supplied by some publication that will in itself contain a library, and be the literary coffee-house of public conversation." In their humble estimation, *The United States Magazine* met the challenge by including a variety of articles designed to make one a better citizen, thus appealing to "the honest husbandman, the industrious labourer, and the mechanic." They believed that their magazine substantially improved the lot of these individuals regardless of their background: "It will supply the want of early education, and enable them to speak with great propriety and fluency on any subject." In fact, the opportunities offered by periodicals such as theirs made them "nurseries of genius" for the cultivation of "moderately knowing and instructed persons." In no other medium, claimed the printers, could such a benefit be found.[8]

An essayist in *The Universal Magazine* emphasized these sentiments in his article entitled "On the Advantages of Periodical Publications." According to the author, one of the most compelling reasons for the "general diffusion of knowledge in the present age" was closely connected to the rise of periodical literature: "nothing seems to have been of more importance than the circulation of so many different periodical papers." This author even suggested that putting a "well conducted periodical pamphlet in the way of ingenious youth" would likely contribute to their "great and rapid improvements in the science of life and manners." He argued that periodicals also had the ability to educate the masses: "In the country particularly, how many thousands receive what they read in a periodical publication as oracular decisions, and to whom knowledge of social or moral duty could not otherwise be communicated, as they too often neglect other means of instruction." Thus the main object of these periodicals was to "illuminate and reform." The essayist then concluded that newspapers and magazines had been quite successful in this endeavor:

> They commonly tend to convey instruction, and to generalize knowledge. By giving intelligence from every quarter of the globe they excite enquiries; by displaying good and bad qualities of other nations, they remove ill founded prejudices. . . . They communicate beneficial discoveries which would otherwise be lost; they record transactions which engage admiration, or rivet disgust; they warn by example, and instruct by censure. They diffuse taste; they correct prevailing absurdities.[9]

For this author, periodicals had become one means of achieving the ideals of the republic by reaching and transforming thousands of Americans into better citizens.[10]

After the American Revolution, periodicals took on an added significance in preserving the new republic. How exactly was the new nation to survive? And how did religion figure into the equation? Periodicals answered these questions by emphasizing three key themes to periodical readers. The first theme stressed the connection between education and a successful citizenry. Without exception, every writer in the periodicals declared that the survival of the state was predicated on an educated citizenry. Because power was dispersed in a republican government, each citizen was expected to live virtuously, and it was through education that virtue was cultivated. For many, failure in education literally spelled the demise of the new nation.[11] One writer in the *Boston Magazine* emphasized this point by arguing how "highly important" it was "that each individual be enabled to judge of those things which concern the public good." The only way this could be achieved was through "the knowledge of letters" which was so "necessary to preserve their freedom."[12] The need for an education applied to people of all ranks, not just a select wealthy few. In fact, it was necessary to crusade against the ignorance prevalent in the lower orders. One Philadelphia resident declared in *The American Museum, or Universal Magazine* that "in short, when the common people are ignorant and vicious, a nation, and, above all, a republican nation, can never be long free and happy."[13]

An essay in *The Universal Asylum and Columbian Magazine* went so far as to call for a public tax to ensure the educational future of America. "Education should not be left to the caprice, or negligence of parents, to chance, or confined to the children of wealthy citizens," the author declared. Rather, the future of the nation depended upon government securing an education "to every class of citizen, to every child in the state." In fact, one of the primary duties of government was to enact legislation mandating the establishment of public schools. By his calculations, a "land tax of three pence or four pence on every acre would be sufficient to defray all the expenses of such an establishment."[14] Perhaps the author, "Alfred," best summed up this connection between education and society in a 1797 article published in *The South Carolina Weekly Museum*. There he warned of dire social and political consequences facing Americans:

Ignorance is the parent of every national evil, it is the means by which every tyrant, since the earliest date of history, has mounted the throne of power, and bore down the necks of his subjects with the galling yoke of slavery and oppression. It has also been the bane of republics, both ancient and modern. It attacks the very vitals of government, and unless suddenly and vigorously arrested in its devouring progressing, never fails of producing entire destruction: Nothing can escape its contaminating influence—it saps the foundation of people's power, and makes the strong pillars of the monarch's throne to totter.[15]

Education, therefore, was literally the foundation of a free government; without it, a free citizenry would collapse.

A growing number of writers emphasized the need to incorporate females into the educational processes. One commonality that most authors shared was their despair over the general malaise of female education in America. Historians such as Mary Beth Norton and Linda Kerber have emphasized how the issue of educational reforms for women had become an integral part of American society after the American Revolution. The necessity of having an intellectually competent mother raising virtuous republican children necessitated an overhaul in the traditional constraints that had been placed upon female education. Because education began at home with the mother, it was essential that women be prepared for this enormous responsibility.[16] As teachers of virtue, it became necessary for women to receive a greater education, even at the public's expense. Periodicals contributed significantly toward defining the contours of "Republican Motherhood." As "The Dreamer" professed in *The Massachusetts Magazine*, "Are our sons alone worthy of care, and our female offspring meriting of total neglect? . . . ought not these mothers to receive in early life, such instruction as may be profitable to their children?"[17] The political climate of the late eighteenth century mandated that female education be expanded to provide women with the proper training for virtuous mothers and wives. By breaking away from the educational restraints of the past, female intellectual capacities would be expanded instead of restricted. "Women," announced one essayist in the magazine *The Nightingale*, "[are] no longer condemned to the narrow sphere of domestic drudgery—no longer confined in the contracted circle of housewifely and culinary sciences." Rather, because of the new educational opportunities afforded to women, a female now could assume "her proper station in society." With such profound changes, the future of America could only be bright: "Happy America, where the wives and mothers, are instructors and exemplars of Wisdom and Virtue."[18] This author and others believed that through the achievement of academic success, women would become guardians of virtue and morality, thus ensuring them a crucial civic duty in the new republic.

Moral formation was the second key message emphasized to periodical readers. Because humans were not born with virtue, it had to be taught. Periodicals proved useful because they outlined for the public the connection between virtue and good citizenship. In *The South Carolina Weekly Museum*, one essayist expounded upon the need to educate children in virtue: "Under the direction of an able and faithful instructor, the first motions of vice and extravagance are checked and discounted," he contended. While discouraging immoral behavior, education would also introduce "noble pursuits and worthy motives" to the untrained mind, as well as foster "efforts of genius and virtue."[19] In *The Massachusetts Magazine*, the "Friend of Liberty" pointed out the moral implications of a proper education:

> A RIGHT education of children has [always] been esteemed by the best philosophers and wisest legislatures, as the most certain source of happiness, not only to families, but to states and kingdoms; and is, on all moral and civil considerations, the first blessing in order and necessity, the highest in value and importance, and, in these united republics, the grand basis on which their future happiness and prosperity depend.[20]

The conflation of morality and national progress became one of the major cornerstones of the educational process. In fact, the future of the nation depended upon the inculcation of virtuous principles in the younger generation.

All agreed that education was crucial to the survival of the United States, but what was the foundation of that education? The answer was religion. The third key theme found in periodicals is the religious nature of American education. The religious education espoused in newspapers and magazines was a very practical education, one reflecting the influence of the Enlightenment. The religious content of periodicals was clearly informed by the principles of rational Christianity, or what Henry May terms the "Moderate Enlightenment."[21] Influenced by such thinkers as Locke, Newton, and the Scottish "common sense" philosophers, colonial elites reconciled new scientific thinking with religion. Periodical authors argued that science and religion complemented each other, and the use of one's rational faculties buttressed faith in a benevolent God. For most periodical authors, the combination of reason and revelation provided the basis of a stable society, resulting in balance, harmony, and order.

Numerous articles and essays addressed the pragmatic direction that religious education should take. *The Pennsylvania Magazine or American Monthly Museum* published "A New Plan of Education," which argued that the successful future of America rested upon training its children properly. "Many schemes have been formed by ingenious men for this purpose," the author declared, but his personal solution lay in a curriculum "by which science and morality are planted in the youthful mind." The same magazine also published "A Series of Letters on Education" which explored the concept of youthful education in greater depth, this time focusing on the religious dimensions of a proper education. The anonymous contributor of these letters encouraged both husbands and wives "to conspire and co-operate in every thing relating to the education of their children." When training their children, parents should "be purified by the principles, and controuled or directed by the precepts, of religion." A religious education could be valued as "profitable" for a child, concluded the author, since religion was "a venerable thing in itself, and it spreads an air of dignity over [a] person's whole deportment." Most importantly, "the real dignity of religion" lies in its ability to create an "excellence" of character where individuals choose a life of virtue rather than that of "dissolution."

Writers insisted that, because of the virtue it instilled, religious education must begin at an early stage. One author in *The Independent Chronicle and Universal Advertiser* proclaimed that an early education was absolutely necessary "towards laying a foundation of religion, which dignifies the man, and crowns him with glory, honor, and immortality."[22] Over and over again, authors emphasized how the combination of religion and education was the key ingredient in developing a virtuous citizenry. "But there is one point in the article of education, which is more essential than any of the rest," concluded an essayist in *The Boston Gazette and Weekly Republican Journal*: all learning should be based upon the "principles of religion" because they taught children "virtue, and a sense of their duty to God."[23]

Several authors emphasized the innate religious character of females. One declared that women had "a much clearer notion of their religious duties" given their spiritual strength. The author urged that religious education be an integral part of female schooling because their "natural" disposition made them better students of it.[24] An essay published in *The Massachusetts Magazine* by a female student lauded the religious dimensions of an education for women. A female education, she wrote, was "conducive to piety," which consequently led to greater morality and happiness. Religious education created a cultivated female mind allowing her to see "a thousand instances of perfection of the Deity, which would be unobserved or unnoticed by an uncultivated mind." She insisted that an education would "fill our souls with reverence and awe for that all powerful Being" and would help those instructed "see such innumerable instances of his holiness, justice, wonderous mercy and transcendent love." Armed with this knowledge, women would thus become active soldiers for God and transform the nation into one of love and virtue. From this viewpoint, a female education had truly revolutionary consequences for American society.[25]

Periodicals also educated its readers about the principles of religious toleration. The basic argument for religious toleration suggested that tolerance bred stability within the community. These authors contended that all religions emphasized positive behavior and were the foundations of a moral, stable society; thus, readers learned that religious intolerance prevented the realization of a greater good. In an article written by the author "A.Z.," religion was declared to be a matter of personal choice, and no civil law should interfere with "the concern of a man individually." A person "ought to have a free choice" to pursue the path he believes will procure for him "celestial felicity." In addition, no "enlightened" state had the right to dictate one's personal conscience, even if that meant practicing a non-Christian faith. The author "J. F." concurred, suggesting in the *Massachusetts Magazine* that all individuals have the right to determine their own religious course. After all, he argued, "the object of all publick worship is the same, it is that great eternal Being who created every thing. The different manners of worship are by no means subjects of ridicule; each thinks his own the best." In fact, no standard existed with which to measure the accuracy of religion, for "every man seeks for truth, but God only knows who has found it." At worst, he argued, "extreme religious viewpoints should be pitied rather than punished or ridiculed."[26] One enterprising essayist suggested that Jesus Christ himself tacitly demanded toleration and accommodation by his disciples. To go against this dictate interfered with God's own designs: "Genuine religion is a concern, that lies entirely between God and our own souls," he theorized.[27]

Regardless of the religion or denomination, religious practice had the salutary effect of creating a moral society. Beginning in October 1789, *The Gentlemen and Ladies Town and Country Magazine* published "The Friar's Tale," a story describing the trials and tribulations of Albert and Matilda. Throughout their adventures, they encountered various religious figures, some adhering to the "true" tenets of Christianity, others mocking its practice. The moral of the story suggested that true religion transcended any particular denominational belief. Indeed, religious practice called for moral reformation and a universal love of humanity. "True religion," concluded the main character of the story, "howsoever it may vary in outward ceremonies or articles of faith, will always teach you to do good, to love and help each other."[28] The foundation of morality was a love and respect of all people, or as one essayist quoted from the Bible, "Whatsoever you would that Men should do to you, do ye even so to them." Virtuous behavior embodied actions that contributed towards these goals. Benevolence, forgiveness, compassion, generosity, and toleration encompassed what "Philanthropist" called "propriety of conduct." Through "right action," individuals can "mend the morals of others" and help "regulate the world."[29]

Periodicals also educated readers that reason and science were crucial components of religious understanding. A number of articles stressed reason as the basis for decision making in religious and moral formation. Most writers uniformly described a rational God whose universe ran according to just and reasonable notions. In arguments expressing deistic thought, writers declared that God had given man the ability to rationally solve many of his own problems. An essayist encapsulated this thought in his article published in *The Columbian Magazine*, where he tentatively offered a definition of the "law of religion." According to his theory, religion was not simply comprised of profound revelations from God. Instead, religion worked in logical ways, and through the use of reason an individual could actually figure out the "religious laws" as created by God. The author defined the laws of religion as those "impressed on a man's heart, as a guide to his actions." To further hone his definition, he quoted from an Anglican bishop, who defined religious law as "that which man might know and should be obliged unto by mere principle of reason, without the help of revelation."[30]

The application of rational religion implied that individuals had the ability to make the world a much better place, given the abilities with which they were provided at birth. The "Philanthropist," a columnist in the *Massachusetts Magazine*, criticized the Calvinist interpretation of Christianity. He railed that so many people had focused upon the sinful nature of humanity and the concomitant problems faced throughout history. The problem with this, advised the Philanthropist, was that humans had forgotten that "God created man in his own image." By striving to improve themselves, humans could possibly return to the time when they were "pure and uncorrupt." To behave in the manner God intended for them, it was their duty and responsibility to exercise those gifts God had provided. Philanthropist declared that "reason" was the foundation of man's ability to perfect himself: It was man's rational capacity that "connects him with higher orders of beings in the intellectual world" and pushes him to achieve "the things that are excellent," including the "exercises of piety and the practice of virtue."[31]

The use of reason contributed more than virtue; it also helped to explain God's universe. The greatest application of human reason was to the growing field of scientific research and its connection with religion. Science was touted as God's special gift to humanity. With it, the mysteries of God's creation could be unveiled. Even human behavior could be analyzed and explained, leading authors to speculate over how best to create a stable society.[32] Science, thus, became an integral part of the public's religious education. The combination of religion and science was far from antithetical; instead, both represented intrinsic pieces of the puzzle of God's universe. In many ways, the study of science was a religious pursuit. As one writer in the *Boston Magazine* concluded: "It is a pleasing idea, that science will beam forth with increasing lustre until the revolutions of nature are ended, and the glories of the celestial realms are laid open to our ravished spirits."[33]

If science contributed to religious formation, then it was necessary to educate the public on basic scientific principles. A variety of articles informed readers about the various scientific explanations of the universe.

Periodicals proved invaluable in conveying this new scientific thought because, as one author in *The Pennsylvania Magazine* pointed out, "the bulk of mankind have neither leisure nor opportunity to apply to books of science for information." Instead, newspapers and magazines provided "a means of conveying some degree of philosophical truth to those who would never look for it in any other place."[34] Periodicals thus facilitated a close connection between science and Christianity. When applied to religion, science had the potential to dispel any false notions about the Christian faith. Advocates of this new "scientific" religion soundly criticized superstitions because they shrouded the true nature of religion. The author "Eugenio" echoed these sentiments when he exclaimed in *The Boston Magazine*: "Knowledge humanizes the mind—Reason inclines to mildness. . . . No longer does superstition debar us from the enjoyment of rational delights. . . ." Instead, Eugenio claimed that "The beatific influences of science have enlarged our views—inspired us with liberal sentiments—and taught us to imitate the great exemplar of human conduct. In short, USEFUL KNOWLEDGE now forms the soul."[35] While praising the merits of rational Christianity, the "Moralist" from *The Nightingale* denounced the adulterating nature of superstition within religious belief: "In a word, superstition fetters the understanding, depresses the spirits, embitters the temper, disturbs the passions, and spoils the manners."[36]

The author "Zara" best summed up in *The Massachusetts Magazine* the dual role of religious education in both secular and spiritual terms:

> certainly, every church and religious assembly, with an able teacher at its head, must be acknowledged and prized as a most important school, in a political view to fit men to be useful members of society on earth, and in a religious view, to complete their education for the refined employments and intercourses of heaven.[37]

The knowledge thus learned from religious studies could be practically applied to daily living, truly making one a "useful member" of society. An article by one Dr. Price offered similar thoughts regarding the transformation of religious thought and practice over the course of the eighteenth century. In 1789, he published an essay discussing the nature of religion in *The American Museum, or Universal Magazine*. According to Price:

> It is indeed only a rational and liberal religion—a religion, founded on just notions of the Deity, as a being who regards equally every sincere worshipper . . . a religion which consists in the imitation of the moral perfections of an almighty but benevolent governor of nature, who directs for the best, all events . . . it is only this kind of religion that can bless the world, or be an advantage to society. This is the religion that every enlightened friend to mankind will be zealous to promote.[38]

Overall, periodicals served many useful functions to Americans in the eighteenth century. This chapter has explored how newspapers and magazines created a forum where religion and education could be discussed, and how authors of these periodicals believed that the fate of the United States depended on the nation's ability to create a virtuous citizenry. Periodicals were crucial in conveying this valuable information to a public that had limited access to learning. While we know much about the attitudes of famous eighteenth-century Americans like Washington, Adams, and Jefferson, our understanding of what an "average" American believed is still lacking and often difficult to discern. Periodicals help to uncover the values that circulated among the middling ranks of American society, and the content conveyed in newspapers and magazines are crucial to understanding how Americans connected religious behavior to the future success of the United States.

An essayist from the *Nightingale* eloquently articulated the transformative powers of American periodicals when he declared in 1796: "Among the various means of promoting useful knowledge, a periodical paper is not the most inconsiderable. Such a paper, well executed, would greatly contribute to refine the taste, correct the manners, and improve the virtue of the people among whom it circulates."

All sorts of people would contribute to periodicals, ranging from the "gentlemen of education and leisure" to those of "common understanding and education," combining to make periodicals a paragon of knowledge.[39] It is clear that in looking back at eighteenth-century America, periodicals did indeed contribute significantly to the intellectual and educational formation of the American republic. A contributor in *The Philadelphia Monthly Magazine* argued such when he opined that periodicals "effect the most proper means that ever yet have been contrived for raising human nature to its highest degree of exaltation." In fact, he concluded, the success of a nation is in large part tied to its development of the periodical press: "we shall in general find, that the progress of nations in knowledge . . . will keep pace with the number of periodical publications allowed to circulate."[40] This author, and others like him, believed that periodical print had the power to alter the course of the nation through the material published on its pages; by the end of the eighteenth century, many had come to view periodicals as indispensable to the survival of the new nation.

REFERENCES

The American Museum or Universal Magazine, April 1787.
———, December 1789.
The American Universal Magazine, January 2, 1797.
———, January 9, 1797.

———, April 3, 1797.

———, July 24, 1797.

———, September 4, 1797.

The Boston Gazette and Republican Weekly Journal, September 25, 1797.

Boston Magazine, January 1784.

———, February 1784.

———, March 1784.

———, June 1784.

———, February 1785.

———, July 1785.

Brown, Richard. *The Strength of a People: The Idea of an Informed Citizenry in America, 1650–1870.* Chapel Hill, NC: University of North Carolina Press, 1996.

Clark, Charles. *The Public Prints.* New York: Oxford University Press, 1994.

Cohen, I. Bernard. *Science and the Founding Fathers: Science in the Political Thought of Jefferson, Franklin, Adams, and Madison.* New York: Norton, 1995.

Columbian Magazine, May 1787.

Gaustad, Edwin S. *Faith of Our Fathers: Religion and the New Nation.* San Francisco: Harper and Row, 1987.

The Gentlemen and Ladies Town and Country Magazine, December 1789.

Hall, David. *Cultures of Print: Essays in the History of the Book.* Amherst, MA: University of Massachusetts Press, 1996.

Heyerman, Christine. *Southern Cross.* New York: Knopf, 1997.

Hoffer, Peter. *When Benjamin Franklin Met the Reverend Whitefield: Enlightenment, Revival, and the Power of the Printed Word.* Baltimore: Johns Hopkins University Press, 2011.

The Independent Chronicle and Universal Advertiser, January 26, 1795.

Kerber, Linda. *Women of the Republic.* Chapel Hill, NC: University of North Carolina Press, 1980.

The Ladies Magazine, October 1792.

———, February 1793.

Lambert, Frank. *Inventing the "Great Awakening."* Princeton, NJ: Princeton University Press, 1999.

Massachusetts Magazine, January 1789.

———, February 1789.

———, May 1789.

———, "Letter from The Dreamer." June 1789.

———, October 1789.

May, Henry. *The Enlightenment in America.* New York: Oxford University Press, 1976.

The Nightingale, July 7, 1796.

———, July 16, 1796.

Norton, Mary Beth. *Liberty's Daughters.* Boston: Little, Brown, 1980.

Pacholl, Keith. "American Access to Periodical Literature in the Eighteenth Century." *The International Journal of the Book,* 4 (2007).

The Pennsylvania Magazine, or American Monthly Museum. August 1775 edition.

———, November 1775.

The Philadelphia Magazine and Review, January 1799.

———, February 1799.

The Philadelphia Minerva, August 27, 1796.

———, October 8, 1796.

———, November 26, 1796.

———, November 28, 1795.

The Philadelphia Monthly Magazine, January 1798.

———, February 1798.

Philoctetes. "Letter from a Reader." *The Dessert to the True American,* April 6, 1799.

Purvis, Thomas. *Revolutionary America, 1763-1800.* New York: Facts on File, 1995.

Ramsay, David. *The American Monthly Review,* 1794, volume 3.

Remer, Rosalind. *Printers and Men of Capital: Philadelphia Book Publishers in the New Republic*. Philadelphia: University of Pennsylvania Press, 1996.

The Royal American Magazine, January 1774.

The South Carolina Weekly Museum, March 4, 1797.

———, March 11, 1797.

———, "Letter from Alfred." April 1, 1797.

———, May 13, 1797.

The State Gazette of South Carolina, March 2, 1789.

The United States Magazine, January 1779.

The Universal Asylum and Columbian Magazine, February 1791.

The Universal Magazine. "On the Advantages of Periodical Publications." January 2, 1797.

Warner, Michael. *The Letters of the Republic*. Cambridge, MA: Harvard University Press, 1990.

Ziff, Larzer. *Writing in the New Nation: Prose, Print, and Politics in the Early United States*. New Haven, CT: Yale University Press, 1991.

NOTES

1. *The Dessert to the True American*, April 6, 1799.
2. This chapter focuses on periodicals published in Boston, Philadelphia, and Charleston, since they were the major publishing centers in their respective regions in the late eighteenth century. I would like to thank Gordon Bakken, Brenda Farrington, Steven Gable, and Dan Williams for reviewing this chapter and offering constructive comments. This chapter has greatly benefitted from their insights and suggestions.
3. Peter Hoffer, *When Benjamin Franklin Met the Reverend Whitefield: Enlightenment, Revival, and the Power of the Printed Word* (Baltimore: Johns Hopkins University Press, 2011), 5–6. The literature regarding the power of the printed word and the influence of eighteenth-century periodicals is vast. Some of the key works include Richard Brown, *The Strength of a People: The Idea of an Informed Citizenry in America, 1650–1870* (Chapel Hill, NC: University of North Carolina Press, 1996); Charles Clark, *The Public Prints* (New York: Oxford University Press, 1994), 249–251; Michael Warner, *The Letters of the Republic* (Cambridge, MA: Harvard University Press, 1990); Frank Lambert, *Inventing the "Great Awakening"* (Princeton, NJ: Princeton University Press, 1999); David Hall, *Cultures of Print: Essays in the History of the Book* (Amherst, MA: University of Massachusetts Press, 1996); Rosalind Remer, *Printers and Men of Capital: Philadelphia Book Publishers in the New Republic*. Philadelphia: University of Pennsylvania Press, 1996); and Larzer Ziff, *Writing in the New Nation: Prose, Print, and Politics in the Early United States* (New Haven, CT: Yale University Press, 1991).
4. Keith Pacholl, "American Access to Periodical Literature in the Eighteenth Century," *The International Journal of the Book* 4 (2007), 1–2.
5. Thomas Purvis, *Revolutionary America 1763–1800* (New York: Facts on File, 1995), 277.
6. Pacholl, "American Access to Periodical Literature." City Tavern quote from page 3.
7. David Ramsay, *The American Monthly Review*, 1794, Appendix, volume 3.
8. *The United States Magazine*, January 1779, 9–11.
9. *The Universal Magazine*, January 2, 1797, 9–10.
10. The Querist of *The Pennsylvania Magazine, or American Monthly Museum* declared much of the same in the August 1775 edition of that magazine, 353: "Very few of us are possessed of libraries—and if we were, we could not spare time to search the voluminous works of the learned. . . . We shall, therefore, consider your Magazine as our oracle, and apply to it, as occasion may offer, for instruction and information."
11. For an expanded treatment on the interaction between knowledge and republicanism, see Brown, *The Strength of a People*. This chapter is indebted to the overall insights offered in Brown's book.

12. *Boston Magazine*, March 1784, 176–177, and June 1784, 318.
13. *The American Museum, or Universal Magazine*, April 1787, 326–329.
14. *The Universal Asylum and Columbian Magazine*, February 1791, 110–112.
15. *The South Carolina Weekly Museum*, April 1, 1797, 431.
16. *See* Mary Beth Norton, *Liberty's Daughters* (Boston: Little, Brown, 1980), chapter 9; and Linda Kerber, *Women of the Republic* (Chapel Hill, NC: University of North Carolina Press, 1980), chapter 7, for an examination of the overall change to female education in America after the American Revolution.
17. *The Massachusetts Magazine,* June 1789, 370–373.
18. *The Nightingale*, July 7, 1796, 300–301.
19. *The South Carolina and Weekly Museum*, March 11, 1797, 302–303. See also *The South Carolina and Weekly Museum*, April 1, 1797, 430–432. *American Universal Magazine*, July 24, 1797, 116–118.
20. *The Massachusetts Magazine*, June 1789, 381. For similar types of sentiments, see *The State Gazette of South Carolina*, March 2, 1789.
21. Henry May, *The Enlightenment in America* (New York: Oxford University Press, 1976). May offers a concise view of the variations of "Enlightenment" thinking, pointing out that it is inaccurate to assume the Enlightenment meant the same to all people. Instead, different gradations of enlightenment thought existed throughout the eighteenth century, ranging from the moderate applications of Locke and Newton, to the radical skepticism of Voltaire and Paine. The arguments found in late-eighteenth-century periodicals reflect the ideas found in May's book, particularly the first section on the "Moderate Enlightenment," I would question his chronology for the demise of the moderate enlightenment, which May suggests subsided by the time of the American Revolution. My research suggests that this thinking was alive and well in magazines throughout the 1790s (see pages 3–101, 307–357). To see how rational Christianity affected public figures, see Edwin Gaustad's religious biography on Thomas Jefferson: *Sworn On the Altar of God* (Grand Rapids, MI: William B. Eerdman, 1996).
22. *The Independent Chronicle and Universal Advertiser*, January 26, 1795.
23. *The Boston Gazette and Republican Weekly Journal*, September 25, 1797.
24. *The Philadelphia Minerva*, November 26, 1796.
25. *The Massachusetts Magazine*, January 1789, 28–29.
26. *Columbian Magazine*, May 1787, 402; *Massachusetts Magazine*, May 1789, 283. For a sampling of other articles arguing the same, see *The Ladies Magazine*, February 1793, 152; *Massachusetts Magazine*, February 1789, 77–78; *Boston Magazine*, January 1784, 92–95, February 1784, 149–152, March 1784, 175–176; *The American Universal Magazine*, April 3, 1797, 41–42; *The Philadelphia Minerva*, November 28, 1795.
Even Catholicism received support from several of the more liberal contributors. According to these writers, a greater openness toward Catholicism must be realized if universal toleration was to be successful. This interest in Catholicism by no means suggested an interest in wholesale conversion. Rather, after years of bitter dispute, periodical authors believed that stability of the new nations depended on an accommodation with all religious beliefs, even those that had generated tremendous controversy. For examples of positive discussions on Catholicism, see *South Carolina Weekly Museum*, March 4, 1797, 314–315; *The Philadelphia Magazine and Review*, February 1799, 120; *The Philadelphia Minerva*, October 8, 1796; *The American Universal Magazine*, September 4, 1797, 342–344; *The Nightingale*, July 16, 1796, 357. See also *The Ladies Magazine*, October 1792, 237.
Ironically, the one group that seemed to be left out of the equation were evangelicals, whose perceived radicalism and extremism seemed to upset the balance of personal choice, particularly with their charges against the "unconverted ministry." According to these critics, in an age of reason, evangelical culture and its anti-intellectual trends had a limited place in the new nation. See Christine Heyerman, *Southern Cross* (New York: Knopf, 1997) on the various ways evangelical culture was deemed "aberrant" during the eighteenth century.
27. *American Museum, or Universal Magazine*, December 1789, 446–447.
28. *The Gentlemen and Ladies Town and Country Magazine*, December 1789, 641. See also *The American Universal Magazine*, January 2, 1797, 12–13.

29. *The Royal American Magazine*, January 1774, 7; *Massachusetts Magazine*, October 1789, 609–610; see also the essay by "Moralis" on virtue in the same edition, 601–602. For other discussions of virtuous attributes, see *South Carolina and Weekly Museum*, May 13, 1797, 591–593; *The Philadelphia Minerva*, August 27, 1796.

30. *Columbian Magazine*, May 1787, 405.

31. *Massachusetts Magazine*, June 1789, 337–338.

32. *See* I. Bernard Cohen, *Science and the Founding Fathers: Science in the Political Thought of Jefferson, Franklin, Adams, and Madison* (New York: Norton, 1995), for an example of how individuals like Jefferson, Franklin, and Adams applied scientific principles to guide social and cultural behavior.

33. *Boston Magazine*, June 1784, 226. See also *The Pennsylvania Magazine and Review*, January 1799, 7–9; *Boston Magazine*, July 1785, 261–262; *The American Universal Magazine*, January 9, 1797, 54–57, for similar types of arguments.

34. *The Pennsylvania Magazine*, November 1775, 503.

35. *The Boston Magazine*, February 1785, 56–57.

36. *The Nightingale*, 4 June 1796, 135.

37. *The Massachusetts Magazine*, January 1790, 23.

38. *American Museum, or Universal Magazine*, December 1789, 447.

39. *The Nightingale*, July 16, 1796, 349–352.

40. *The Philadelphia Monthly Magazine*, January 1798, 21–23, and February 1798, 71–74.

Chapter Ten

Fighting over the Founders: Reflections on the Historiography of the Founders' Faiths

Matt McCook

Arguments over America's "Founding Fathers," their views on religion and the role of religion in the public and political sphere are as old as the United States itself. One might think that an argument this old would have run its course or at least lost the public's interest. However, even a cursory search for titles on "church and state in America" or the various "faiths of the Founding Fathers" reveals that the opposite is true. Recent decades have shown a dramatic increase in such publications and, since 2002, a virtual onslaught. Historians and activists from both sides of the political spectrum have weighed in, often with disappointing results. Conservatives railing against the left and devoted secularists decrying the religious right carefully select their evidence or favorite founders to support their case. On the surface, disparity in their conclusions suggests that no interpreters of America's founding religious principles (or lack thereof) can see beyond their own biases. Yet a closer analysis of recent historiography restores history's trust and credibility, thanks to the work of scholars who, although they do not always agree, have shed light on the complexities of religion's role in the personal and public lives of America's founding generation.

As America's founders were varied, so too are those who have interpreted them. Interpretive and quality differences make classification more difficult than one might imagine. Whereas much of the argument centers on binary values—the influence of Protestant Christian thought and the Enlightenment, the original intent of strict separation versus accommodation—writers do not divide easily into secularist and Christian camps, or the friends and enemies of church–state separation. Personal religious views are not always manifest

159

in one's scholarship and I have not attempted to uncover each author's beliefs, although a few state them explicitly. Certainly there are Christians who favor church–state separation and secularists who recognize the influence of religion in the founding generation.

It is useful, then, to think of writers as falling into one of four groups. The first two are polemicists, who ardently champion a secularist or Christian perspective. The others are more exemplary scholars whose arguments, whether for strict separation or a government more friendly to religion, are less like a call to arms. Based on the most recent scholarship, the following presentation will describe and analyze these groups, their methodologies, and—by way of example—their treatments of a few of America's founders.

First, however, it is important to point out the common inspiration that has caused this scholarly outpouring, the culture wars of the late-twentieth and early-twenty-first centuries. The timing of so many publications makes this fairly obvious; authors in all camps confirm the suspicion. In 1987, popular Christian author and activist Tim LaHaye attacked the American Civil Liberties Union (ACLU) and liberal historians as secular humanists for the "deliberate rape of history" in his *Faith of Our Founding Fathers.*[1] In her book *The Moral Minority: Our Skeptical Founding Fathers*, Brooke Allen suggests that America's tolerably balanced civil religion crossed the line in the Reagan era when the president declared 1983 "the Year of the Bible."[2] Her work was inspired by President George W. Bush, who claimed a Judeo–Christian basis for American heritage, an assertion Allen set out to deny.[3] A pair of respected academic historians, Isaac Kramnick and R. Laurence Moore, admit that culture wars, or rather the religious right, inspired their work, entitled *The Godless Constitution.*[4] As they analyze the founders' intentional and wise silence on religion in the Constitution, they criticize culture warriors Pat Robertson, Pat Buchanan, and Ralph Reed and defend Bill Clinton, likening religious criticism of him to that of the "infidel" Thomas Jefferson.[5] More recent works often cite 9/11 or its immediate aftermath as their reason for exploring the roots of America's unique religious and political heritage.[6] Stephen Mansfield suggests that a religious awakening since 9/11 forces a reexamination of religion's role in public life.[7] Scholars from the more moderate camps attribute their work to culture wars subtly; they write primarily to clarify distortions perpetrated by extremists. And there seems to be no shortage of distortions that must be corrected. Interestingly, both sides write as if the deck were stacked against them. Thus authors share not only an inspiration from culture war politics but also a sense of urgency and victimization.

Such feelings are most apparent among the first group to be analyzed: Christian polemicists. This group comprises Christian authors, philosophers, and activists, often with ministry backgrounds, who write primarily for a Christian audience. Among them are David Barton, John Eidsmoe, Tim La-

Haye, Stephen Mansfield, Michael Novak, and a number of others. Although some of them have written insightful and thought-provoking histories, this group is generally characterized by skepticism toward professional, academic historians and, in some cases, a misunderstanding of the discipline itself. Tim LaHaye most vociferously attacks history "experts" and their rewriting of history, claiming that liberal foundations funded these "left wing scholars for hire."[8] Ironically, after urging his readers to avoid history written in the last fifty years, he cites mainly secondary sources of recent origin. David Barton is a prolific author, lecturer, and founder of WallBuilders, "a national pro-family organization that presents America's forgotten history and heroes, with an emphasis on our moral, religious, and constitutional heritage."[9] He frequently suggests that America's Christian heritage was widely taught in schools and known nationwide until revisionist historians distorted the past with untruths, omissions, and psychobabble.[10] He shares documents and other evidences of America's Christian heritage that have supposedly been suppressed by historians. Brion McClanahan echoes this conspiracy theory in *The Politically Incorrect Guide to the Founding Fathers*. He asserts that the founders have been minimized by modern education standards and frequently mentions "books they don't want you to read."[11] Michael Novak similarly expresses dismay that the "guardians" of national memory have too little interest in religion and have willfully ignored the overwhelming evidence that religion played a major role in the individual and collective work of the founders.[12]

Favorite evidentiary sources among these writers are the words of the founders. This in itself represents no deviation from professional standards, but more than any other group of writers, the Christian polemicists assume that the founders' words and historical "facts" speak for themselves. For example, Glen Gorton insists that in his work "our founders are not interpreted, nor are their opinions subjected to any creative exposition." They are simply "given the floor to speak as they please."[13] Gorton says nothing about the selectivity or contextualization of quotes while he has eighteenth-century gentlemen speak to a host of turn-of-the-twenty-first-century hot-button political topics, including patriotism, gun control, welfare, federal power, and religion. Before criticizing the interpretive and speculative nature of history, Gorton proclaims the U.S. Constitution the greatest political document from the greatest assembly in world history as if this were undeniable fact.[14] Christian polemicists thus often see historical sources as many Protestants see Scripture—as something that can be taken at face value without interpretation or help from source specialists.

Quite often, history writers deal with the unhistorical as they speculate on how the founders would respond to modern issues. This exercise in imagination is so reminiscent of the popular question "What would Jesus do?" that some Christian polemicists find it irresistible to apply to George Washington and company. Again, Glen Gorton's *What Would They Say* uses the Founders' quotes to address modern political issues. Brion McClanahan is more explicit and politically assertive in arguing what the Founders would do. They would cut spending and taxes, reduce the debt and military, limit immigration, restore federalism, and protect the Constitution.[15]

The most unique characteristic of this group's writing, absent from all others, is closing with a call to action. Joseph Kulbacki urges readers to pray for America.[16] LaHaye adds to this simple request registering, voting, and recruiting other political activists.[17] John Eidsmoe, whose work is well researched and balanced enough to be associated with the more scholarly group, also ends with the admonition for Christians to get involved, because "America's legal and political system needs a massive transfusion of Christian blood."[18] David Barton's lectures, books, and videos typically end in the same way, with the equivalent of a religious activist altar call. Like a preacher's sermon that moves from biblical text to theological principle to practical application, these writers often move from documents to historical truths to ways in which their audience can set the record and culture straight.

The barrage of literature produced by political conservatives and evangelical Christians who argue that the Founders were generally Christians and that we have taken church–state separation too far has inspired more than a few liberal Christians, secularists, and scholars to retort in equally controversialist ways. Among scholars, Isaac Kramnick and R. Laurence Moore stand out in this group. They admit to writing a polemic for a godless constitution and godless politics.[19] While emphasizing God's absence in the Constitution, they fail to recognize James Madison's acknowledgment of God in the *Federalist Papers*. They also underestimate the percentage of churchgoers, because they fail to account for strict membership requirements, thus making the United States appear more secular than it was.[20] Among lay historians in this group are Brooke Allen and Gary Kowalski. Even famed atheist and evolutionary biologist Richard Dawkins joins their ranks, with a few historical comments in his *The God Delusion*. He is not too purely historical to ask "What would the founders do?" He just arrives at different conclusions than do Christian polemicists; he declares that if the greatest founders of the United States were not atheists in their day, they certainly would be in ours, and they would be horrified by today's political climate.[21] Kowalski asserts that the founders were unbelievers in a sense because, as children of the Enlightenment, they questioned orthodox views, with no use for traditional creeds.[22] Never mind that the founders on whom he focuses all came from the most traditional Protestant groups. Kowalski is certainly a better historian than Dawkins, but his shortage of citations fails to meet professional standards. Allen portrays the founders in the image of her father, whom she describes as a skeptic and freethinker.[23] Personal backgrounds and political and religious views influence these writers no less than they do the Christian polemicists.

Writers within this group have a limited definition of *Founding Fathers*. Technically, the list could include signers of the Declaration of Independence and the Constitution, members of the Continental and First Congress, and other principal state leaders, a list that would include some two or three hundred men. Brooke Allen's *Moral Minority*, however, includes only Benjamin Franklin, George Washington, John Adams, Thomas Jefferson, James Madison, and Alexander Hamilton. Rather than portraying these men as unique, she uses these "principal" founders as representative of all. Curiously and casually, Allen mentions that these main founders' images, minus Adams and Madison's, dominate our money. It is not clear whether this is meant to justify her selection or to imply that mammon was and is America's god.[24] Kowalski substitutes Thomas Paine, a more acknowledged deist, for Hamilton, but otherwise writes on the same men. This is not uncommon; most works on the founders' religious beliefs concentrate on this same short list, but writers who argue that the founders were Christians are more likely to include a number of "forgotten founders," like John Jay, John Witherspoon, Roger Sherman, Benjamin Rush, Elias Boudinot, Patrick Henry, and Samuel Adams.[25] Secularists and separatists prefer the short list.

Once defined, this group tends to portray the founders in their own image by ignoring or explaining away religiosity. Kowalski depicts the founders as modern multiculturalists, dreaming of a "land where strangers were welcome and differences could thrive," a description that hardly fits the Federalist Era.[26] While describing the founders as good men of science, Kowalski assumes a greater antagonism between it and religion than actually existed and downplays the role of religion in their lives. He mentions Benjamin Rush as a man of modern medicine, not as a Christian activist and president of a Bible society.[27] Similarly, he emphasizes John Adams's rejection of orthodox Calvinism, but says nothing of the influence of Calvinism on Adams's political views or his religious proclamations as president.[28] Brooke Allen minimizes the personal religiosity of most founders, with a skeptical interpretation of civil religion. She dismisses John Adams's religious pronouncements made while in office, assuming that frank speech comes only after retirement from politics.[29] She places Alexander Hamilton within the tradition of "Bible thumping" to influence opinion, interpreting his support of public religiosity as merely a political strategy.[30] If Christian polemicists have a tendency to take the founders at their word when it comes to religious pronouncements, secularists are too dismissive of anything religious these men ever said.

Allen and Kowalski emphasize the influence of Enlightenment thinking on the founding generation, and Kramnick and Moore focus more on the influence of Roger Williams and the English liberal tradition, but they all agree that America's political and intellectual culture took a turn for the worse, thanks to the rise of evangelicalism in the early nineteenth century. Kramnick and Moore highlight evangelicals' attempts to Christianize politics in ways contrary to the founders' intent.[31] Kowalski holds religious revivals responsible for undermining reason in America.[32] Brooke Allen mentions both rationalism's decline and a breach in the wall of separation. She says the Second Great Awakening brought the Enlightenment to an "abrupt" end, and that religious political activists like Timothy Dwight turned to "fundamentalism," a term used about a century out of place.[33]

The next group of scholars is composed primarily of professional historians and public intellectuals. They are more even-handed than the polemicists and often write as moderators between extreme evangelicals and secularists. They emphasize religious pluralism in the founding era and make clearer that there was not a single, unified faith among the founders. Still, they typically examine only a small number of founders to explore the variety of religious opinions. They are not in complete agreement on how religious the founders were but are held together by their insistence that the separation between church and state has been good for both. Because they all raise valid issues, a brief sketch of the key features of their individual works is provided here.

In 2006, David Holmes published *The Faiths of the Founding Fathers*, a fairly conventional work except for a few unique features. As the title implies, Holmes emphasized the plurality of religious beliefs among the founders and throughout the Colonial Period. He devoted chapters to the usual suspects, but included chapters on James Monroe, the wives and daughters of the founders, and "three orthodox Christians," Samuel Adams, Elias Boudinot, and John Jay. He uses these orthodox Christians and women, however, as a contrast to the founders, whom he generally describes as deists.[34] To make such an assertion, he uses a broad definition of deism that does not disallow church membership, attendance, or belief in sin and life after death.[35] Those who claim the founders as Christians have a much narrower conception of deism that would not include anyone who believed in divine intervention in human affairs. Because Holmes and his book were subjected to a roundtable critique at the 2007 Conference on Christianity and American History hosted by Liberty University, he received plenty of scrutiny from evangelical critics. They challenged his broad definition and argued that abstaining from certain religious rites was no more confirmation of being a deist than church attendance made one orthodox—neither was using certain language to describe God as "the supreme lawgiver" or other terms found also in orthodox creeds.[36] Whether Holmes applied the label *deist* appropriately or if he unfairly attached it to all Unitarians and theologically liberal Christians, his work is a reminder that agreement on definitions for *founders*, *Christians*, and *deists* is necessary if one is to have meaningful debate on the subject of the founders' religious beliefs.

A pair of religious history scholars and a popular contemporary author and editor whose works are separated by two decades tried to moderate between extremists in the culture wars of the 1980s and 2000s. Edwin Gaustad's *Faith of Our Fathers* dismantled the myth that church–state issues were simpler in the early national period. In fact, Gaustad asserts, because they were not as certain of the nation's survival as contemporary Americans are, their questions over the role of religion in the public arena were tougher.[37] After detailing the beliefs of Madison, Washington, Franklin, Adams, and Jefferson twice, Gaustad plays the role of peacemaker, acknowledging that the United States is a very religious nation despite or rather because of its founders' insistence on separating it from government.[38] Frank Lambert, author of *The Founding Fathers and the Place of Religion in America*, also takes a middle position and criticizes secularists and the religious right for their presentist efforts to find a "useable past."[39] Whereas Gaustad devotes one chapter, Lambert uses half of his book to describe church–state relations in the Colonial Period in order to illustrate the Revolutionary generation's abandonment of religious establishments. Certainly one must bear in mind the differences between America's founders and the Puritan founders on church-state issues, groups that Christian polemics too often lump together to claim America as a Christian nation.[40] In his *American Gospel*, Random House editor Jon Meacham also conciliates between cultural combatants. He asserts that America was not established as a Christian nation but that secularists who decry all public expressions of faith go too far and are unrealistic in their expectations. For Meacham, religion has been positive in America's public life. Civil religion is not a substitute for private faith, but neither is it a Trojan horse filled with evangelicals. Therefore extremists should focus on real questions over how much and what kinds of public religious expression is appropriate.[41]

Lest anyone think that this academic debate is neatly divided between Christians and secularists, theologian and minister Forrest Church and founder of Belief.net Steven Waldman have contributed significant counterexamples. While Church and Waldman personally and professional promote faith and spirituality, their works celebrate religious freedom and the separation of church and state. In *So Help Me God*, Church vividly describes battles over church and state through the first five presidents' administrations. He details controversial religious acts by the national government, like the appointment of chaplains, designation of national days for prayer and fasting, and public debates over the religious intentions of candidates John Adams and Thomas Jefferson. Ultimately, Church contends, as the New England states were associated with being unpatriotic in the War of 1812 and their religious establishments discredited, and as churches grew through voluntary efforts, there was a greater balance in the relationship between church and state. Civil religion protected the nation from moral relativism, but church–state separation allowed both religion and the government to thrive. [42]

In a similar way, Steven Waldman praises the founding faith, which was neither Christianity nor secularism but religious freedom. Waldman criticizes polemicists for distorting history through their "custody battle" over the founders. He challenges several of the widely held myths, including the idea that America was established as a Christian nation and that the first Amendment was intended to separate church and state everywhere. [43] Although he focuses on the usual list of founders, he treats their religious views more subtly and with more nuance than most. He points out that the First Amendment was a compromise between different opinions on church–state relations and that it built "a wall that looks good from all sides." [44] He closes by praising the founders for being right but suggests that they did not resolve church–state issues once and for all; he urges contemporary Americans to consider not just what is constitutional but what is wise. [45] For its narrative, argument, and balance, Waldman's work is probably the best single-author contribution to the literature.

Also noteworthy is Alf Mapp's *The Faiths of Our Founding Fathers,* which predates David Holmes's reminder of religious pluralism by three years. Because he focuses on the individual beliefs of a number of founders with little effort to generalize or detail intentions at the Constitutional Convention, his work is difficult to categorize. On one hand, his treatments of Franklin and Jefferson place him in the camp just described. However, his inclusion of orthodox Christians like Patrick Henry, John Marshall, and George Mason and the generation's leading Catholic, Charles Carroll, do not. A chapter on Haym Solomon, a Polish Jew, illustrates the realities of religious pluralism in America and connections between government and religion. Although Solomon took issue with Pennsylvania's law requiring representatives to accept the Old and New Testaments, he expressed no concern for atheists' rights. [46] Mapp's selection of subjects thus connects him with the last group, who, for lack of a better term, shall be called "accommodationists," because they emphasize that, contrary to popular notions of the strict separation between church and state, the founders were comfortable with the government accommodating churches by encouraging religion and morality generally.

Accommodationists are serious scholars of history and the law published by prestigious university and trade publishers; they are not merely Christian polemicists writing for the Christian press. They include Daniel Dreisbach, Mark David Hall, Jeffry Morrison, Anthony Munoz, and James Hutson. Often they focus on forgotten founders or forgotten features of the founding, but they also contribute significantly to a fuller understanding of the best-known leaders and church-state documents. Although they are academic scholars, accommodationists make clear that the debate over the founders' religion is not simply an academic matter; it is a subject of wide-ranging importance because it is used as a basis for significant Supreme Court decisions.[47] These scholars offer alternative interpretations for the court.

Munoz does this more thoroughly than any others through his analysis of Madison, Washington, and Jefferson and the application of their views to modern court decisions. Munoz details the church–state doctrines of these founders: Madison's noncognizance of religion, Washington's emphasis on civic good, and Jefferson's anticlerical push for religious freedom. With a bit more certainty, he then deals with the question, "What would the founders do?" in modern religious establishment and free exercise cases and compares their views with thise of individual jurists. Madison proves to be the modern court's favorite, but conservative justices find Washington most useful.[48] Whereas Munoz argues that the founders' views on religion and government are poorly understood and demand further study, he does not simply defend original intent. Like Steven Waldman, he believes that they deserve attention because of the "profundity of their thought," not because they shaped the Constitution.[49]

Daniel Dreisbach deals with the familiar and with court implications in *Thomas Jefferson and the Wall of Separation Between Church and State*. Dreisbach argues that Jefferson's "wall of separation" metaphor has been misunderstood and overused. His Jefferson did not intend to establish a universal principle of church–state separation at all levels of government; he carefully crafted a statement of his views on federalism and limitations on the national government, not limitations on religion.[50] Dreisbach admits the positive arguments for church–state separation—the protection of religious minorities and reliance on voluntarism—but suggests that the "wall" metaphor, taken too literally, leads to a strictly secular state, where separation is prized over religion's free exercise.[51]

The Founding Fathers on God and Government, edited by Daniel Dreisbach, Mark Hall, and Jeffry Morrison, provides a perspective different from those already mentioned. For one thing, it is a collaborative work from ten scholars. It includes chapters on the most studied individuals but also on John Witherspoon, George Mason, James Wilson, and two prominent Catholics, the Carrolls of Maryland (Charles and John). Accommodationists use these founders to illustrate alternative views to those most often referenced from Madison and Jefferson. George Mason, for example, still supported church establishment and thought that religious tolerance was enough. Witherspoon found religion necessary for virtue, and virtue essential for a republic—an idea he passed on to those who attended the College of New Jersey, including James Madison. He did not favor a Protestant establishment but supported the "public provision for worship" and led the nation in three Thanksgiving proclamation prayers. James Wilson, a major voice at the Constitutional Convention, promoted a particularly Christian-based concept of natural rights. John and Charles Carroll supported church–state separation but, more importantly for accommodationsits, also remind readers that religious differences in the founding era were mainly between different Christian faiths, not between believers and atheists. [52] This volume closes with the reminder that the Enlightenment was not a mass intellectual movement in the United States and that therefore its influence at the founding should not be overemphasized. Further, it manifested itself differently in America than in France; here it was more skeptical of human nature and less hostile to religion. [53]

Inspired by a history conference, Dreisbach and friends followed up with a similar volume, *The Forgotten Founders and Religion and Public Life*, providing even more examples of church–state philosophies contrary to Madison's. These "forgotten founders" are designated as such and should not be ignored simply because they came from smaller, less consequential states, wrote less, or died sooner than other founders. Certainly Roger Sherman deserves attention as a founder, Mark Hall argues. He not only signed the Declaration, Articles of Confederation, and Constitution but also debated the First Amendment, argued theological points with Calvinist Samuel Hopkins, and argued for religious tolerance as well as government support for days of fasting. [54] Another noteworthy inclusion is Oliver Ellsworth, Madison's counterpart in the Senate who helped shape the First Amendment. He fully endorsed state support for religion and national religious proclamations and, accommodationists say, anyone studying original intent must include his thought as well. [55]

Finally, James Hutson has contributed significantly to the accommodationists' arguments without compromising scholarly integrity. In *Forgotten Features of the Founding,* Hutson details ideas that were common in the early republic but that have received scant attention from scholars because they are not seen as progressive. The founders generally regarded the belief in a future state of rewards and punishments to be of great political utility, essential for maintaining order and good citizenship. [56] They also believed that governments should be the "nursing fathers" of the churches, whether Anglican, Congregationalist, or Presbyterian. [57] Hutson asserts also that "rights" in America were originally seen as a power from God, but now rights are a raw power to satisfy appetites, and the conception of rights is detached from morality. [58] In a chapter on William Penn, Hutson asserts that modern Americans are losing their grounds for religious liberty; for all of his emphasis on religious liberty, Penn still outlawed gambling, fornication, sodomy, and other practices that are allowed today for the sake of liberty. [59] Hutson considers Madison's views on the church–state relationship to be the most radical and challenges the notion that disestablishment was good for religion; he points out that the Second Great Awakening started in Connecticut, where state support fostered the rapid growth of religion.[60] In another volume, Hutson provides yet another book of quotations on religion from the founders. Yet instead of arranging it according to individuals, as most have done since Norman Cousins's 1958 compilation, Hutson moves topically and shows what a significant number of founders, both forgotten and recognized, had to say about the afterlife, atheism, the Bible, chaplains, and so on.[61] Organizing quotes in this way makes it easier to deduce what the founders in general said about religion. In his preface, Hutson tries to assuage the fears that some conservative Christians have about academic historians by pointing out that sound scholarship is no enemy.[62]

This point is reiterated by John Fea in the latest book on the founders and religion. His 2011 publication asks but never definitely answers the age-old question, *Was America Founded As a Christian Nation?* There is no easy answer to this question. The terms *Christian, founding*, and *national* must be clearly defined first of all. And more importantly, those truly interested in the question must know how to think historically. Fea, more than any other author, tries to educate readers about thinking historically and understanding the "five Cs" of history—change, context, causality, contingency, and complexity.[63] The public, unfortunately, has little understanding, patience, or interest in deeply nuanced history. Thus, authors who provide easy answers to complex questions, even when they do not provide complexity, contextualization, or citations, will continue to have an audience, especially when their message resonates with readers' deeply held but historically uninformed political convictions. Public discussions on the faiths of the founders and on religion in American public life will be deeper and more informed the more people read exemplary histories, such as those by John Fea.

This is the encouraging point one should take in reading on the founders and religion. Despite the political inspiration and partisan motivation behind many works, there are thought-provoking and compelling arguments on both sides of the issue that should be considered. Interest in the topic shows no signs of declining. Those anxious for universally accepted portraits of the founders as individuals or as a group will not be satisfied any time soon. Citizens and their government must continually and honestly educate themselves on the founders for understanding original intent or to glean from the collective wisdom of the first generation. People of faith should take solace in the words of Thomas Jefferson, because as far as their own salvation and the present state of religion in America are concerned, it matters not if the founders believed "in one god, twenty gods, or no gods." And historians can take comfort in noting that some in their scholarly fellows exemplify the craft in ways that engage the public and inform citizens.

REFERENCES

Allen, Brooke. *The Moral Minority: Our Skeptical Founding Fathers*. Chicago: Ivan R. Dee, 2006.

Barton, David. *Original Intent: The Courts, the Constitution, and Religion*. Aledo, TX: Wall-Builder Press, 2010.

Brookhiser, Richard. *What Would the Founders Do? Our Questions, Their Answers*. New York: Basic Books, 2006.

Church, Forrest. *So Help Me God: The Founding Fathers and the First Great Battle Over Church and State*. Orlando, FL: Harcourt, 2007.

Cousins, Norman (ed). *"In God We Trust": The Religious Beliefs and Ideas of the American Founding Fathers*. New York: Harper, 1958.

Dawkins, Richard. *The God Delusion*. Boston: Houghton Mifflin, 2006.

Dreisbach, Daniel L. *Thomas Jefferson and the Wall of Separation Between Church and State*. New York: New York University Press, 2002.

———, Mark David Hall, and Jeffry H. Morrison (eds). *The Forgotten Founders on Religion and Public Life*. South Bend, Indiana: University of Notre Dame Press, 2009.

———, Mark David Hall, and Jeffry H. Morrison (eds). *The Founders on God and Government*. Lanham, Maryland: Rowman and Littlefield, 2004.

Eidsmoe, John. *Christianity and the Constitution: The Faith of Our Founding Fathers*. Grand Rapids, MI: Baker Book House.

Fea, John. *Was America Founded as a Christian Nation? A Historical Introduction*. Louisville, KY: Westminster John Knox Press, 2011.

Gaustad, Edwin S. *Faith of Our Fathers: Religion and the New Nation*. San Francisco: Harper and Row, 1987.

Gorton, Glen (ed.). *What Would They Say? The Founding Fathers on Current Issues*. Lafeyette, LA: Huntington House, 1998.

Holmes, David L. *The Faiths of the Founding Fathers*. New York: Oxford University Press.

Hutson, James. *Forgotten Features of the Founding: The Recovery of Religious Themes in the Early American Republic*. Lanham, MD: Lexington Books, 2003.

——— (ed.). *The Founders on Religion: A Book of Quotations*. Princeton: Princeton University Press, 2005.

Kowalski, Gary A. *Revolutionary Spirits: The Enlightened Faith of America's Founding Fathers*. New York: Blue Bridge, 2008.

Kramnick, Isaac, and R. Laurence Moore, *The Godless Constitution: The Case Against Religious Correctness*. New York: Norton, 1996.

Kulbacki, Joseph V. *America . . . A Nation That's Lost Its Way: What's Wrong With America!* Potter, KS: International Localization Network, 2009.

LaHaye, Tim. *Faith of Our Founding Fathers*. Brentwood, TN: Wolgamath and Hyatt, 1987.

Lambert, Frank. *The Founding Fathers and the Place of Religion in America*. Princeton, NJ: Princeton University Press, 2003.

Mansfield, Steven. *Ten Tortured Words: How the Founding Fathers Tried to Protect Religion and America and What's Happened Since*. Nashville, TN: Thomas Nelson, 2007.

Mapp, Alf J. Jr. *The Faiths of Our Fathers: What America's Founder Really Believed*. Lanham, MD: Rowman & Littlefield, 2003.

McClanahan, Brion. *The Politically Incorrect Guide to the Founding Fathers*. Washington, DC: Regency, 2009.

Meacham, Jon. *American Gospel: God, the Founding Fathers, and the Making of a Nation*. New York: Random House, 2006.

Miller, William Lee. *The First Liberty: America's Foundation in Religious Freedom*, expanded and updated edition. Washington, DC: Georgetown University Press, 2003.

Munoz, Vincent Philip. *God and the Founders: Madison, Washington, and Jefferson*. Cambridge, MA: Cambridge University Press, 2009.

Nash-Marshall, Siobhan. *What It Takes to Be Free: Religion and the Roots of Democracy*. New York: Crossroads, 2003.

Novak, Michael. *On Two Wings: Humble Faith and Common Sense at the American Founding.* San Francisco: Encounter Books, 2002.
Smith, Sam, Garrett Sheldon, and Mark McGarvie. Roundtable on *The Faiths of the Founding Fathers* by David Holmes. Presented at the Liberty University Conference on Christianity and American History, April 2007.
Waldman, Steven. *Founding Faith: Providence, Politics, and the Birth of Religious Freedom in America.* New York: Random House, 2008.

NOTES

1. Tim LaHaye, *Faith of Our Founding Fathers* (Brentwood, Tennessee: Wolgamath and Hyatt, 1987), 5.
2. Brooke Allen, *The Moral Minority: Our Skeptical Founding Fathers* (Chicago: Ivan R. Dee, 2006), 147.
3. Ibid, xi.
4. Isaac Kramnick and R. Laurence Moore, The Godless Constitution: The Case Against Religious Correctness (New York: W.W. Norton, 1996), 11–12.
5. Ibid, 21, 88, 156–64.
6. *See* Siabhan Nash-Marshall, *What It Takes to Be Free: Religion and the Roots of Democracy* (New York: Crossroads, 2003), 9; William Lee Miller, *The First Liberty: America's Foundation in Religious Freedom, Expanded and Update ed.* (Georgetown University Press, 2003), vii–xii.
7. Stephen Mansfield, *Ten Tortured Words: How the Founding Fathers Tried to Protect Religion and America and What's Happened Since* (Nashville: Thomas Nelson, 2007), xix..
8. LaHaye, 4–6.
9. http://www.wallbuilders.com/ABTbioDB.asp (accessed March 20, 2011).
10. *See* David Barton, *Original Intent: The Courts, the Constitution, and Religion* (Aledo, Texas: WallBuilder Press, 2010), 285–324.
11. Brion McClanahan, *The Politically Incorrect Guide to the Founding Fathers* (Washington: Regency, 2009), 1–4, 41. This title further illustrates the mutual identification as outsiders, for if McClanahan and Bill Maher can both claim to be "politically incorrect," one wonders what political correctness is or how strong its hold on culture is.
12. Michael Novak, *On Two Wings: Humble Faith and Common Sense at the American Founding* (San Francisco: Encounter Books, 2002), 1–2.
13. Glen Gorton, ed., *What Would They Say? The Founding Fathers on Current Issues* (Lafeyette, Louisiana: Huntington House Publishers, 1998), 10–12.
14. Ibid, v.
15. McClanahan, 329–333. *See also* Richard Brookhiser, *What Would the Founders Do?: Our Questions, Their Answers* (New York: Basic Books, 2006). Although Brookhiser is not among the Christian polemicists, his book is notable for addressing this theme. It emphasizes disagreement among the founders on religious matters and that the United States was a very religious country founded on moral principles, but not explicitly Christian.
16. Joseph V. Kulbacki, *America . . . a Nation That's Lost Its Way: What's Wrong With America!* (Potter, Kansas: International Localization Network, 2009), 284.
17. LaHaye, 199–201.
18. John Eidsmoe, *Christianity and the Constitution: The Faith of Our Founding Fathers* (Grand Rapids, Michigan: Baker Book House), 406.
19. Kramnick and Moore, 11–12.
20. James Hutson, *Forgotten Features of the Founding: The Recovery of Religious Themes in the Early American Republic* (Lanham, Maryland: Lexington Books, 2003), 113–116. Hutson suggests that Kramnick and Moore's admission of writing a polemic is an excuse for inaccuracy.
21. Richard Dawkins, *The God Delusion* (Boston: Houghton Mifflin, 2006), 38–39, 45.

22. Gary A. Kowalski, *Revolutionary Spirits: The Enlightened Faith of America's Founding Fathers* (New York: Blue Bridge, 2008), 6.

23. Brooke Allen, *The Moral Minority: Our Skeptical Founding Fathers* (Chicago: Ivan R. Dee, 2006), viii.

24. Ibid, xiii–xvi.

25. *See* Daniel L. Dreisbach, Mark David Hall, and Jeffry H. Morrison, eds, *The Founders on God and Government* (Lanham, Maryland: Rowman and Littlefield, 2004); Daniel L. Dreisbach, Mark David Hall, and Jeffry H. Morrison, eds, *The Forgotten Founders on Religion and Public Life* (South Bend, Indiana: University of Notre Dame Press, 2009); Alf J. Mapp, Jr., *The Faiths of Our Fathers: What America's Founder Really Believed* (Lanham, Maryland: Rowman and Littlefield, 2003) for examples. Eidsmoe also uses a large number of founders in his *Christianity and the Constitution.*

26. Kowalski, 6.

27. Ibid, 39–41.

28. Ibid, 116–123.

29. Allen, 49–69.

30. Ibid, 130.

31. Kramnick and Moore, 132–142.

32. Kowalski, 186–191.

33. Allen, 143.

34. David L. Holmes, *The Faiths of the Founding Fathers* (New York: Oxford University Press), 109–112, 143–157.

35. Ibid, 135–141.

36. Sam Smith, Garrett Sheldon, and Mark McGarvic, "Roundtable on The Faiths of the Founding Fathers by David Holmes" at the Liberty University Conference on Christianity and American History, April 2007.

37. Edwin S. Gaustad, *Faith of Our Fathers: Religion and the New Nation* (San Francisco: Harper and Row, 1987), 2–11.

38. Ibid, 134–140.

39. Frank Lambert, *The Founding Fathers and the Place of Religion in America* (Princeton: Princeton University Press, 2003), 5–7.

40. Ibid. *See* the first five chapters.

41. Jon Meacham, *American Gospel: God, the Founding Fathers, and the Making of a Nation* (New York: Random House, 2006), 18–23, 31–32.

42. *See* Forrest Church, *So Help Me God: The Founding Fathers and the First Great Battle Over Church and State* (Orlando: Harcourt, 2007).

43. Steven Waldman, *Founding Faith: Providence, Politics, and the Birth of Religious Freedom in America* (New York: Random House, 2008), ix–xi.

44. Ibid, 141–158.

45. Ibid, 197–199.

46. Mapp, 80–96, 124–152.

47. Dreisbach, Hall, and Morrison, *The Forgotten Founders on Religion and Public Life*, xvi.

48. Vincent Philip Munoz, *God and the Founders: Madison, Washington, and Jefferson* (Cambridge University Press, 2009), 197, 201.

49. Ibid, 6, 206–207.

50. Daniel L. Dreisbach, *Thomas Jefferson and the Wall of Separation Between Church and State* (New York: New York University Press, 2002), 55–70.

51. Ibid, 118–125.

52. *See* Dreisbach, Hall, and Morrison, *The Founders on God and Government*; and Jeffrey H. Morrison's own *John Witherspoon and the Founding of the American Republic* (South Bend, Indiana: University of Notre Dame Press, 2005).

53. Dreisbach, Hall, and Morrison, *The Founders on God and Government*, 273–292.

54. Dreisbach, Hall, and Morrison, *The Forgotten Founders on Religion and Public Life*, 248–268.

55. Ibid, 93–94.

56. Hutson, *Forgotten Features of the Founding*, 10–33.

57. Ibid, 45–62.

58. Ibid, 73–100.

59. Ibid, 146.

60. Ibid, 177.

61. Norman Cousins, ed. *"In God We Trust": The Religious Beliefs and Ideas of the American Founding Fathers* (New York: Harper, 1958). Although it is considerably older than the other volumes analyzed in this essay, Cousin's compilations and commentary are still valuable for their breadth of coverage and balanced insights.

62. James Hutson, ed., *The Founders on Religion: A Book of Quotations* (Princeton: Princeton University Press, 2005), x.

63. John Fea, *Was America Founded as a Christian Nation? A Historical Introduction* (Louisville, Kentucky: Westminster John Knox Press, 2011), xvii, xxii.

About the Contributors

Sargon G. Donabed is Assistant Professor at Roger Williams University, where he teaches Middle Eastern history and religious studies. He serves on the advisory board of the journal *Chronos*, published by the University of Balamand in Lebanon. His work has been published in journals such as *Folklore* and *National Identities*. He is a recipient of The American Academic Research Institute Iraq (TAARII) grant for his work on Assyrian folklore of Iraq and is the coeditor of *The Assyrian Heritage: Threads of Continuity and Influence* (2012).

Rebeca Vázquez Gómez, PhD, is a State Ecclesiastical Law Researcher at the University of A Coruña (Spain). Her recent publications focus on the presence of religious symbols in public spaces as well as religious and civil powers in the English colonies of North America. She has completed research stays, among others, at the University of North Carolina at Chapel Hill and presented papers at several national and international conferences.

Lawrence B. Goodheart, Professor of History at the University of Connecticut, is author of *The Solemn Sentence of Death: Capital Punishment in Connecticut* (2011). He was a Senior Fulbright Lecturer in Turkey during 2009–2010.

Matthew S. Hedstrom is Assistant Professor of American Studies and Religious Studies at the University of Virginia. He teaches and researches the history and culture of religions, both official and popular, in the nineteenth- and twentieth-century United States, and is the author of *The Rise of Liberal Religion: Book Culture and American Spirituality in the Twentieth Century* (Oxford University Press, 2012).

James Hitchcock is Professor of History at St. Louis University. He is a graduate of St. Louis University and holds master's and doctor's degrees from Princeton University. His books include *Catholicism and Modernity*

(1978), *Years of Crisis* (1985), and *The Supreme Court and Religion in American Life* (2004). His *History of the Catholic Church* will be published in the fall of 2012. His articles have appeared in *Archiv fuer Reformationsgeschichte, Catholic Historical Review, Bulletin of the Institute for Historical Research, Bulletin of the History of Medicine, Law and Contemporary Problems, The New Catholic Encyclopedia, New York Times Magazine, Commentary, Commonweal, America, Yale Review, American Scholar, National Review, South Atlantic Quarterly, First Things,* and other journals.

Sara C. Kitzinger is a doctoral candidate in early modern history at the University of St. Andrews, United Kingdom. She is currently completing her dissertation on the discourse of sovereignty in terms of church and state in sixteenth- and seventeenth-century England. She is a Visiting Fellow at Thomas More College of Liberal Arts, New Hampshire.

Matt McCook has been a professor at Oklahoma Christian University for the past ten years, teaching a wide variety of history courses. His favorites are centered on religious and intellectual history in the early American republic. His research interests include the Second Great Awakening and church–state relations.

Keith Pacholl received his doctorate from the University of California, Riverside. He is the author of several articles, and his research examines the interaction of religion and periodical literature in eighteenth-century America. Dr. Pacholl is currently Associate Professor of History at the University of West Georgia.

Noah Shusterman is Assistant Professor of Intellectual Heritage at Temple University. A specialist in the history of Old Regime and Revolutionary France, he is the author of *Religion and the Politics of Time: Holidays in France from Louis XIV through Napoleon.*

Brent S. Sirota is Assistant Professor of History at North Carolina State University. He is the author of the forthcoming book *The Christian Monitors: The Church of England and the Age of Benevolence, 1680–1740.*

Holly Snyder has been Curator of American Historical Collections at Brown University Library since July 2004. She previously taught college courses in American history and Judaic Studies and worked as an archivist at the U.S. Holocaust Memorial Museum, the American Jewish Historical Society, and the John Nicholas Brown Center. She has authored numerous articles on Jews in the colonial British Atlantic, including an essay on the religiosity of Jewish merchants, which appeared in *Early American Studies* (Fall 2010). She holds a doctorate in American History from Brandeis University, and received M.S.L.S. and M.A. degrees from The Catholic University of America.

Joshua B. Stein has taught at Roger Williams University since 1969. He received his doctorate from St. Louis University in history and master's degree in religious studies from Brown University. His most recent book is

Commentary on the Constitution from Plato to Rousseau. Currently he is working on a comparative study of the literature of the First World War and the Iliad.

Tara Thompson Strauch is a doctoral candidate in history at the University of South Carolina. She is currently working on her dissertation, entitled "Taking Oaths and Giving Thanks: Religious Rituals in the early American Government, 1776–1800," which considers how rituals such as oaths, thanksgivings, fast days, and congressional prayer shaped the American national identity.